IMAGES
of America

NEW HAVEN

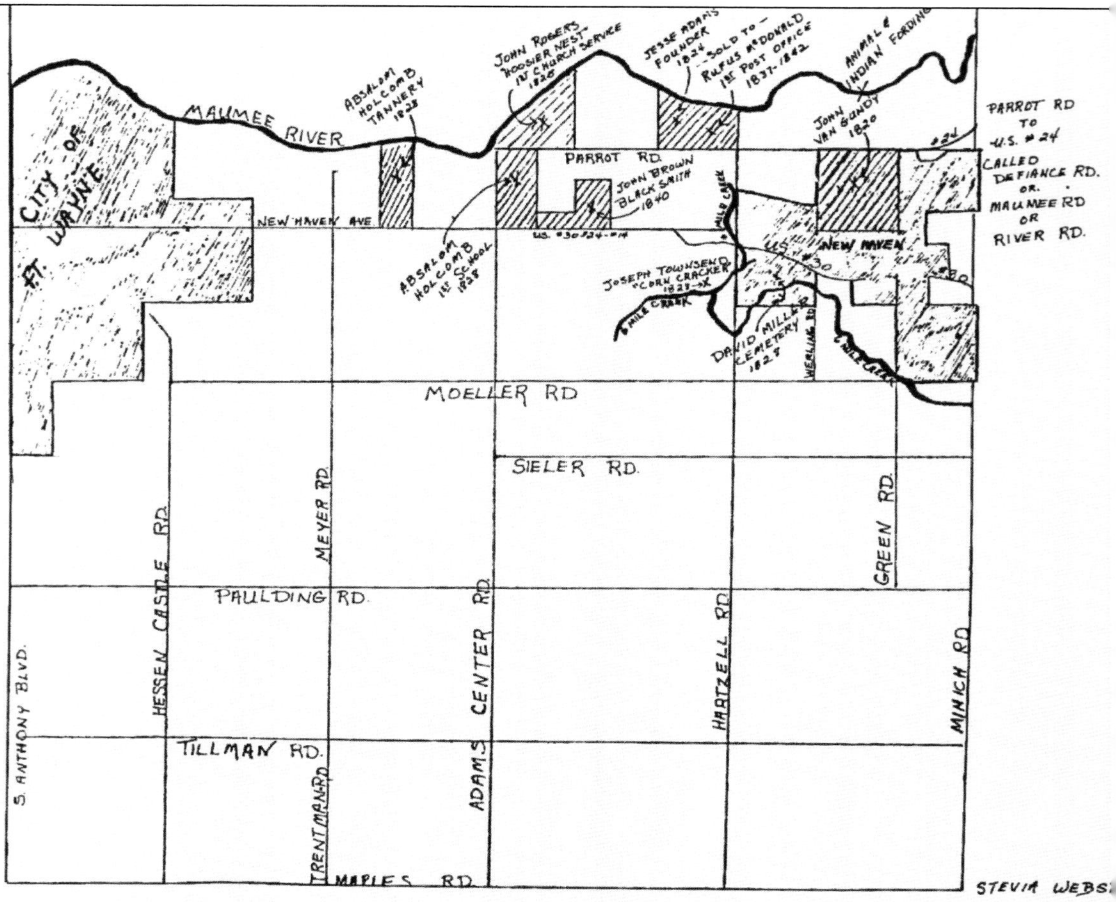

This map shows the first cabins and businesses on the newest frontier of the west in the 1820s. Many talented men came from the east by wagon in 1823, traveling over rutted, muddy forest trails. Settlers included blacksmiths, merchants, and those who contributed their knowledge of government to establish new towns. Farmers were eager to invest in fertile ground and start new lives. Large families and newly married couples looked forward to settling in the new country. (Map from the surveyor's office 1860 plat map; illustration by Stevia Webster.)

On the Cover: Years ago, farmers were like a large family. When one needed help, neighboring families pitched in. Surrounding farmers came together to replace barns, sheds, chicken houses, and smokehouses. When a barn needed to be built and it was time for the walls to be erected, farmers gathered together to raise the heavy timbers. This was also an excuse to celebrate—tables groaned with the weight of delicious food and desserts for everyone. (Rodenbeck family.)

IMAGES
of America

NEW HAVEN

New Haven Area Heritage Association

ARCADIA
PUBLISHING

ISBN 978-0-7385-7800-2

Published by Arcadia Publishing
Charleston, South Carolina

Printed in the United States of America

Library of Congress Control Number: 2009943872

For all general information, please contact Arcadia Publishing:
Telephone 843-853-2070
Fax 843-853-0044
E-mail sales@arcadiapublishing.com
For customer service and orders:
Toll-Free 1-888-313-2665

Visit us on the Internet at www.arcadiapublishing.com

We dedicate this book to the many people who came before us and preserved Adams Township and Jefferson Township histories, and also to those who generously shared their photographs of landmarks and their locations that are long gone. Descendants of homesteaders and those who came decades later have volunteered family histories. It has been a privilege and joy to share in these "olden day" memories.

CONTENTS

Acknowledgments

The New Haven Area Heritage Association has been in existence since December 1984, dedicated to the promotion and preservation of our region's history. We are few but are very enthusiastic about the projects and challenges that have come our way. We recognize Candy Lauber, Dan White, Jeff Hoffman, and Todd Baron for their hours of scanning many photographs. And Mike and Charlene Fromholt and Bill Webster, who served on the book committee. Special thanks to Mike who tirelessly researched addresses and dates of canal houses and others. Alison Adams wrote the cover copy on the back of our book. Above all we recognize and thank Stevia Webster, whose dream long had been to create a local history and without whose persistence this book would never had happened.

Many individuals brought their photographs and family histories.

Contributors include: Maxine (Wolf) Van Horn, Deborah Eidson, Sue Luther, Tom Castaldi, Suzie Schnelker, Rose Stemmler Sweet, Bonnie Schnelker, Katie Day, Walter Sassmannshousen, Hazel Ohneck, Marie Mehring, Hilda Hamilton, Gloria Boles, Jim Pemberton, Lyn Shaw, Zenda Snyder Bateman, Robert and Henrietta Vonderau, Ed Lomont, Warren Messman, Donn Werling, Natalie Seltz, the Virgil and Glenna (Tustison) Asher family, Sue (Asher) Bradley, Jan (Asher) Harnish, Becky (Asher) Hayes, Doug Runyan, Bob Ladig, Helen Smith, Vivian Smith, Mary (Pranger) Ketzler, Nancy Reuille, Bonnie Rinard, Ken Richards, Patricia Davis, Joanne Thoorsell, Hilda Snyder, the Bacon family, Mayor Terry McDonald, and Mike Clendenen of the New Haven Parks Department. Jo Anne Smith sent photographs and information from the state of Georgia. Jeff Hoffman facilitated the sharing of many pictures from the St. Louis Catholic Church library.

Valuable resources included: Mitch Harper's 1980 study of architecture of older homes; Pat Henry's script for a bus tour of New Haven highlighting the historical landmarks; Bob Burn's written family history; the *New Haven Centennial Book* of 1966; articles by Lois Emenhiser, Rod King, and Mark Paloni for the Fort Wayne and New Haven newspapers and the *Old Fort News*. The services of T&D Print Shop and New Haven Print and Copy were of great assistance.

Finally, thank you to John Pearson of Arcadia Publishing for your encouragement and help while creating this book.

We have searched through many resources and hope that our errors are few but welcome any comments about the inevitable inaccuracies. This book is not a definitive history of New Haven, and we invite people to continue sending in family stories and pictures to the New Haven Area Heritage Association at P. O. Box 94, New Haven, Indiana, 46774.

INTRODUCTION

The melting ice of the glaciers in this part of the country formed many lakes. Maumee Lake covered Maumee Valley, which is a part of northeast Indiana and northwest Ohio. It affected Adams Township and the surrounding areas by forming the Van Wert Ridge at its southern shore known as Ridge Road, now U.S. Highway 30 East. The northwestern shore became known as Hicksville Ridge, now State Road 37. The ridge of the roads formed by the glacier is still visible.

When the waters receded, the St. Joseph, St. Mary's, and Maumee Rivers were formed. The moraines that remained became a region covered with a heavy growth of hardwood forests. It lavishly furnished valuable timber such as oak, walnut, beech, maple, ash, elm, sycamore, poplar, hickory, locust, cherry, and many others. There was no other area comparable to these forests.

This was, at the time, the gateway to the far west, and the Maumee and Wabash Rivers were an important route of canoe travel between the Great Lakes and the Ohio River and beyond. The river journey began at the head of the Maumee River at Fort Wayne and a short portage over the little stream, which now occupies the Erie-Wabash Channel and on to the Wabash River.

Before the white man, Native Americans hunted the forests and fished the lakes. This was the home of the Algonquians and the Miami, parts of the Algonquin Nation. Native American lore abounds, and arrowheads, grinding stones, and axe heads are a few of the artifacts still found today.

In 1820, John Van Gundy came to this paradise of abundant fishing and hunting. He found a property that was high and dry and free from the "danged mud." It was located a quarter of a mile from the Native American and animal fording on the Maumee River. Here Gundy girdled the trees with a sure swing of his worthy axe, cutting through the cambium layer and causing the trees to die. Many trees were huge, measuring 90 feet to the first limb. New Haven was known as "Gundy's Deadening." On May 1, 1826, Gundy deposited $236 at the land office in Fort Wayne, Indiana. Pres. John Quincy Adams granted him a deed for his 160 acres of land.

In 1823, one of the first settlers in the area was Jesse Adams, who, with others, founded Adams Township. Adams came from Rochester, New York. He was a prominent and respected businessman who was skilled in medical practices of the time. He served as a doctor at Fort Wayne until his family came from the east to join him. His wife was Laura Edmunds, whom he married in 1821. Many other families came with Adams family. They traveled in covered wagons over the roads, which were few, and they often had to stop to clear trees and brush. Adams bought 97 acres along the Maumee River. In 1824, he became the first person to make a land grant purchase at the cost of $1.25 per acre.

This area was located on the present north side of Rose Avenue, east by the railroad tracks and west beyond Hartzell Road. Adams erected a log cabin hewn from local timber. The windows were made of greased, glazed paper. The floors were logs split lengthwise in two pieces and dropped into furrows with the bark side down. Adams named Adams Township not after himself, but after Pres. John Quincy Adams. Not long after the Adams settled down, Jesse and Laura had a second child, Marcia Loisa, who died in 1824—the first recorded death in the township. She was buried on the Adams' farm.

New Haven has always been known as a transportation town. Because of the pioneers coming to such a fertile land, transportation was of utmost importance. Walking, canoes, and wagons were not fast enough or free from forest growth, slowing down imports and eventually exports. Farmers and businesses were stagnant until the mid-1830s. Canals in the east inspired local politicians to approve the building of a canal here. Soon the Wabash and Erie Canal was hand dug from Toledo, Ohio, to Evansville, Indiana. After the canal came the railroads, interurban train, automobiles, and buses, which encouraged more and better roads. The autobuses and automobile era slowly replaced previous modes of transportation, including the horse.

We hope you will enjoy the many photographs that will bring old New Haven alive again.

One

Pioneers, Founders, and Transportation

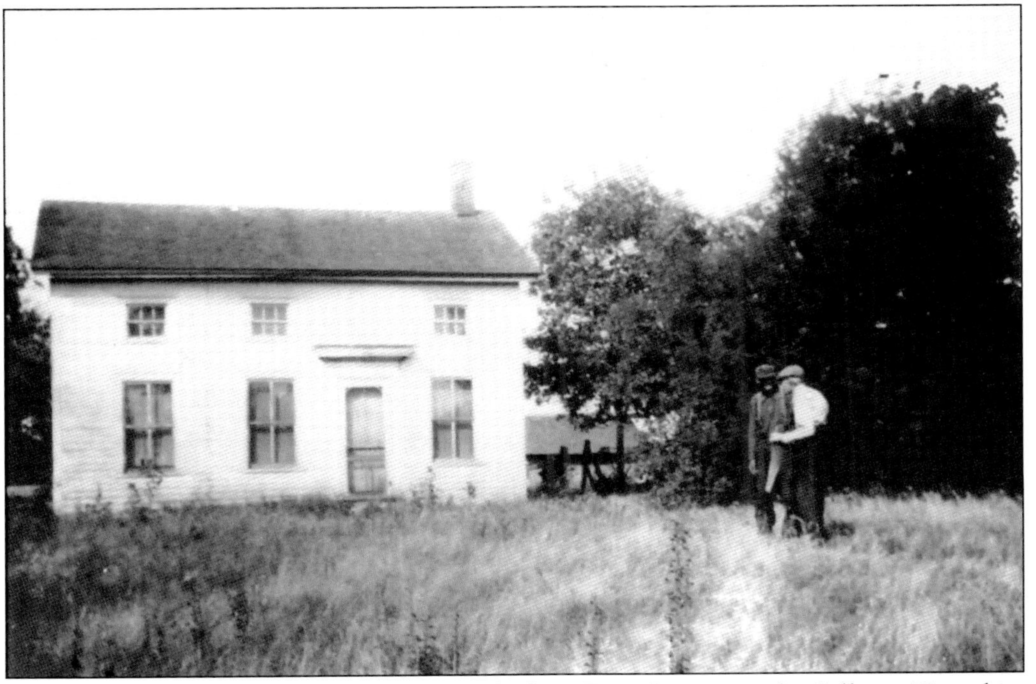

After a few years, Jesse Adams—the founder of Adams Township—moved to Jefferson Township, east of New Haven. His house was near the Highway 469 South ramp. His property consisted of all of the land between U.S. Highway 30 and Dawkins Road. Standing off to one side of Adams's house are his grandson Josiah Adams, left, and grandson-in-law Samuel Burns. (Maxine Van Horn.)

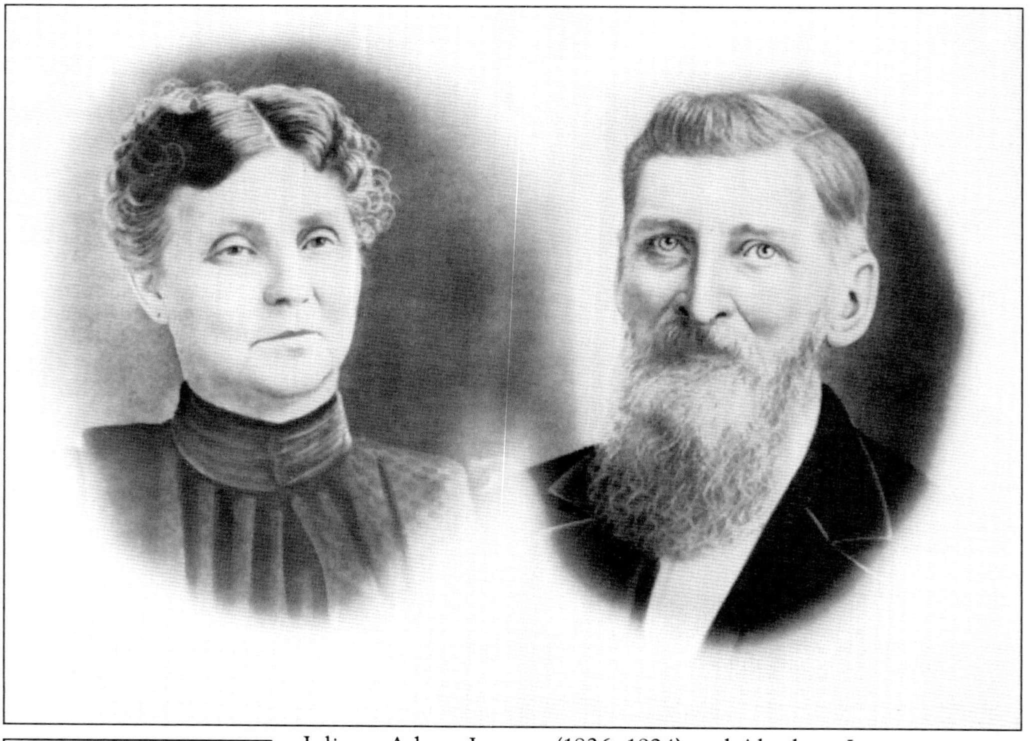

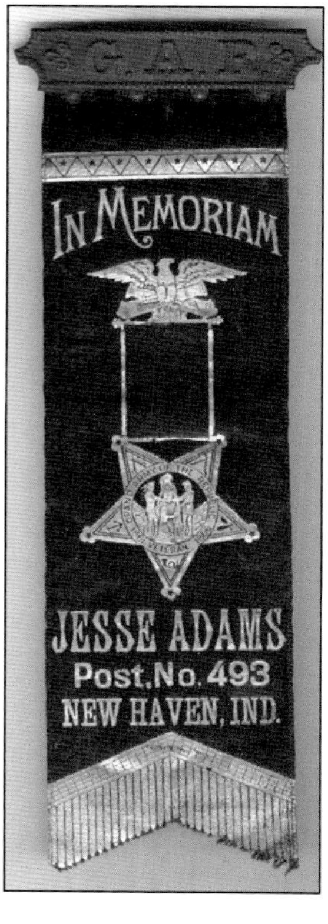

Juliaett Adams Lowrey (1836–1924) and Abraham Lowrey (1828–1905) are pictured above. Juliaett was the sixth child of Jesse Adams. She had property on Dawkins Road. The house stood for four generations before it was torn down (1980s). Abraham Lowrey purchased land in 1863 on 502 Henry Street, perhaps when they were married. (Bob Burns.)

After the Civil War, veterans numbered near 490,000. They formed the Grand Army of the Republic (GAR), founded in 1866 and absolved during 1956 after the last member died. In the early years, a banner was created in honor of Jesse Adams, founder of Adams Township. (Todd Baron).

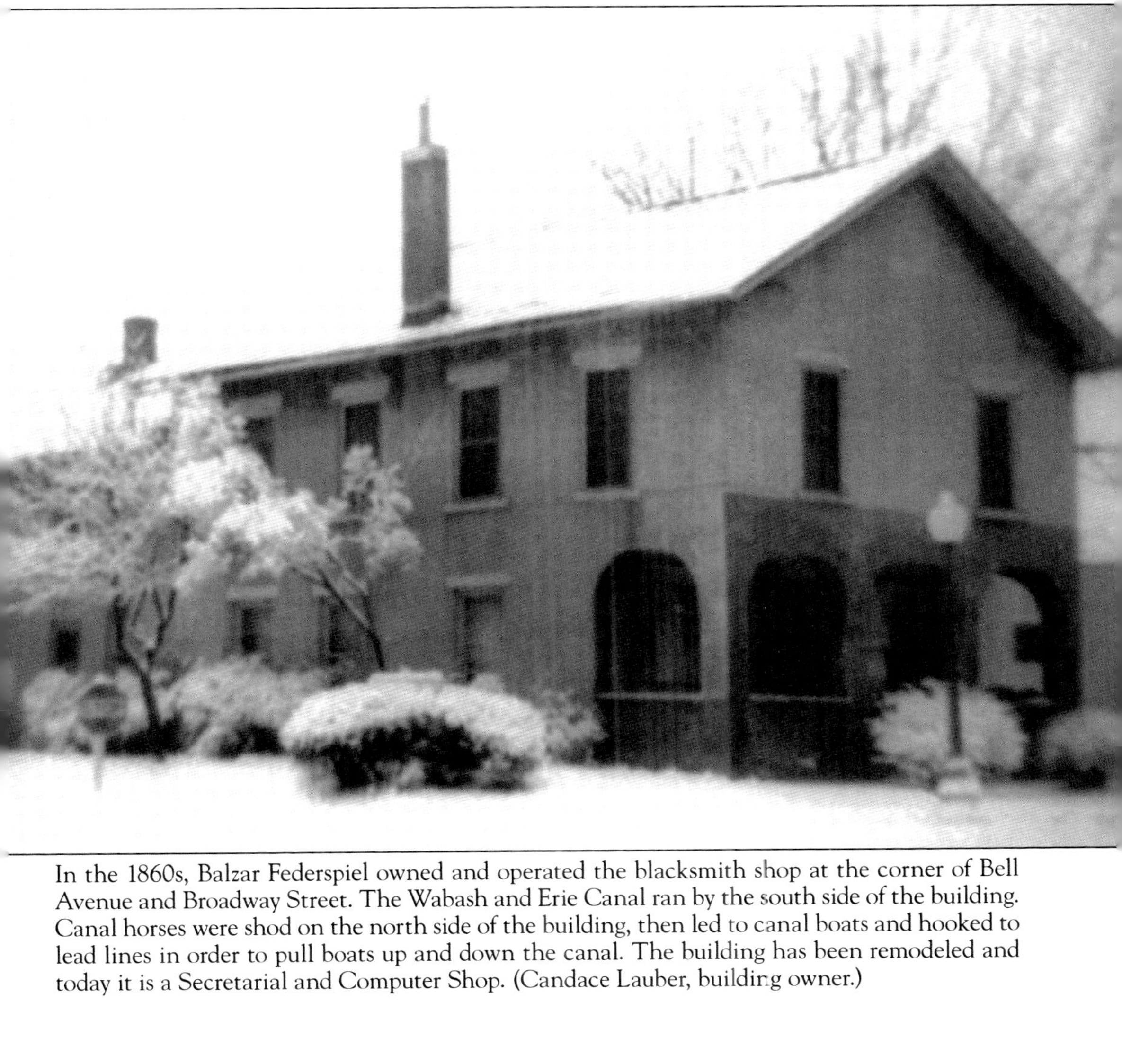

In the 1860s, Balzar Federspiel owned and operated the blacksmith shop at the corner of Bell Avenue and Broadway Street. The Wabash and Erie Canal ran by the south side of the building. Canal horses were shod on the north side of the building, then led to canal boats and hooked to lead lines in order to pull boats up and down the canal. The building has been remodeled and today it is a Secretarial and Computer Shop. (Candace Lauber, building owner.)

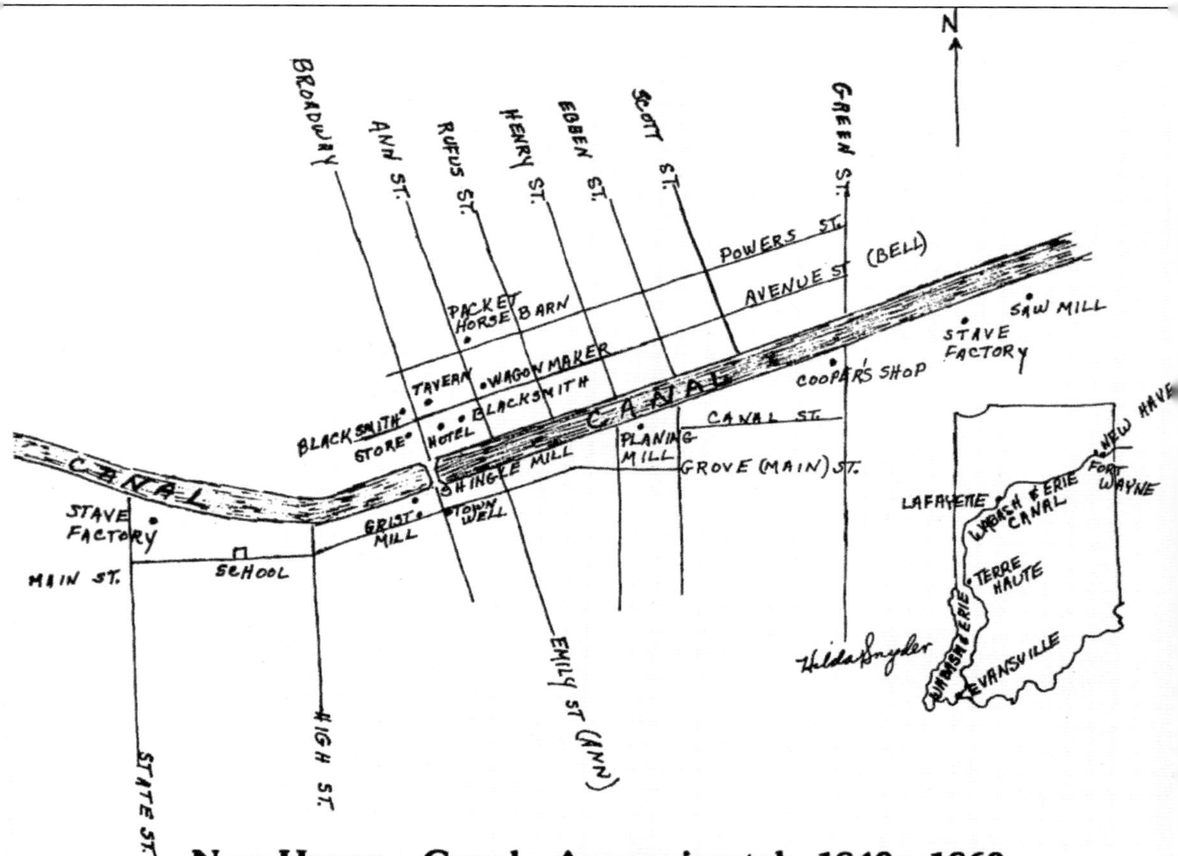

New Haven - Canal - Approximately 1840 - 1860

Before serious attention was directed at building a canal, consideration was given to constructing a railroad. However, railroads required huge quantities of iron, which was not available in the area at that time. But Indiana did have earth, timber, and stone. Ground was broken for the Wabash and Erie Canal on February 22, 1832, in Fort Wayne. This formal ceremony set in motion a course of events that brought the backwoods region of northeast Indiana squarely into the 19th century. In 1835, the first section of the canal opened between Fort Wayne and Huntington. Many of the men who hand dug the canal were from Ireland. They were rewarded with whiskey. Due to disease and injury, one man died per mile of the canal. The map above from 1840–1860 shows the canal and the location of the first businesses in Adams Township. Some of the names of the streets have been changed. The insert of the Indiana map shows the entire canal, 468 miles long. (Illustrated by Hilda Snyder; Mary McCaig, Fort Wayne Newspapers, 1992.)

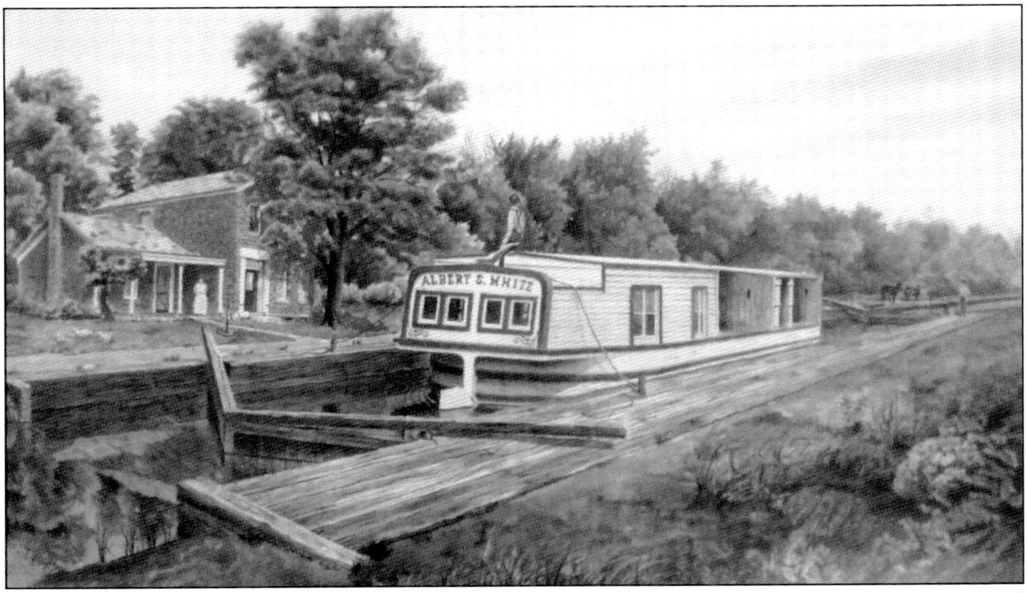

River steamers, called "packets," were 80 to 100 feet long. The interiors were sometimes carpeted in splashy colors, lighted by glass chandeliers, and featured white filigree woodwork trimmed with gold gilding. This painting shows a Wabash and Erie Canal packet, the *Albert S. White*, making her way through the Gronauer lock No. 2, located less than a mile east of New Haven. Joseph Gronauer was the keeper of the lock. His wife is pictured on the porch. Robert Vonderau, a 94-year-old New Haven native, tells of his mother, Emma, and the Harper daughters visiting the lock and watching passengers walk to the house where Mrs. Gronauer served beans and corn bread. (Artist Ralph Lehrman; Dan White.)

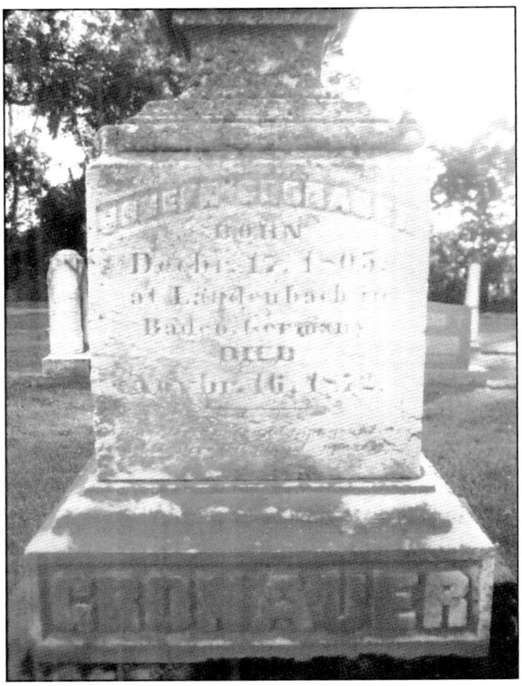

Joseph Gronauer was the lockkeeper on the Wabash and Erie Canal. His house was located in the area of the Highway 469 South ramp on Highway 24, just east of New Haven on U.S. Highway 24 and the south ramp of the 469 bypass. At right is the photograph of Gronauer's impressive marble tombstone, located in the St. John's Catholic Cemetery. He was born in 1805 and died in 1872. (Photograph by Dan White; Alison Adams, Historic Sites, 1992.)

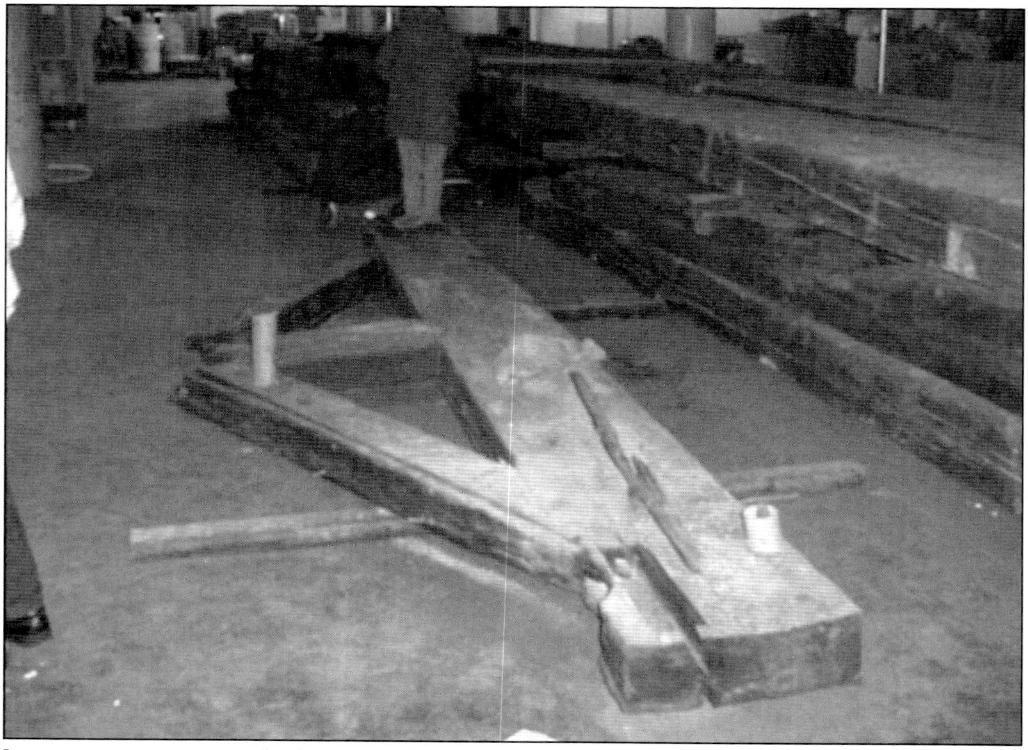

Large trees were cut on the location of the lock to make timbers. Some trees stretched 90 feet to the first limb. One of the timbers taken from the locks was 85 feet long. A large feeder dam was built on the St. Joseph River to provide water. Remains of this dam are visible today. The ideal slope of the canal bed was to be 1 inch per mile, to provide a small current so the water would not become stagnant. (Photograph by Dan White; Mary McCaig, Fort Wayne Newspapers, 1992.)

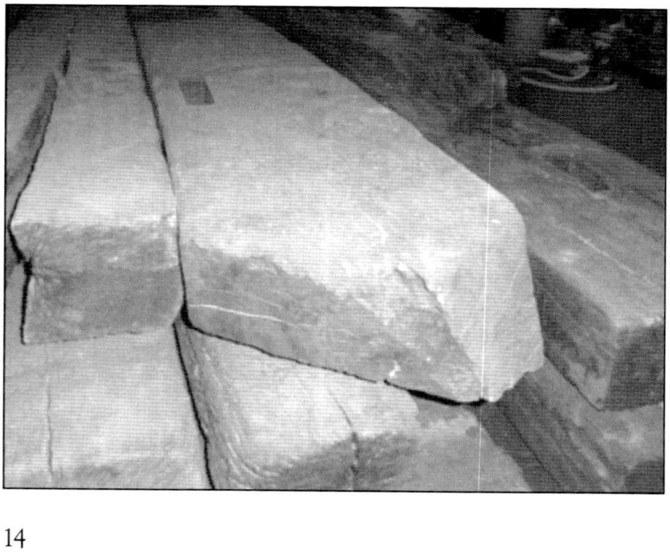

The canal was dug as a series of almost-level stretches connected by lift locks, which made it possible for boats to pass from one level to another. The Gronauer lock was discovered just east of New Haven during excavation for the widening of U.S. Highway 24. Canal locks were usually built of cut stone, but most of these were constructed of wood because there was not good stone available. (Photograph by Dan White; Mary McCaig, Fort Wayne Newspapers, 1992.)

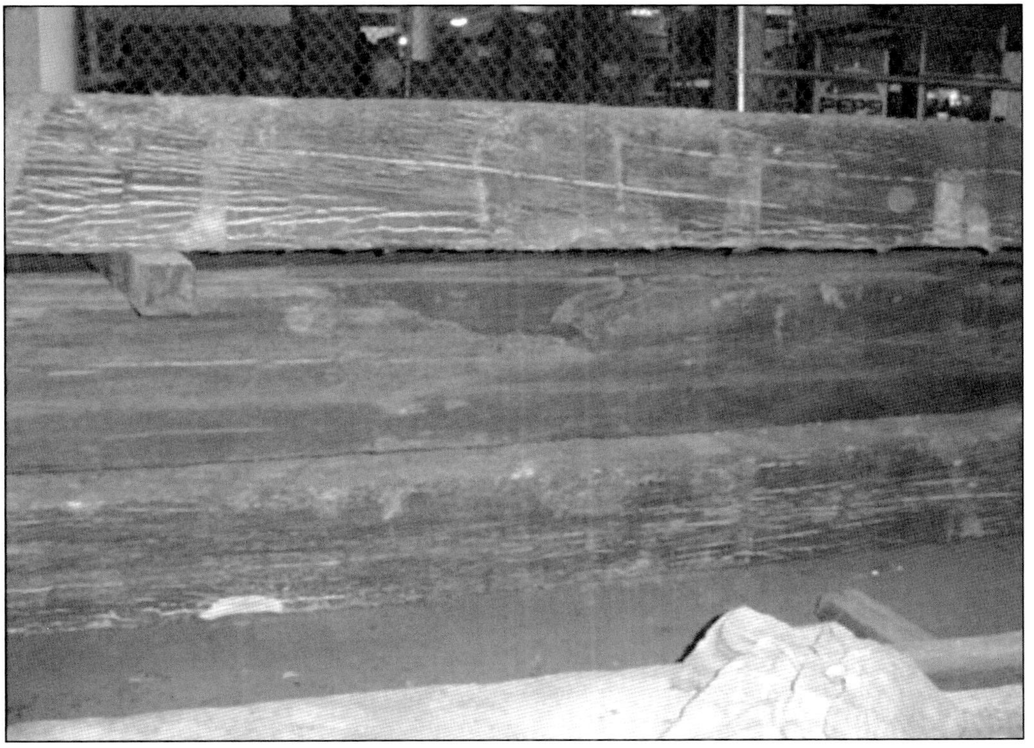

In 1843, the canal opened to New Haven and the city became an important canal town. By 1863, the Wabash and Erie Canal extended from Toledo, Ohio, to Evansville, Indiana, and to the Ohio River, a total of 468 miles. It was the longest man-made waterway in the history of the world. The canals were the cheapest, easiest, and safest mode of transportation. The canal boats could run from Toledo to Evansville in 56 hours. (Photograph by Dan White; Mary McCaig, Fort Wayne Newspapers, 1992.)

The canal caused immense change in northeastern Indiana. The area went from a trackless wilderness to a productive agricultural area in just a few years. Towns grew rapidly as settlers poured in. The benefits of the canal were great for the people, but the backers were on the verge of bankruptcy as floods, ice, and drought closed it, crippling revenue. In 1859–1860, the process of closing the canal began. The section through New Haven was drained and filled by 1882. The Nickel Plate Railroad tracks were laid in the canal bed. (Photograph by Dan White; Mary McCaig, Fort Wayne Newspapers, 1992.)

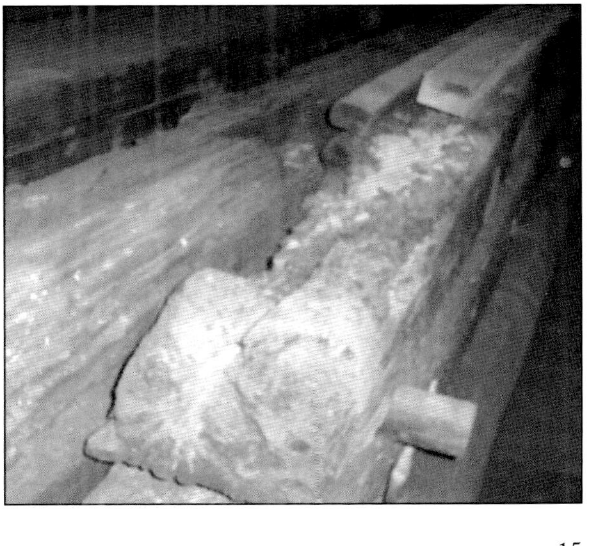

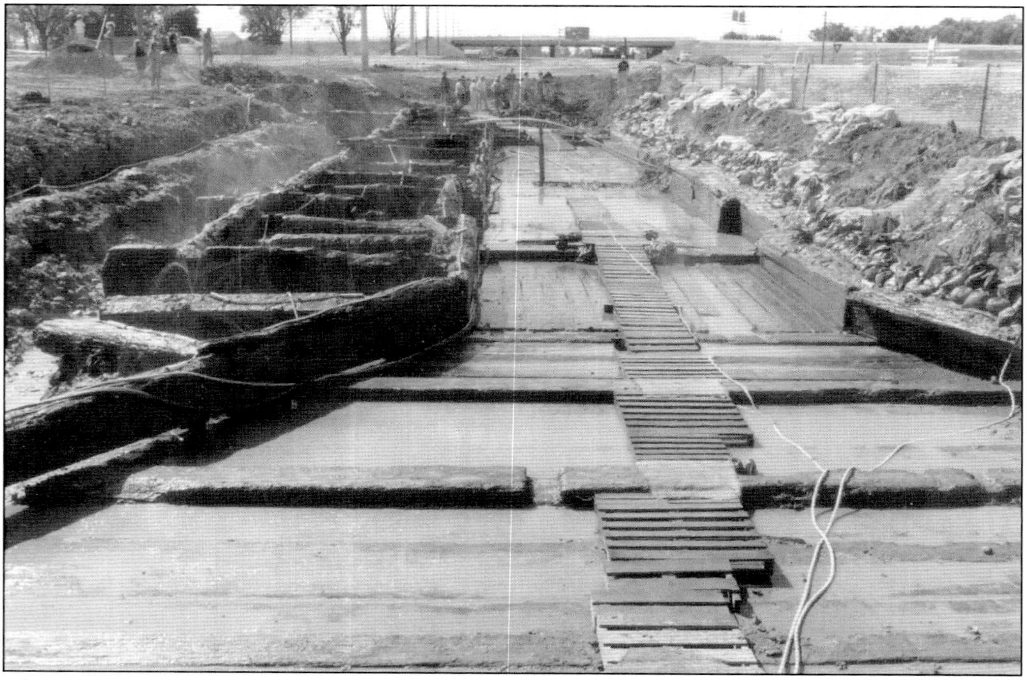

The Gerigs, father and son, were canal buffs. In 1992, during excavation for the installation of a ramp for Highway 469 along U.S. Highway 24, east of New Haven, the Gerigs investigated to see if any of the Gronauer locks were visible. One evening they began digging and unearthed some wooden parts. Searching further, they unearthed the remains of the lock's east and west end. They also cleaned the north side to make sure that it really was the lock. (Photograph by Tom Castaldi; Mary McCaig, Fort Wayne Newspapers, 1992.)

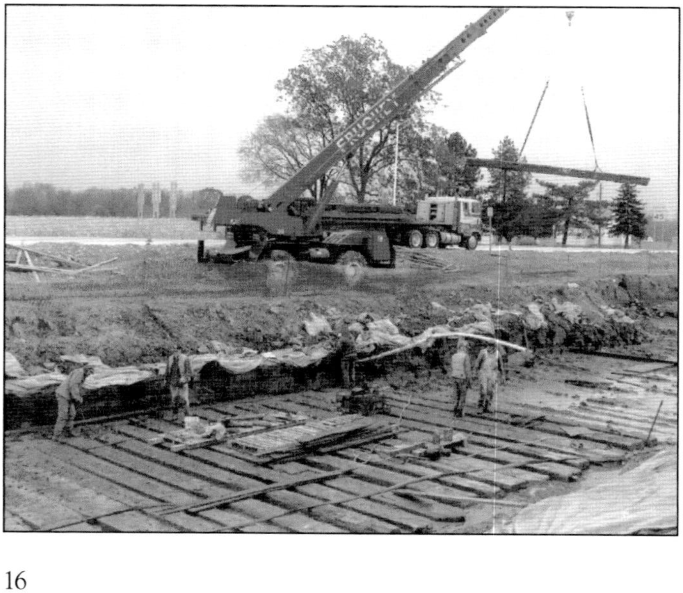

Later that evening, the Gerigs requested a stop work order go into effect. A temporary order went into effect until the lock was verified, then a permanent stop order was issued. The Maumee Valley Wabash Erie Canal Historical Society offered a proposal to support the relocation of the lock. Instead, the state decided the City of New Haven would handle the move. The society agreed to work with New Haven on the project. (St. Louis Catholic Church and Jeff Hoffman.)

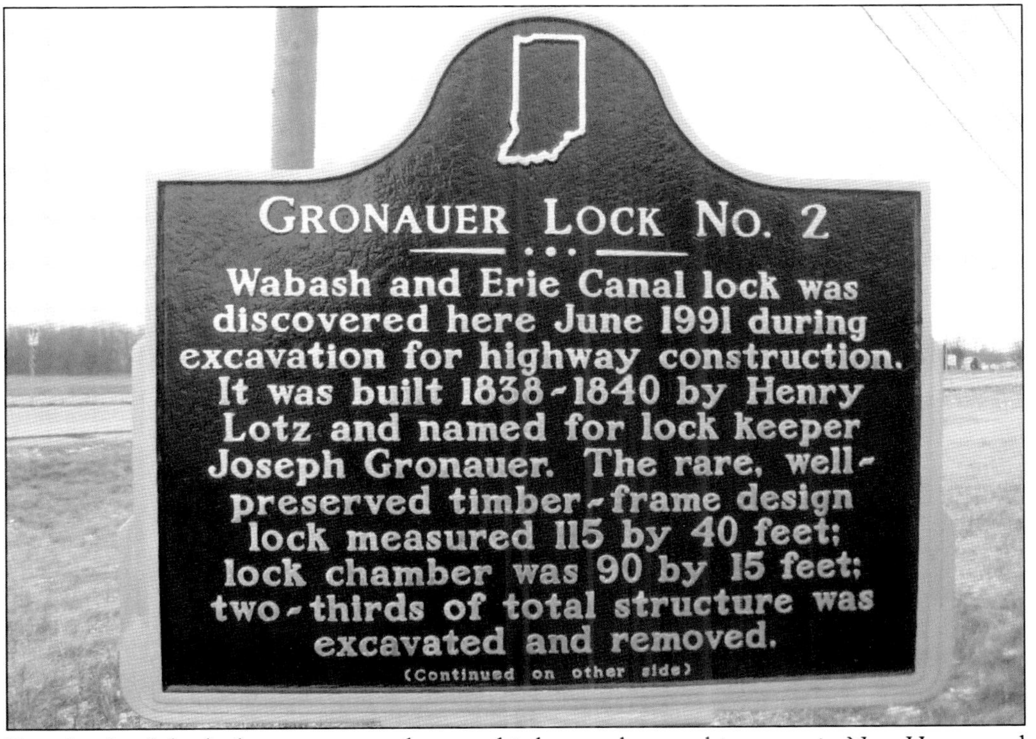

Two-thirds of the lock was excavated—one-third was submerged in water in New Haven and one-third was sent to the South Carolina Institute of Anthropology and Archaeology, which is located in Columbia, for preservation and then sent to Indianapolis to create a display in the new Indiana State Museum. One-third of the lock remained in the ground. The Indiana State Museum in Indianapolis planned to rebuild a large model of the lock but funds prevented them from using all of the material. They called New Haven Area Heritage Association, offering the balance of the lock material if they could transport them home. (Mary McCaig, Fort Wayne Newspapers, 1992.)

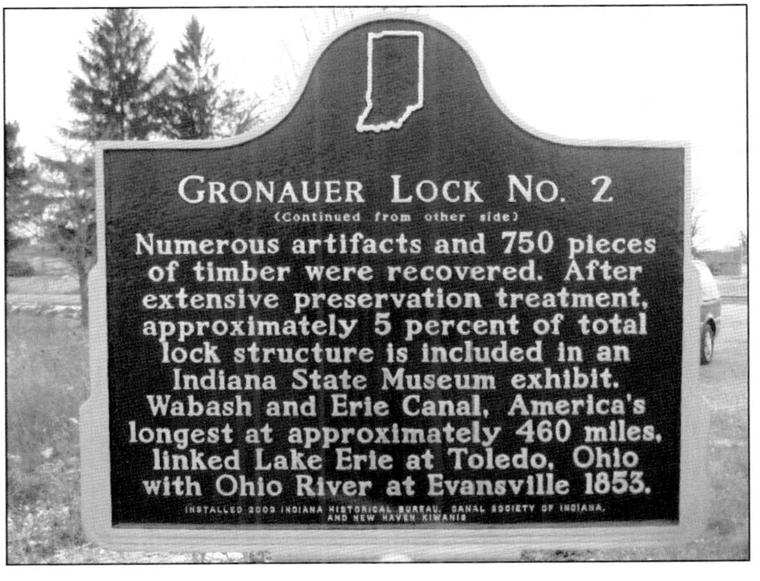

The New Haven Area Heritage Association found a generous and anonymous person who sent two semitruck beds to Indianapolis to bring portions of the lock home and store them. They remain where they are today, awaiting a worthy project that will use them to their advantage and offer protection. (Mary McCaig, Fort Wayne Newspapers, 1992.)

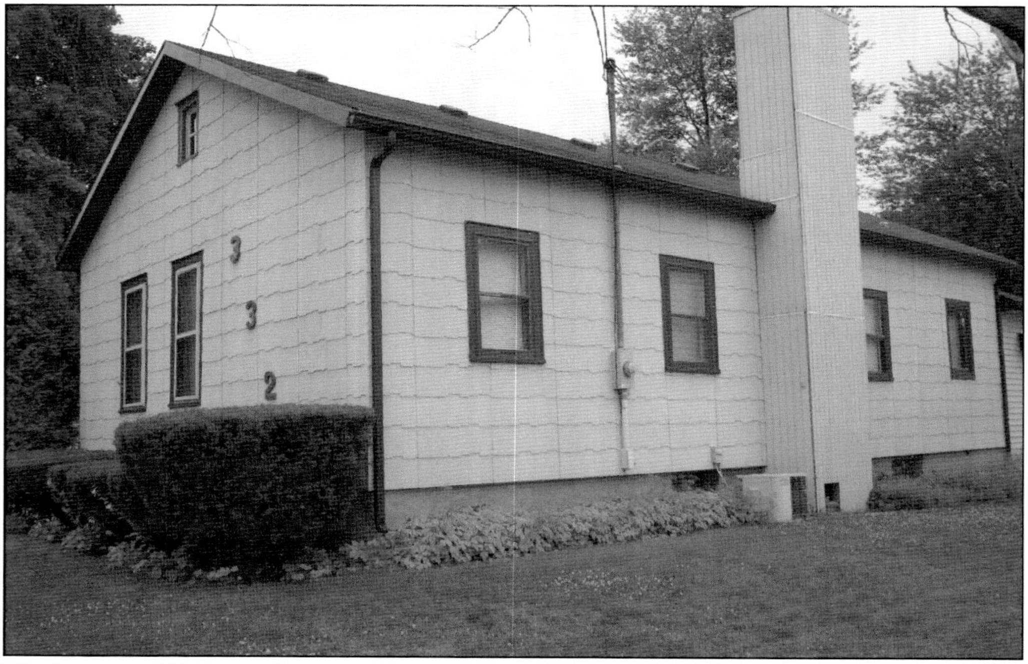

The house at 332 Green Street had been a cooper's shop of the Indiana Stave Company. It was at this location that barrels were assembled and loaded onto canal boats. The canal was located a few feet north of the building. The north side of the present building was the entrance in 1870. (Stevia Webster.)

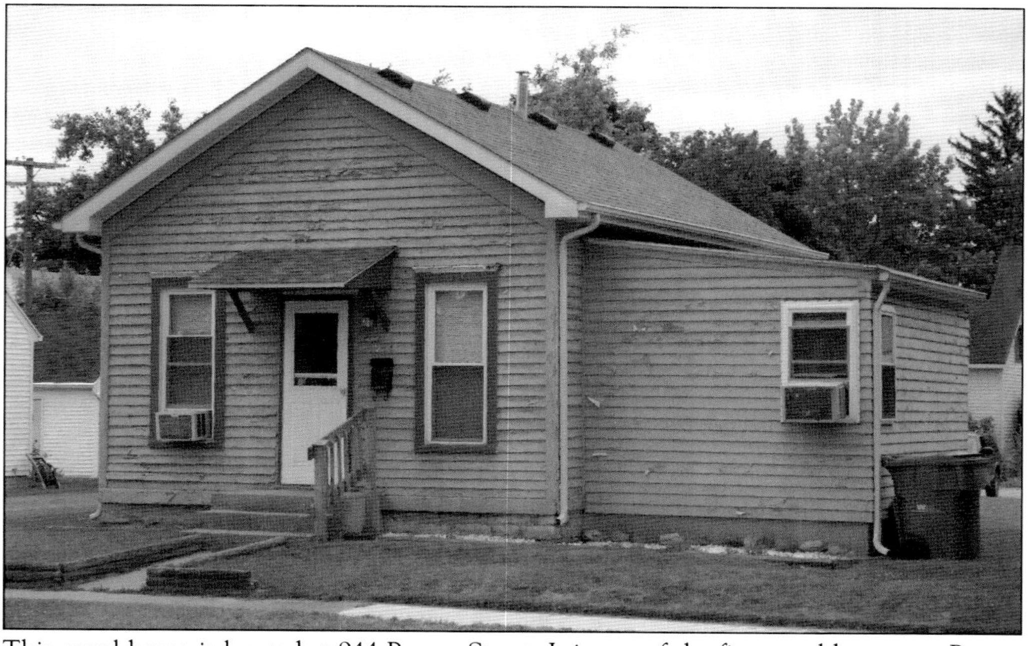

This canal house is located at 944 Powers Street. It is one of the five canal houses on Powers Street listed in Mitch Harper's 1980 study of architecture of older homes. Mitch is from New Haven. (Stevia Webster.)

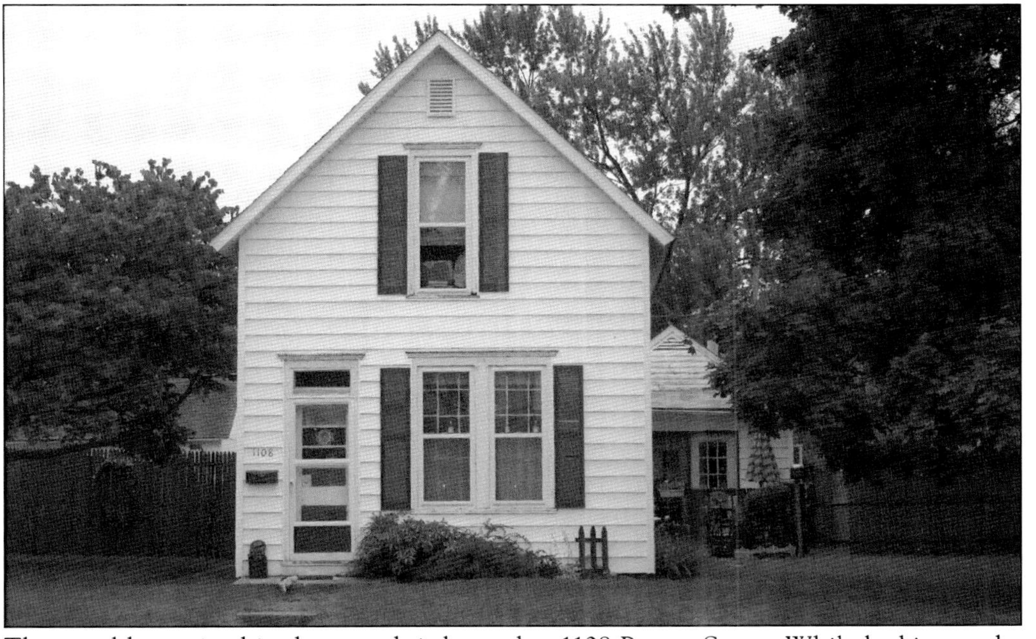

The canal house in this photograph is located at 1108 Powers Street. While looking at the photographs of these three houses, note the likeness of them. They are long and narrow with windows set low to the ground. Some had wings built onto them in later years. (Stevia Webster.)

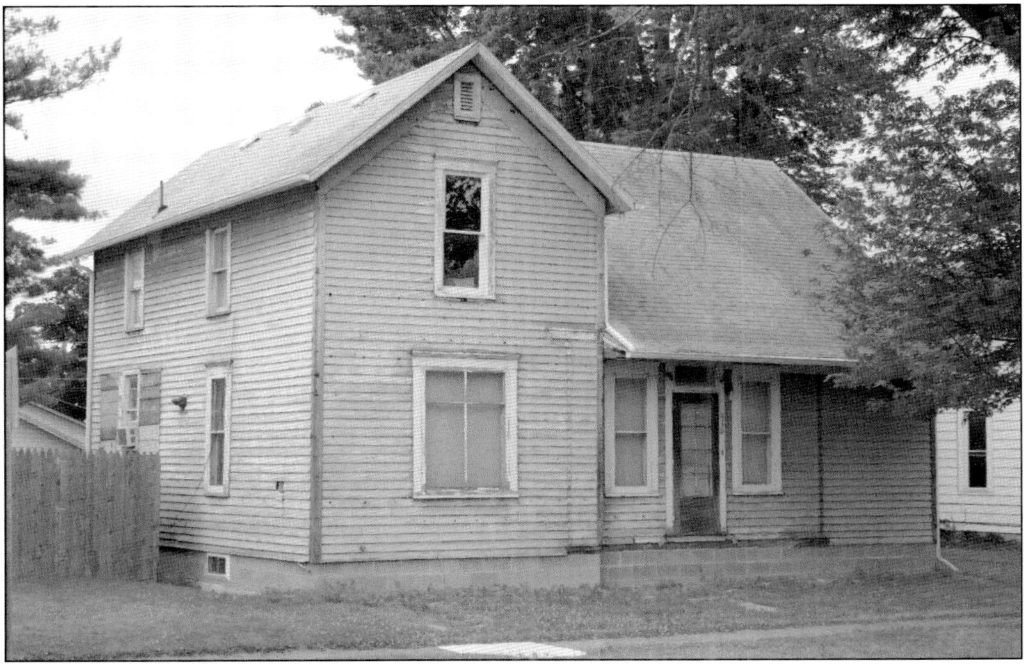

A little different from the two previous houses, the house at 916 Powers Street has been raised within the last three years to accommodate a basement. The windows sit higher because the structure was elevated. The wing on the right side may have been added later. (Stevia Webster.)

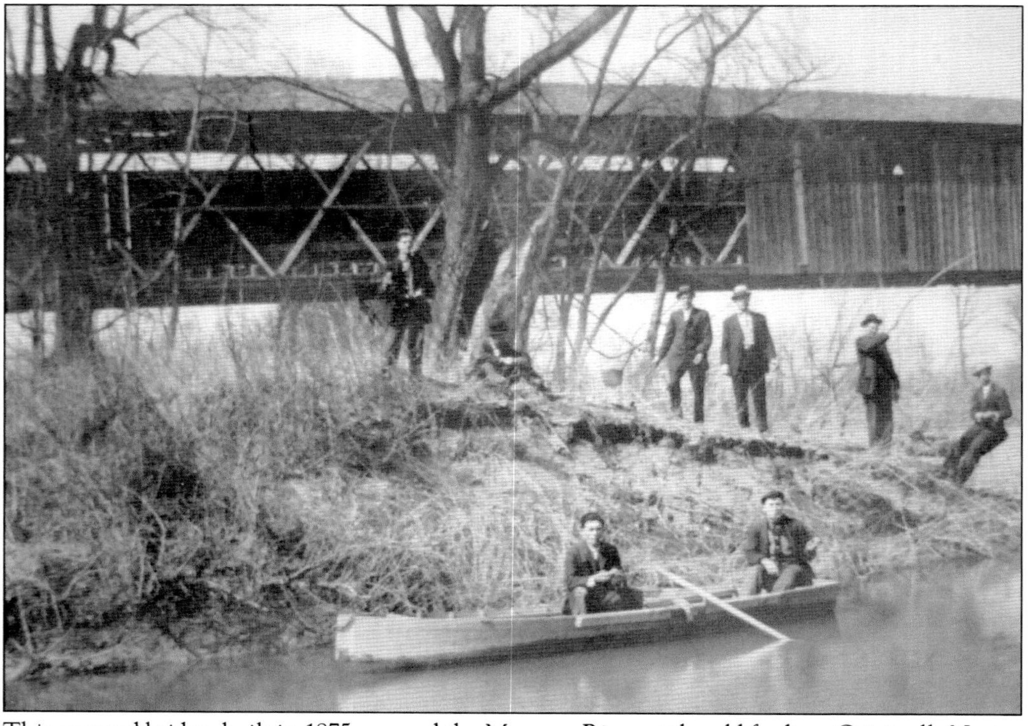

This covered bridge, built in 1875, crossed the Maumee River at the old fording. Originally Native Americans, settlers, and animals crossed here. In 1904, a storm took off the roof and sent it down the river. A newspaper account tells of a dad hoping to surprise his wife by wearing a new suit home. He took off his old clothes on the bridge and threw them into the water. He and his son looked for his new suit in their wagon but found that it was gone. The son asked his dad what he was going to do and his dad replied, "Surprise your mother." (St. Louis Catholic Church and Jeff Hoffman.)

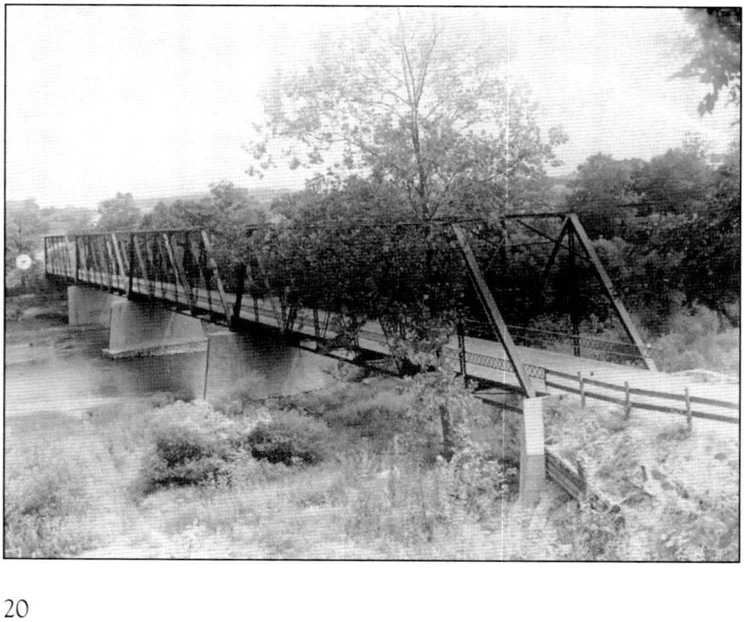

The covered bridge at Rufus Street (left) continued to deteriorate and was not safe, so it was replaced in 1912 with a towering steel bridge. It crossed the Maumee River and the mouth of Trier Ditch with two narrow bridges that had a sharp turn. The old buttresses remain. In 1913, a terrible flood washed out part of the new bridge. Loads of large rocks, helped to shore it up. (Todd Baron.)

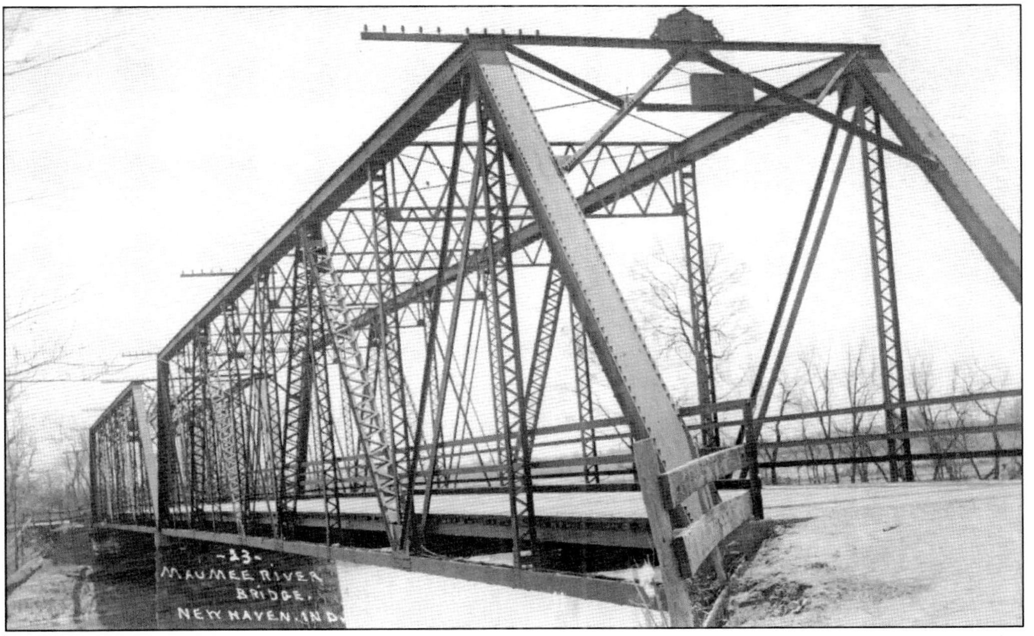

Because of the sustained damage from the 1913 flood, another smaller bridge replaced the Rufus Street bridge in late 1913. In 1966, a new road—Landin Road—extended from Broadway Street to the north. A new concrete bridge was installed, and the steel bridge on Rufus Street was torn down. (Indiana Historical Society, 90391.)

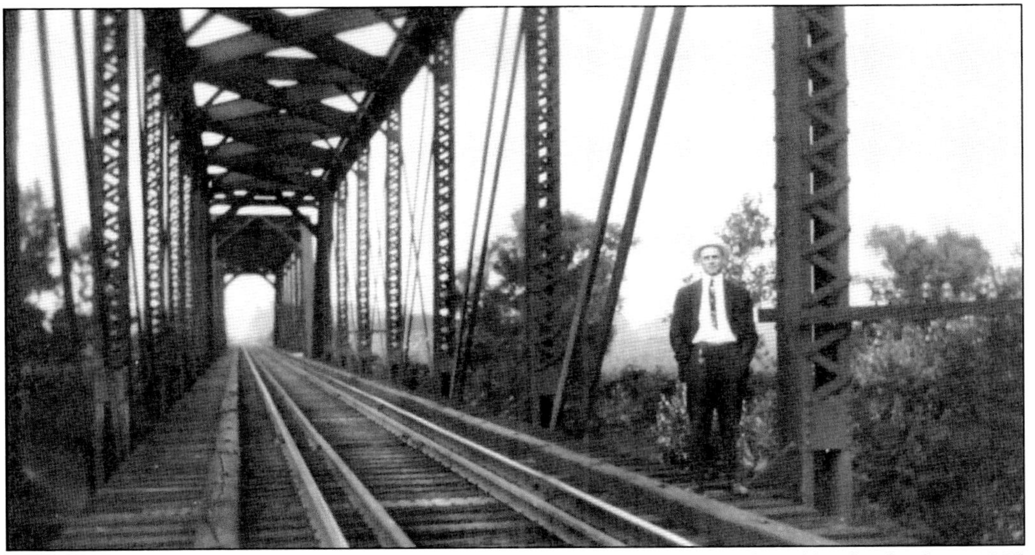

Constructed from a simple structure beam called a truss, this iron railroad bridge built in 1905 spans the Maumee River. A celebration was held at the bridge's dedication. It brought trains into New Haven from the northeast and is still in heavy use today. Its design was influenced by 19th- and 20th-century concepts, making it the oldest type of the iron truss bridges still used today. During the great Maumee Flood of 1913, water rose to the deck of the bridge and threatened to wash it away. A heavily loaded coal train was positioned across the span to weigh it down. (Jo Anne Smith.)

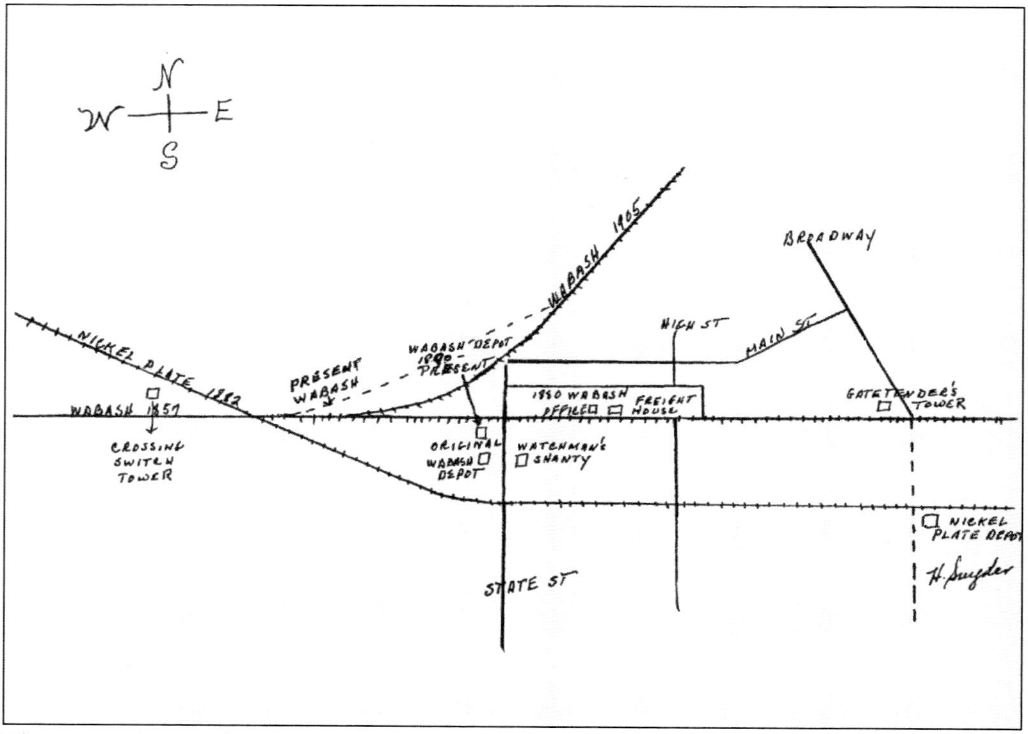

This map indicates where some of the area's railroad buildings were located, but more importantly, it details where two major train accidents occurred. The dotted line illustrates where the tracks were straightened, since two accidents happened on that curve. The first wreck was in 1937 and resulted in one death, that of engineer David Kiracofe of Detroit. The second accident occurred in 1951. (Hilda Snyder.)

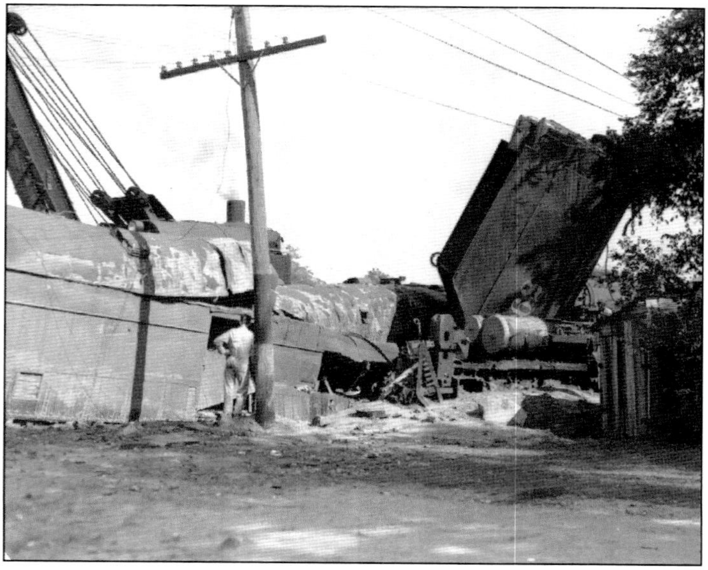

In 1937, the Detroit-St. Louis Wabash Flyer hopped the track east of State Street. The engine and cars left the tracks on an "S" curve; the road was a single track at the site of the disaster. The train plowed along 180 feet of the right-of-way before coming to rest in the backyard of Charles Brandon at 603 West Main Street. (Walter Sassmannshousen.)

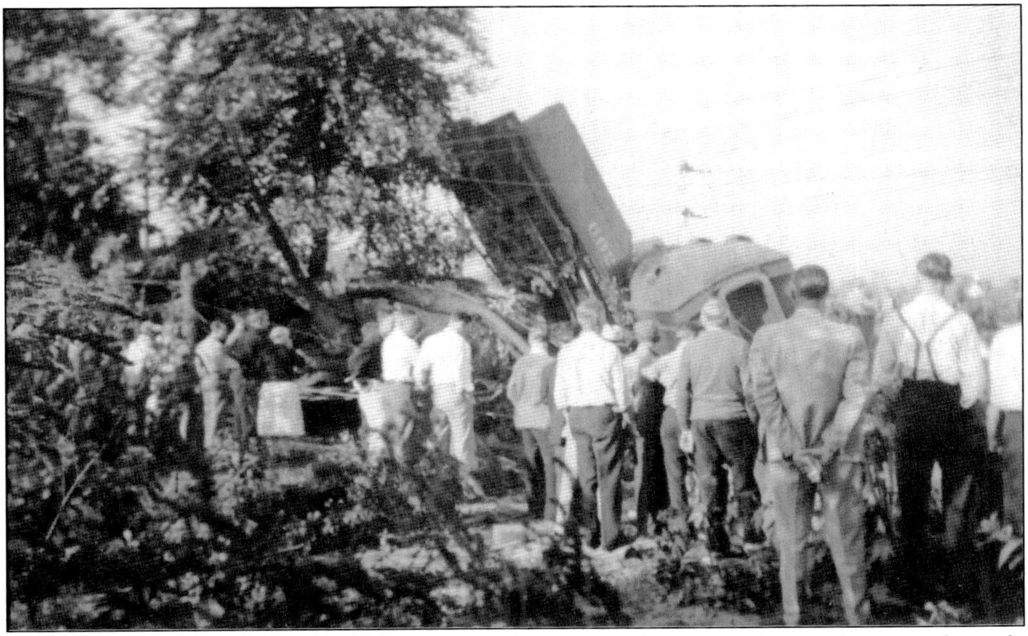

The first mail car was badly damaged in the 1937 train wreck. The engine tender seemed to ride up on the locomotive as the brakes were applied. It came to rest crazily upended against a tree beside the home of Charles Brandon at 603 West Main Street. If the tree had not been there, the house would have been involved in the accident. One set of engine wheels and axle was thrown over a tree as the locomotive tipped on its side. (Todd Baron, Walter Sassmannshousen, and Fort Wayne Newspapers.)

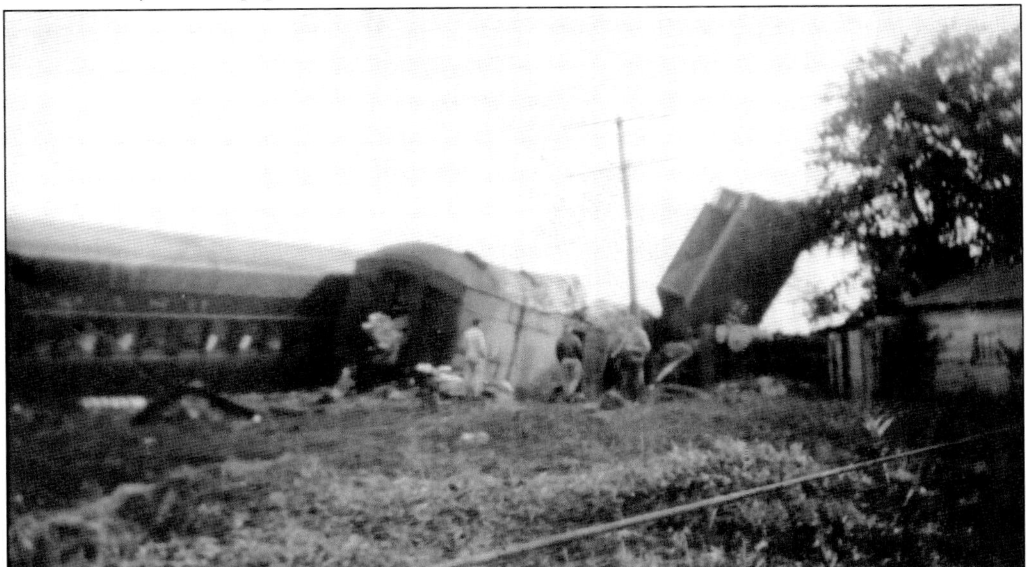

Engine trucks landed between the Brandon house and garage, damaging the garage. The baggage car rolled across Main Street and came to rest many feet from the tracks. Debris from the wreckage was cleared away. The locomotive in which engineer David Kiracofe rode to his death was half-buried in the ground; it was lifted last from the wrecked train. (Todd Baron.)

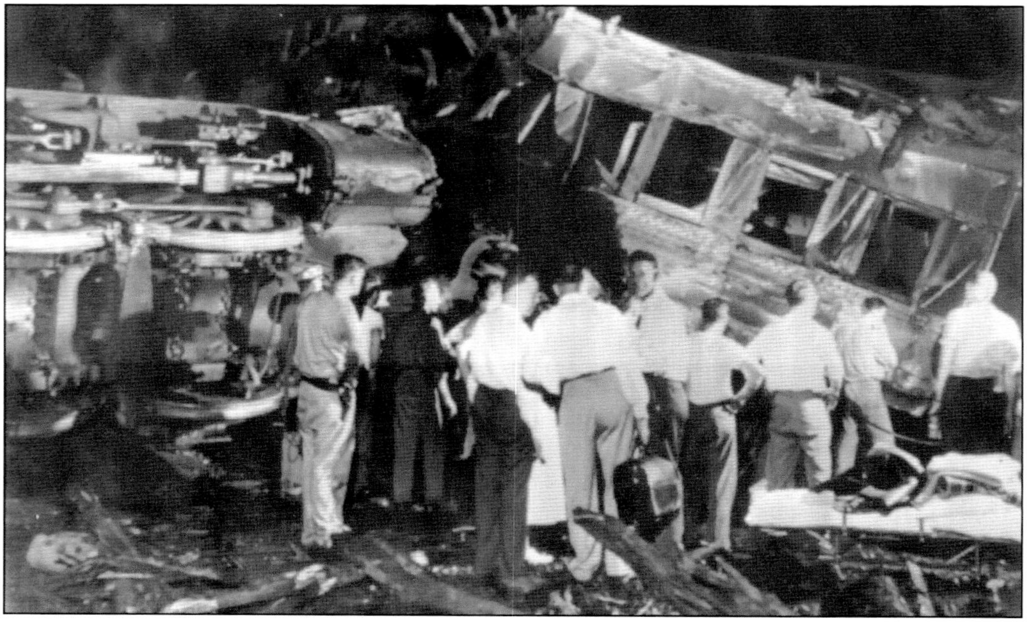

In 1951, this Berkshire 767 from the Nickel Plate Railroad was traveling at 60 miles per hour when it flashed past the New Haven station and entered the home stretch. A dispatcher in Fort Wayne saw from the train control that a wreck was imminent and called ambulances. As the engine cleared the depot, F. J. Hosler, the engineer, was horrified to see a Wabash Railroad passenger train on the crossover, 1,400 feet ahead. (Todd Baron, Walter Sassamannshousen, and Kenneth Keller, *Fort Wayne Journal Gazette*.)

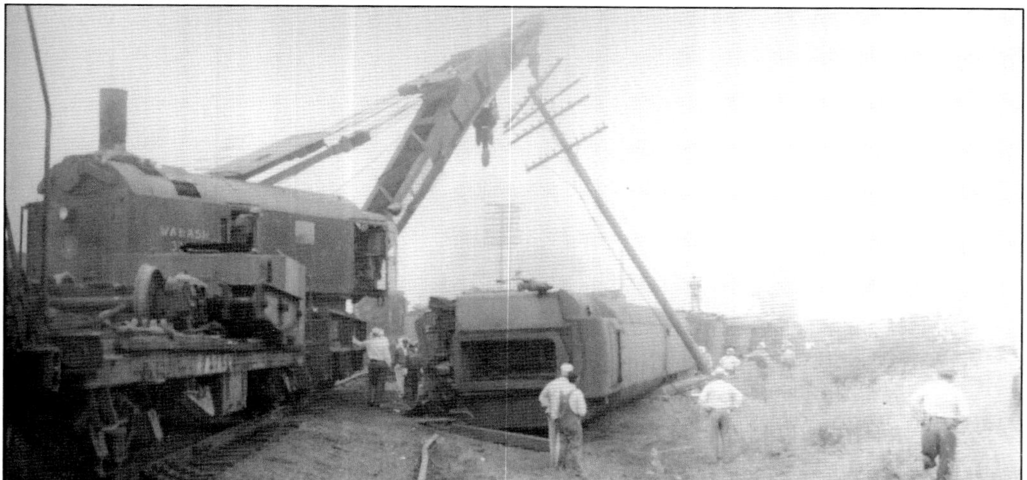

As Hosler recalled, he shut off steam and applied the air brake. Robert L. Kelley, the brakeman, gripped a stoker valve with both hands and then the thunder came as they plowed into the passenger train. The roar of escaping steam awakened most of New Haven. With the first impact, the engineer's side of the cab was compressed, squeezing Hosler against the valves and levers. Then the Berkshire toppled on its side, the steel of the cab bulged, and Hosler was tossed to the other side of the engine. (Todd Baron, Walter Sassamannshousen, and Kenneth Keller, *Fort Wayne Journal Gazette*.)

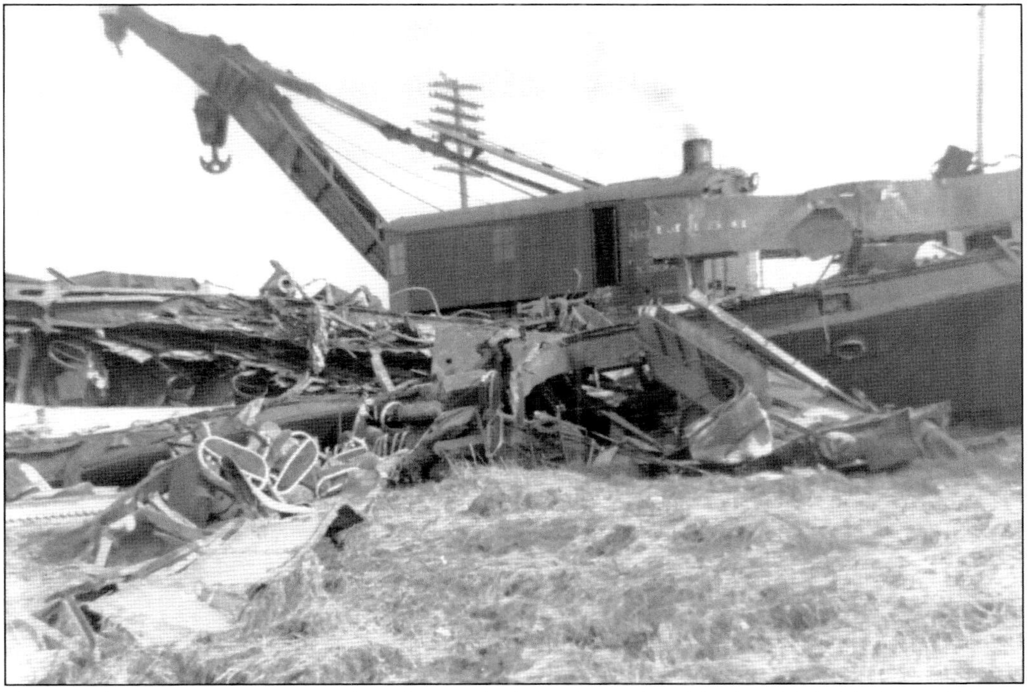

The fire doors gaped open and white-hot coals lighted the shambles in which Hosler and Kelley lay. "Consciousness came and went," Hosler said, "and I tried to reach up and close a steam valve nearby but my legs would not raise me." His hip had been shattered, among other injuries. Kelley stirred and saw flames spurting from the engineers dungarees. He dragged the helpless engineer out of the wreckage. There were four fatalities in the 1951 wreck—all were aboard the Wabash Railroad train. The seven-car passenger train was shattered and tossed. Members of the freight crew included fireman William J. Connors and flagman William Warner and conductor I. C. Bell, who were both riding in the caboose. (Todd Baron, Walter Sassamannshousen, and Kenneth Keller, *Fort Wayne Journal Gazette*.)

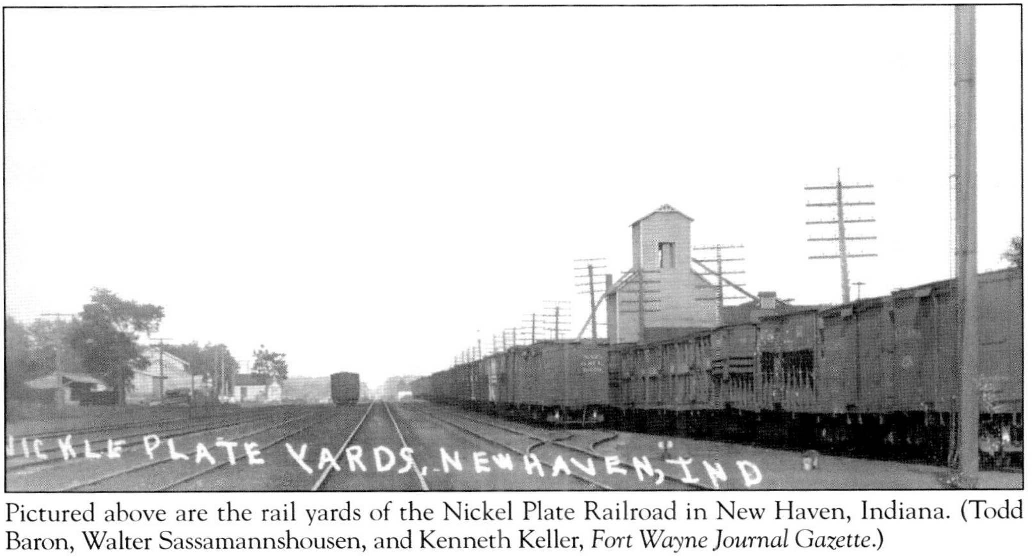

Pictured above are the rail yards of the Nickel Plate Railroad in New Haven, Indiana. (Todd Baron, Walter Sassamannshousen, and Kenneth Keller, *Fort Wayne Journal Gazette*.)

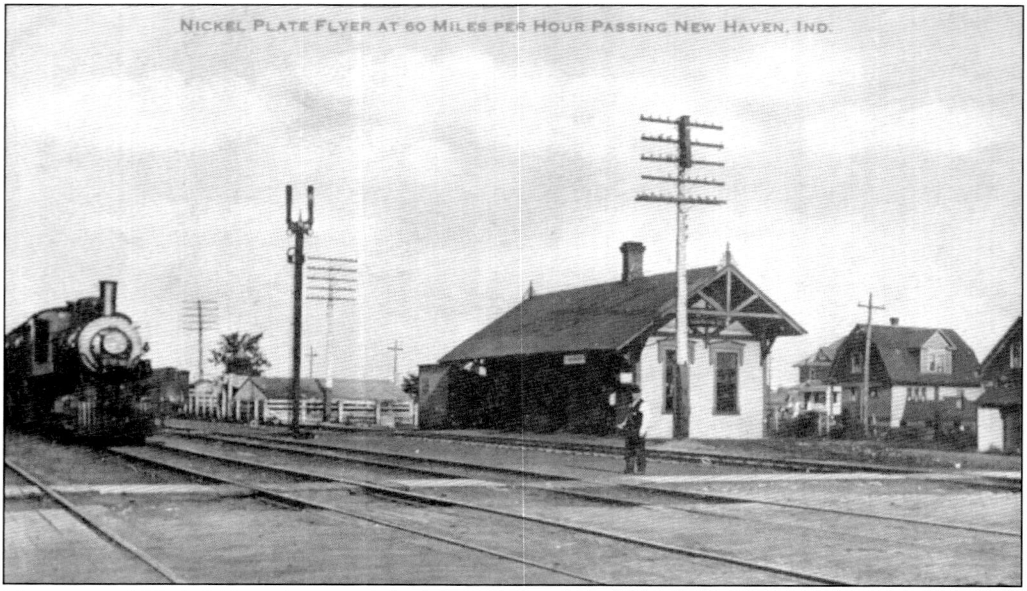

The original Nickel Plate depot was built in 1881 and stood at the southeast side of the tracks on State Street. The second Nickel Plate depot (above) was built in the early 1900s on the southeast side of the tracks on Broadway Street. In this photograph, the Nickel Plate Fast Freight is coming through at 60 miles per hour. Its engine was restored sometime after the 1951 accident. Notice the stockyards sitting along the tracks. (Bonnie Rinard and Terry McDonald.)

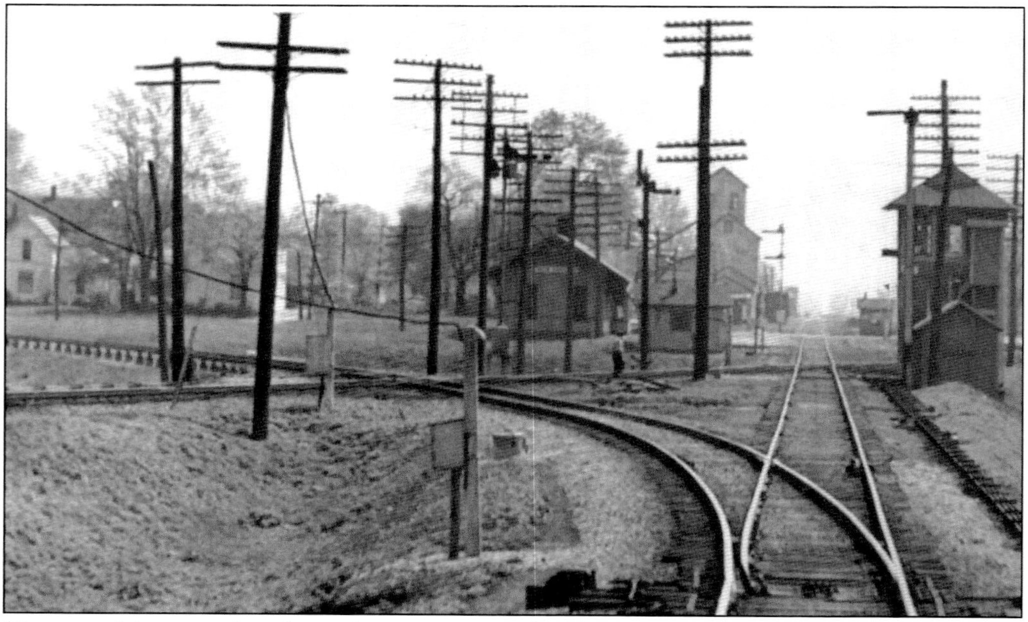

Compare this maze of tracks to the map on page 22. The curve in the track traveling to the left is the beginning of the dangerous turn that caused two accidents. The building on the far right is the watchtower and across the tracks is the Wabash depot; both are located at the State Street crossing. Some buildings have been added or moved since the illustrated map on page 22 was created. (Walter Sassmannshousen.)

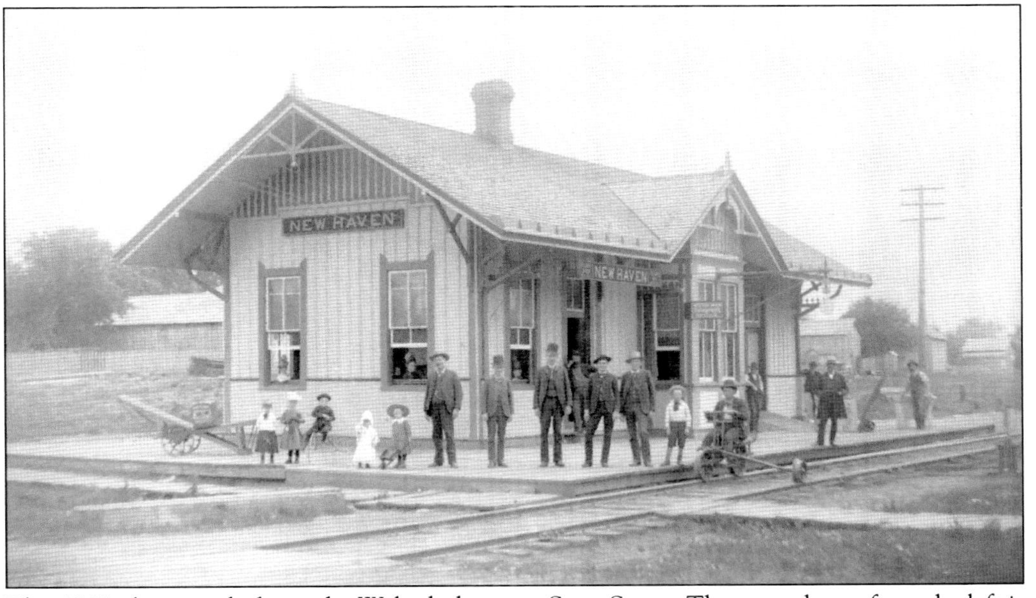

This 1900 photograph shows the Wabash depot on State Street. The second man from the left is station master John Henry Brudi. The fourth child from the left, dressed in white, is his daughter, Esther Brudi Elson. This depot is slated for restoration through grants secured by the New Haven Area Heritage Association. Work will begin during 2010–2011. (Jo Anne Smith.)

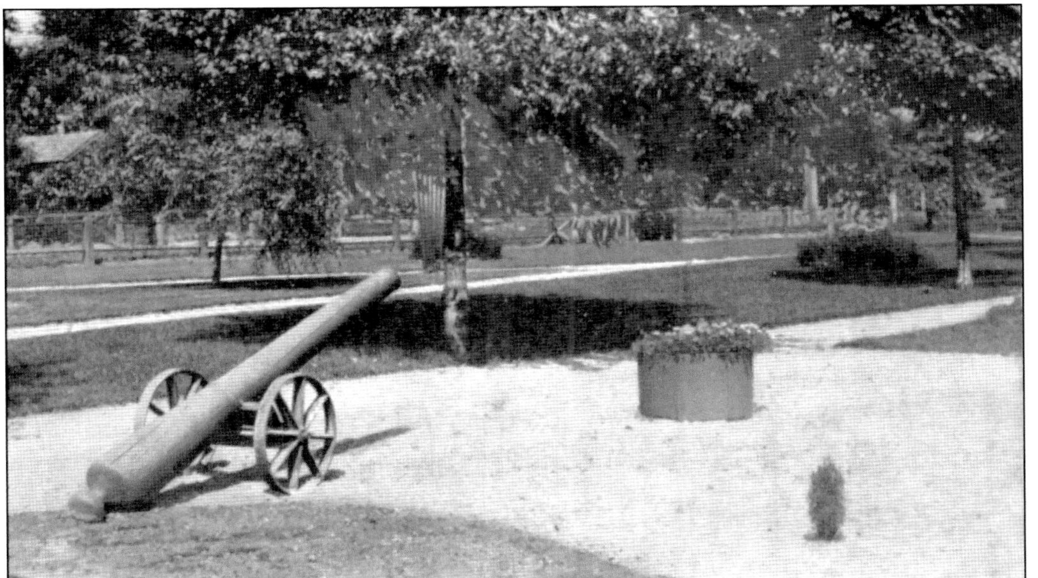

In the mid-1800s, New Haven had one Wabash depot and one station agent who worked 14 hours a day. In 1857, the Wabash Railroad president ordered that all station agents establish a park and maintain it. The park was located on the northeast side of State Street and across from the depot. The soil was very poor due to dumping the cinders from the fired coal that operated the engines, but the station agent was able to grow coleus and cannas. The photograph above shows the park in 1908. Later the park was left to nature, the weeds took over, the cast iron cannon and planter rusted away to nothing, and the park disappeared. (Todd Baron.)

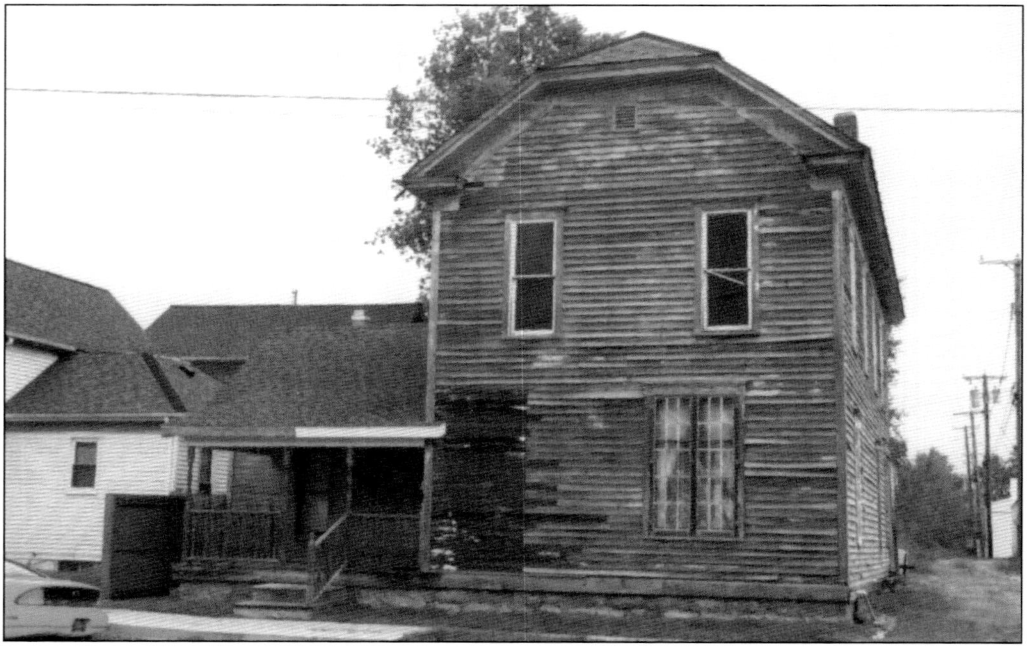

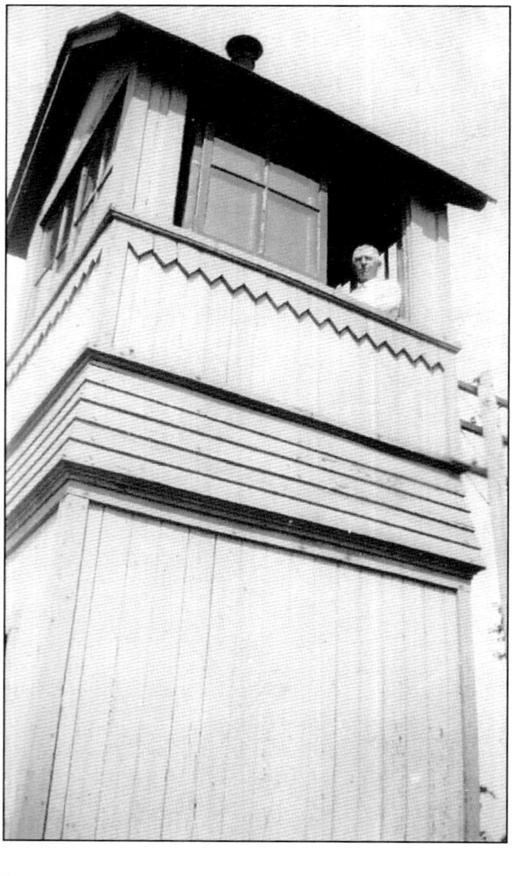

Pictured is the original railroad hotel as it is now, on the east side of State Street. It is across from the Wabash depot and north of what was Wabash Park. It is exciting to see all of these places come alive and know what their original purposes were. (Stevia Webster.)

This watchtower overlooked the Broadway crossing. The man at the window, looking down, is William Richard. He lowered the gates when an oncoming train was approaching the crossing. (Kenneth Richard and Douglas Runyan.)

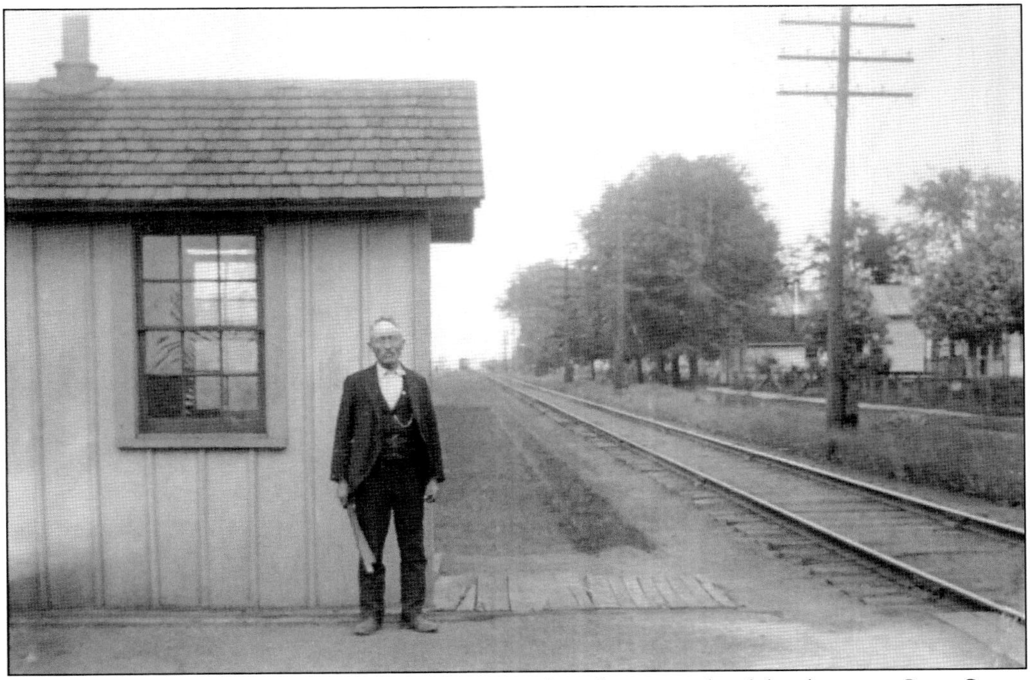

In 1910, before gate crossings, George Dennis stood on the west side of the shanty at State Street and warned road traffic when a train was coming. Notice the houses, to the right, along Center Street. The railroad company built some of the houses for their employees to rent. The Wabash depot is located at this crossing too. (St. Louis Catholic Church and Jeff Hoffman.)

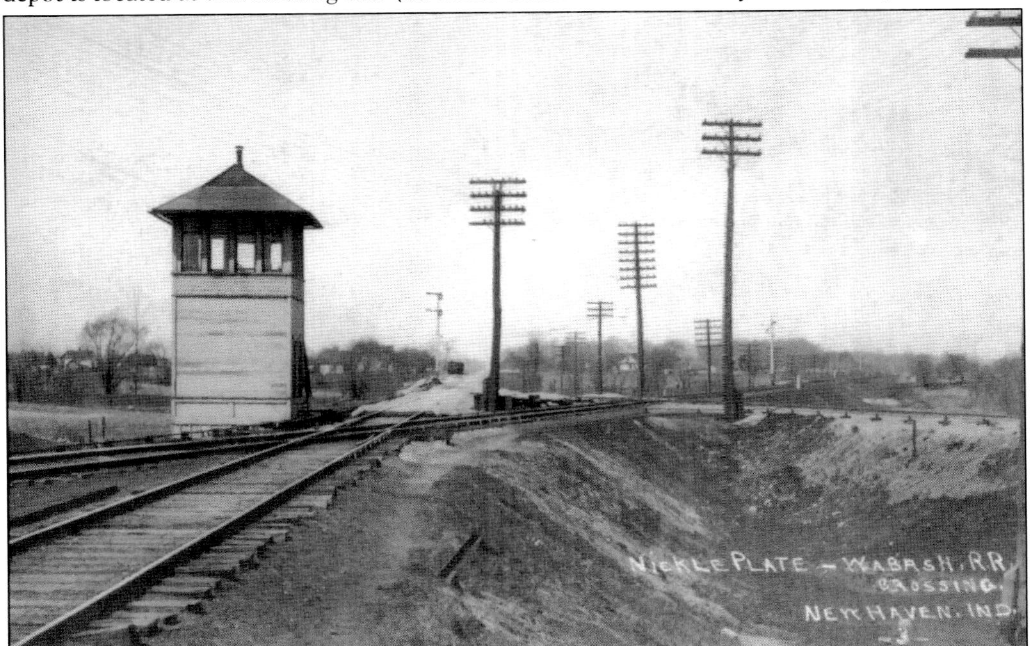

This view shows the Nickel Plate-Wabash Railroad crossing in New Haven. The watchtower is not standing today. (Walter Sassmannshousen.)

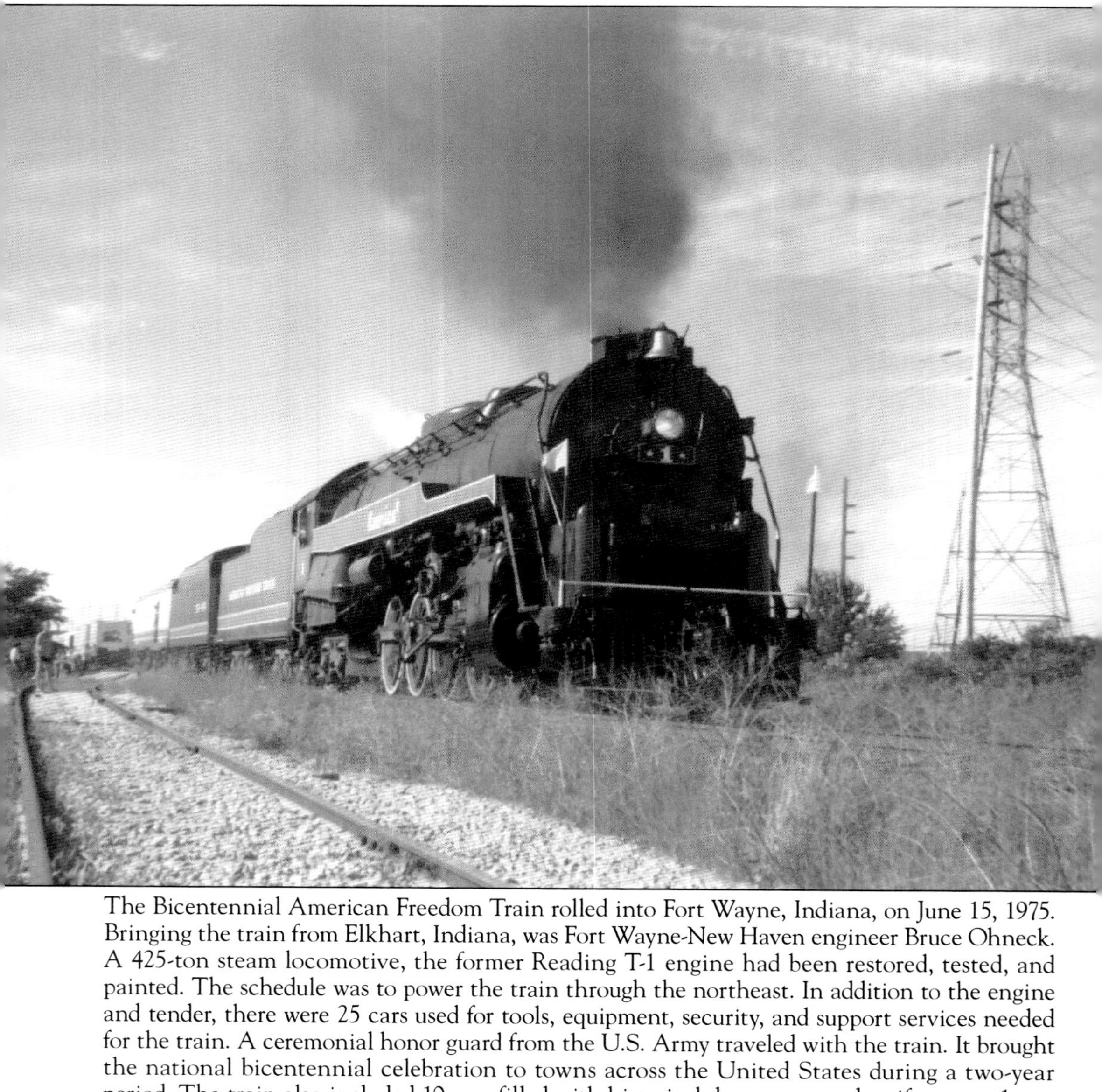

The Bicentennial American Freedom Train rolled into Fort Wayne, Indiana, on June 15, 1975. Bringing the train from Elkhart, Indiana, was Fort Wayne-New Haven engineer Bruce Ohneck. A 425-ton steam locomotive, the former Reading T-1 engine had been restored, tested, and painted. The schedule was to power the train through the northeast. In addition to the engine and tender, there were 25 cars used for tools, equipment, security, and support services needed for the train. A ceremonial honor guard from the U.S. Army traveled with the train. It brought the national bicentennial celebration to towns across the United States during a two-year period. The train also included 10 cars filled with historical documents and artifacts: car 1 was themed the war of independence; car 2, pioneers opening the West and later outer space; car 3, growth and transportation; car 4, immigrants; car 5, review of the inventors and technicians; car 6, creative labor and professions and the diversity of their work; car 7, the sporting American car; car 8, performing arts; car 9, paintings that portray America from the 18th century; car 10, dramatic portrayal of five events in American history; and showcase cars. The second car carried the Freedom Bell, which was twice the size of the Liberty Bell. (Walter Sassmannshousen and Hazel Ohneck.)

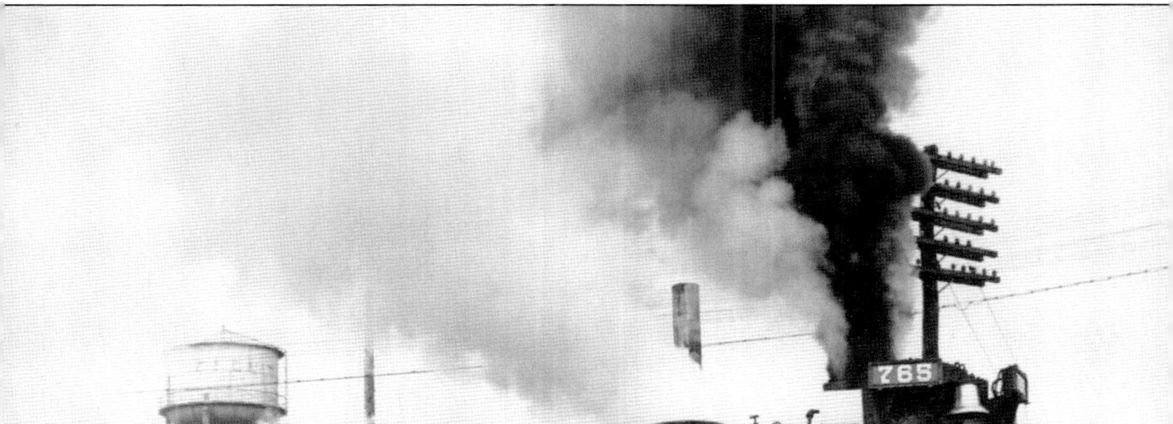

As engine No. 765 belched a plume of black smoke into the October sky, steam billowed out from underneath it and its whistle pierced the air. The photograph shows the train at the Estella Avenue crossing in 1950. Built in 1944 at Lima Locomotive Works, the Berkshire-type steam engine was born. This steam engine was on display in Lawton Park from about 1961 until it was removed in 1974. The Nickel Plate No. 765 then underwent a five-year rebuild by the Fort Wayne Railroad Historical Society. In the early 1980s, No. 765 traveled through the Midwest and East Coast as an excursion train. It was again retired in the early 1990s and rebuilt to its 1944 specifications. On Memorial Day 2010, the engine began the second phase of its career as an excursion train. The engine uses its capacity of 22 tons of coal to travel about 150–200 miles. It can cost between $4,000 and $8,000 a day to operate it, not including insurance and other costs. (Todd Baron and Rebecca Green, *Fort Wayne Journal Gazette*.)

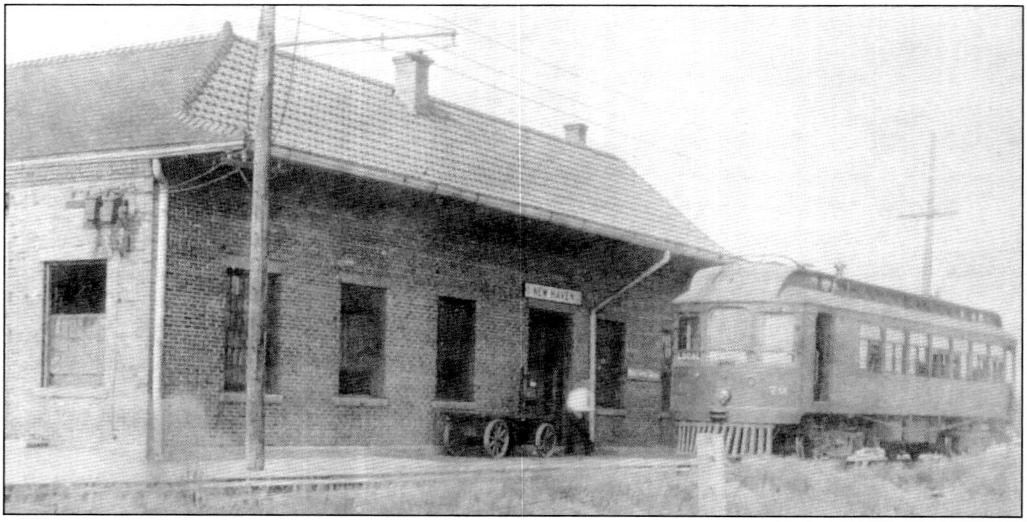

This photograph was taken on March 24, 1904. The Fort Wayne, Van Wert, and Lima Electric Company's interurban train line started rolling in April 1903. The station was located on the northwest corner of Broadway Street and Dawkins Road. The interurban train was replaced by a privately owned bus line in the early 1930s. The Fort Wayne Transit Company now serves the New Haven Area. (Walter Sassmannshousen and the 1966 *New Haven Centennial History* book.)

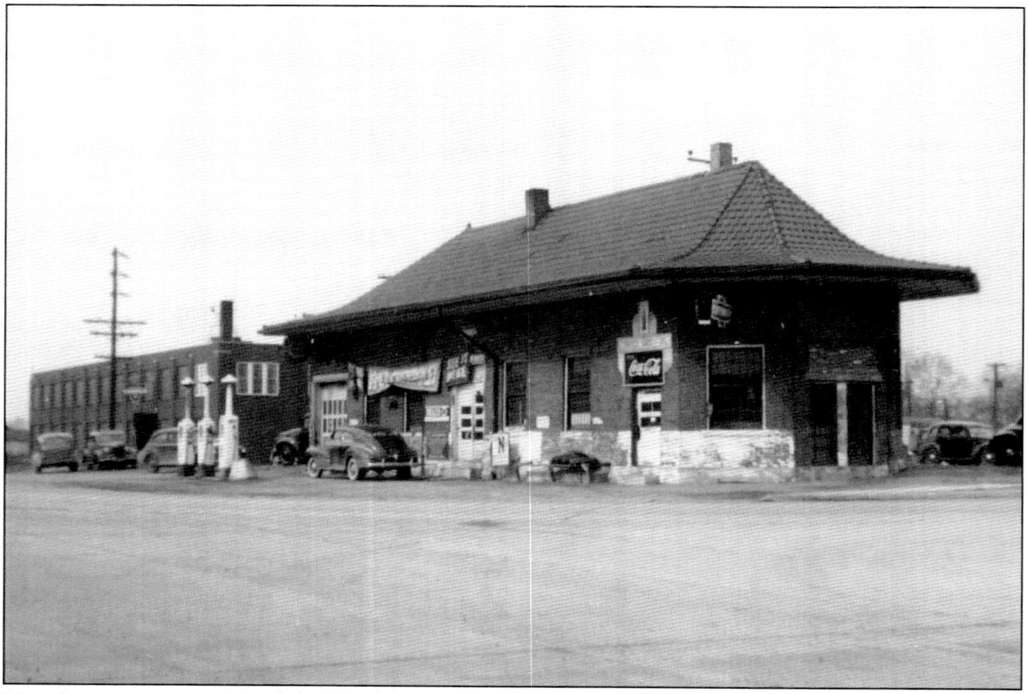

New businesses give new life to old buildings; the interurban train building was about 40 years old in this photograph. In 1942, it hosted a gas station. It is in the same location. The building to the left housed several businesses: the Meyer Pump Company operated there in 1914, then the Knitting Mill, and lastly Bennetts Manufacturing, which produced men's clothing. That structure was torn down to make room for the New Haven City Hall. (Sue Asher Bradley.)

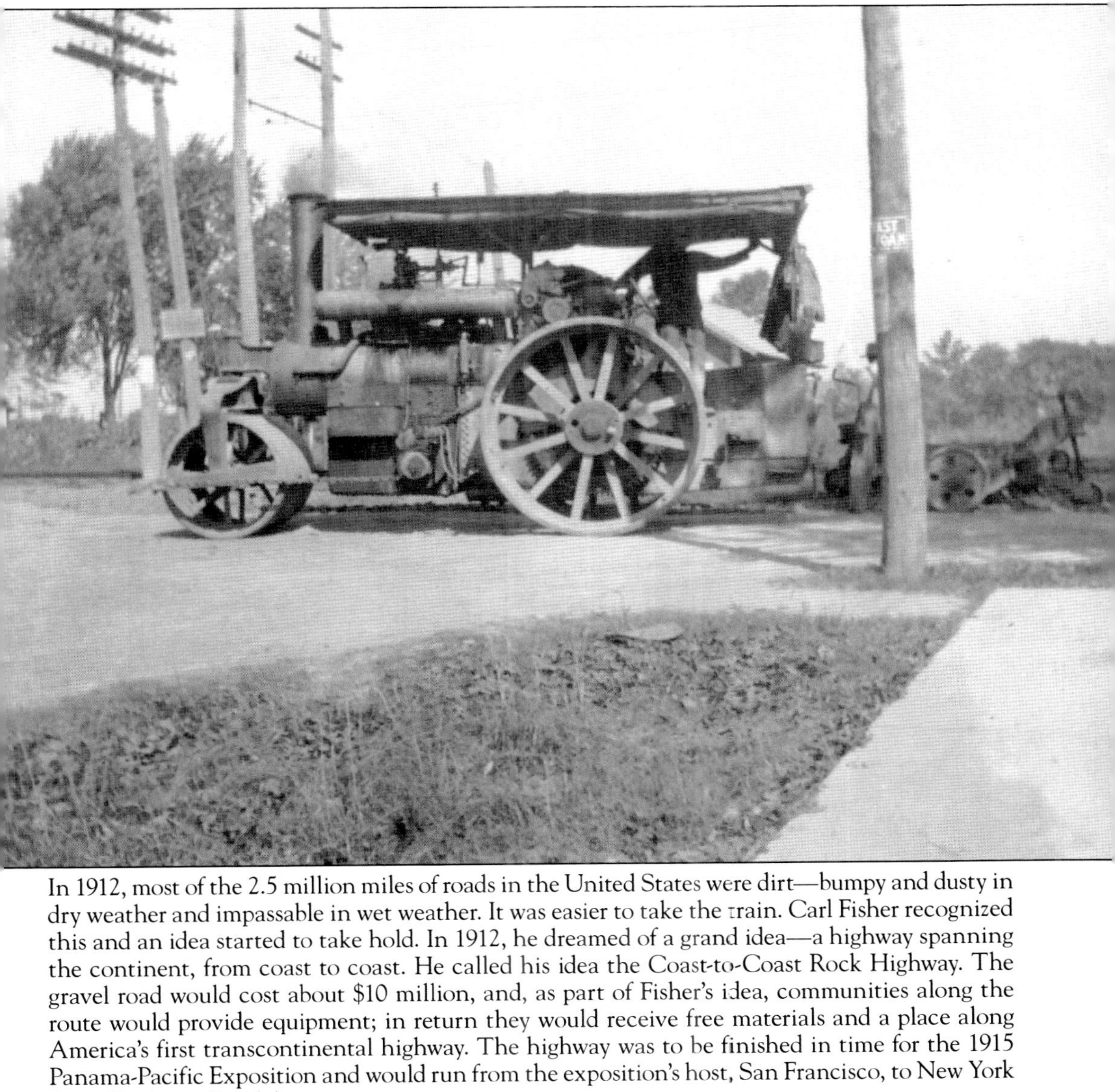

In 1912, most of the 2.5 million miles of roads in the United States were dirt—bumpy and dusty in dry weather and impassable in wet weather. It was easier to take the train. Carl Fisher recognized this and an idea started to take hold. In 1912, he dreamed of a grand idea—a highway spanning the continent, from coast to coast. He called his idea the Coast-to-Coast Rock Highway. The gravel road would cost about $10 million, and, as part of Fisher's idea, communities along the route would provide equipment; in return they would receive free materials and a place along America's first transcontinental highway. The highway was to be finished in time for the 1915 Panama-Pacific Exposition and would run from the exposition's host, San Francisco, to New York City. (Jo Anne Smith.)

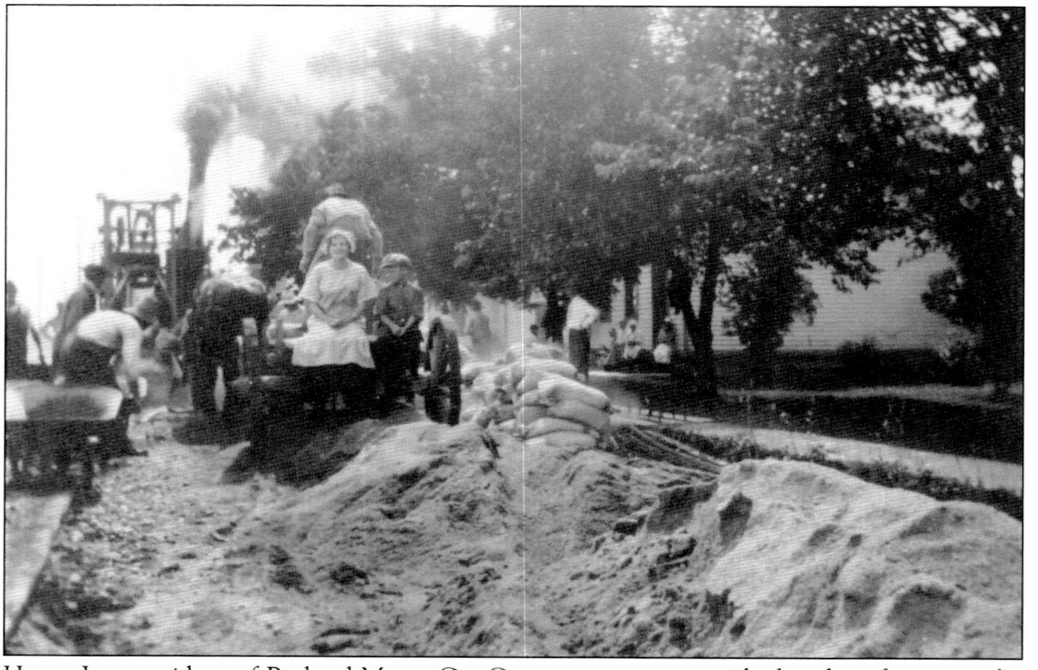

Henry Joy, president of Packard Motor Car Company, came up with the idea of naming the highway after Abraham Lincoln. He wrote Carl Fisher urging him to draft a letter of protest to Congress, which was considering spending $7 million on a marble memorial to Lincoln. The name "Lincoln" captured Fisher's fancy; he realized it would give great patriotic appeal to the highway. Joy became the primary spokesman for the highway project. (Jo Anne Smith.)

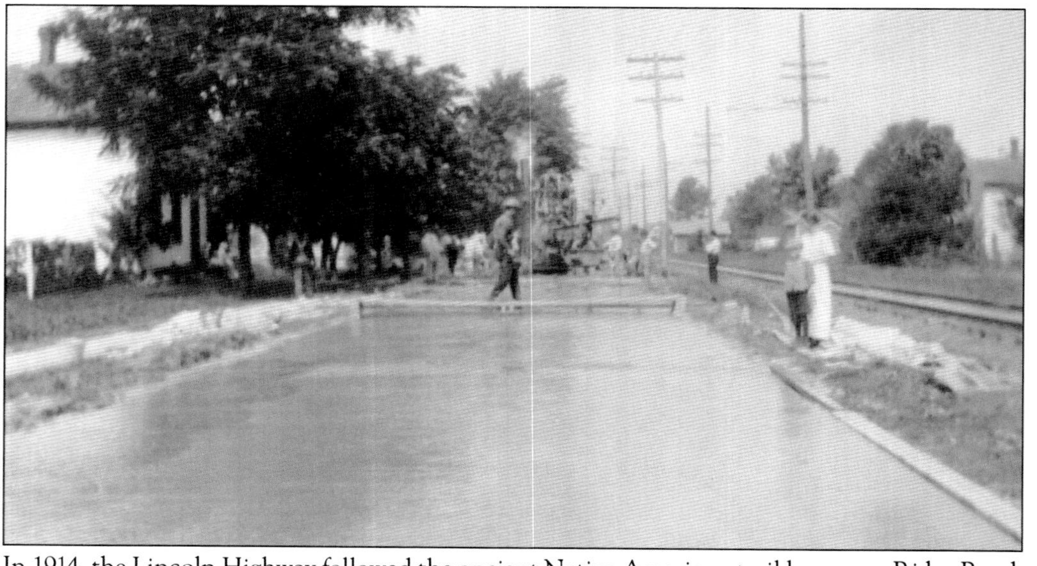

In 1914, the Lincoln Highway followed the ancient Native American trail known as Ridge Road, bringing the highway to New Haven's doorstep from the east. Concrete was laid in the 1920s. The orders were for 110 feet of right-a-way (55 feet on each side of the road) and pavement that was 40 foot wide and 10 inches thick. The load limit was 8,000 pounds. In this photograph, machinery can be seen that is ready to lay the concrete. (Jo Anne Smith.)

Two

Early Businesses in New Haven

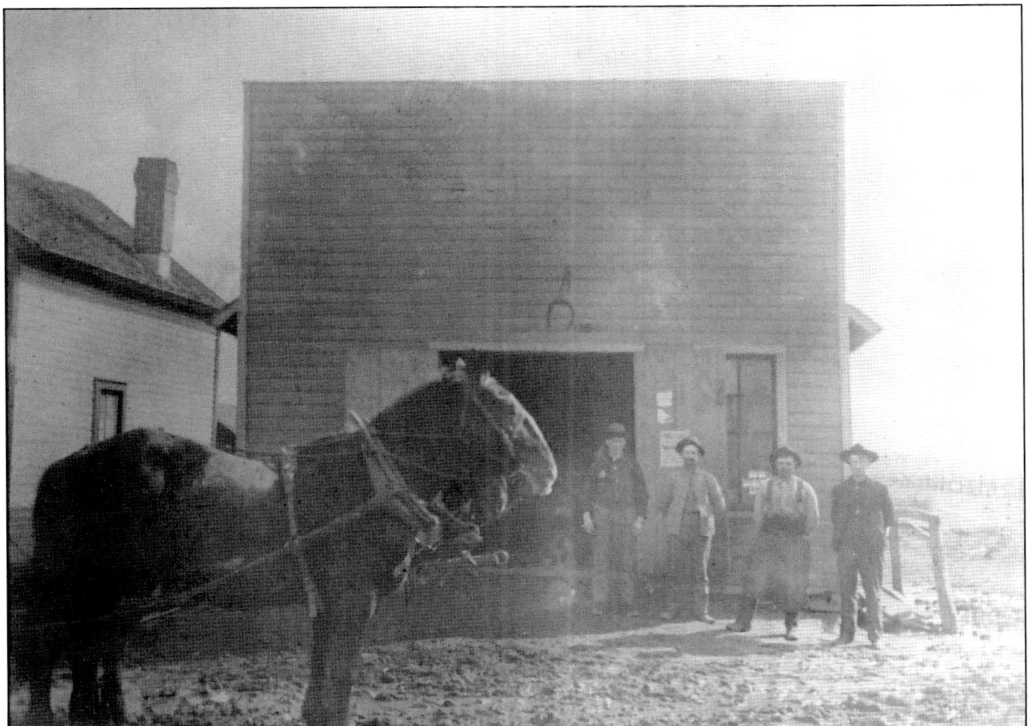

This is one of the first photographs of a local blacksmith shop. In early days, blacksmiths were almost as plentiful as gas stations are today. The horses, farm equipment, and everyday tools of the time period required much upkeep. Four or five blacksmith shops operated in New Haven alone. (Todd Baron.)

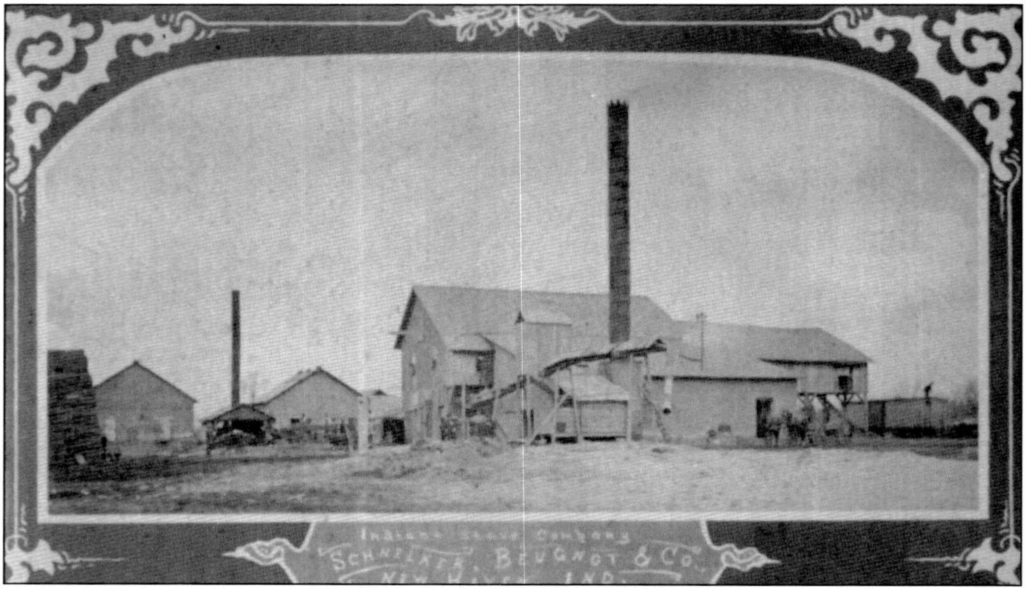

Schnelker and Beugnot, the first industry in New Haven, was the cooper shop started by John Begue in 1854. The business had a stable existence and was enlarged to include stave manufacturing. The Beugnot brothers entered the firm, which in the 1870s was reorganized as Schnelker, Beugnot, and Company and became an establishment of decided importance. This photograph is from the 1890s. (Todd Baron.)

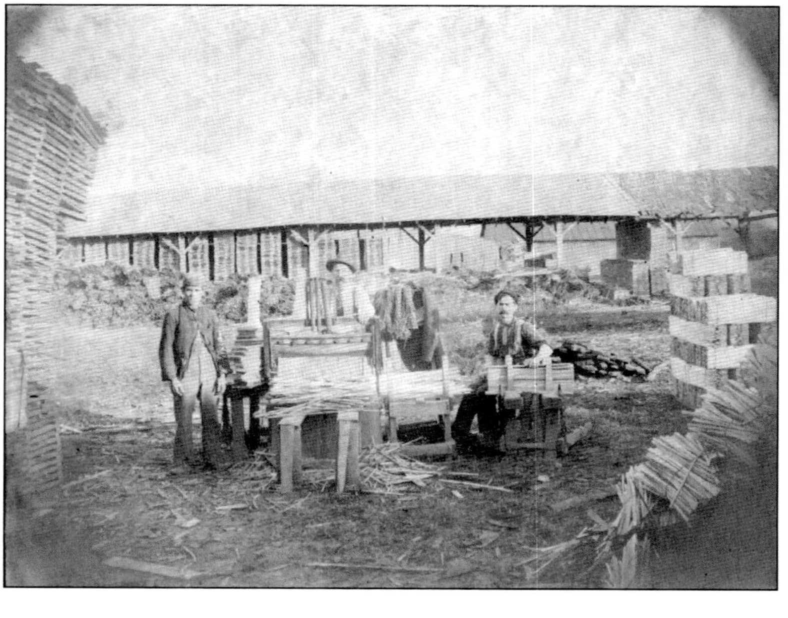

Photographed is the Schnelker Stave Factory and some of the materials employees worked with. Most of the wood was from local trees. The factory employed 95 workers and its engines consumed 12,000 cords of wood per year. The workers are, from left to right, Joe Smith, Amos Rich, and unidentified. (Todd Baron.)

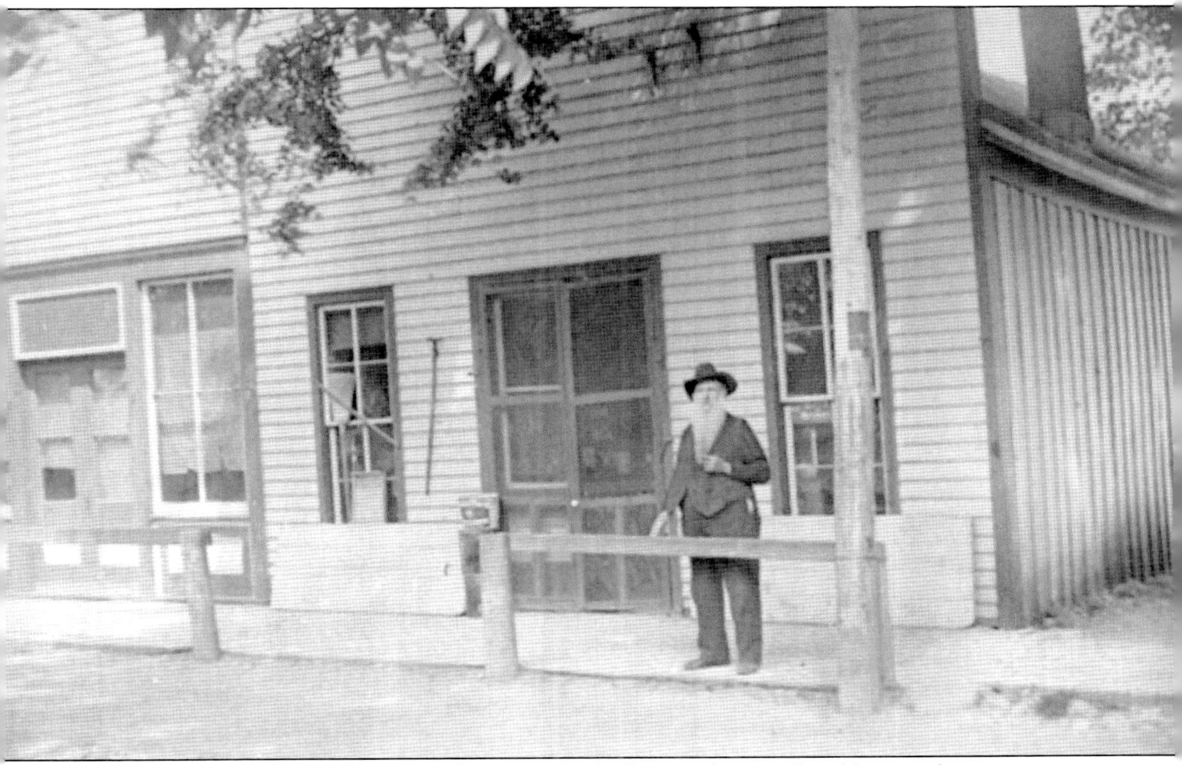

Salvador Peltier is pictured at the age of 81 in 1912. At the time he was the oldest resident in town, born in Fort Wayne on August 15, 1830. Peltier lived in New Haven for more than 30 years. An uncommonly active man for his advanced years, Peltier had his faculties of mind and very little impaired by age. He was tall and heavy built with a long-flowing white beard. His bright eyes and vigorous, easy step made him seem younger. After the Nickel Plate Railroad came through New Haven in 1880, he moved to the town and in 1881 opened the grocery store at the corner of Summit and Green Streets. It was a two-room building with his home at the back of the building. He married Catherine Valiket in 1857 and had three children. Peltier remembered that at the age of 10 he liked listening to men speak of the olden days. He especially enjoyed hearing stories of the construction of the Wabash and Erie Canal. (Fort Wayne Newspapers.)

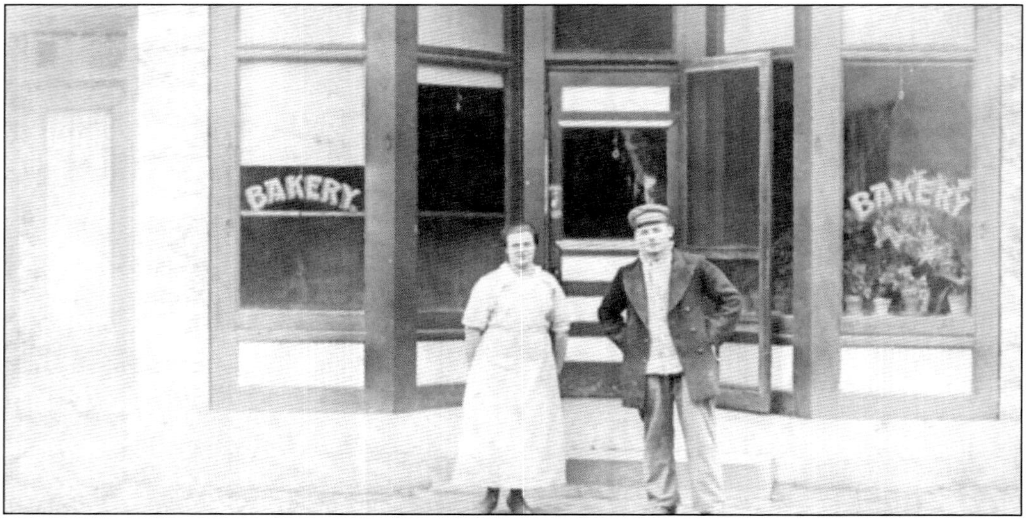

On July 6, 1912, when Conrad Stemmler was 24 years old, he came to America from Germany. He had several unsuccessful jobs in different towns until a yeast salesman told him the New Haven Bakery needed help. In December 1914, he went to work for the Helmicks, who owned the bakery, earning $10 a week plus room and board. Later Conrad bought the New Haven Bakery for $4,000. In 1915, he married Nora Zink after he met her while delivering baked goods. By 1924, the bakery employed 10 people and had six trucks and a horse and wagon. They delivered goods to Ossian, Fort Wayne, New Haven, and surrounding rural areas. The Stemmler family lived in the adjoining rooms of the bakery until 1927, when the bakery was sold because Conrad could no longer lift the heavy bags of flour. He built a gas station at 1307 Rose Avenue, which still stands today but not for commercial use. (Both, Rose Stemmler Sweet.)

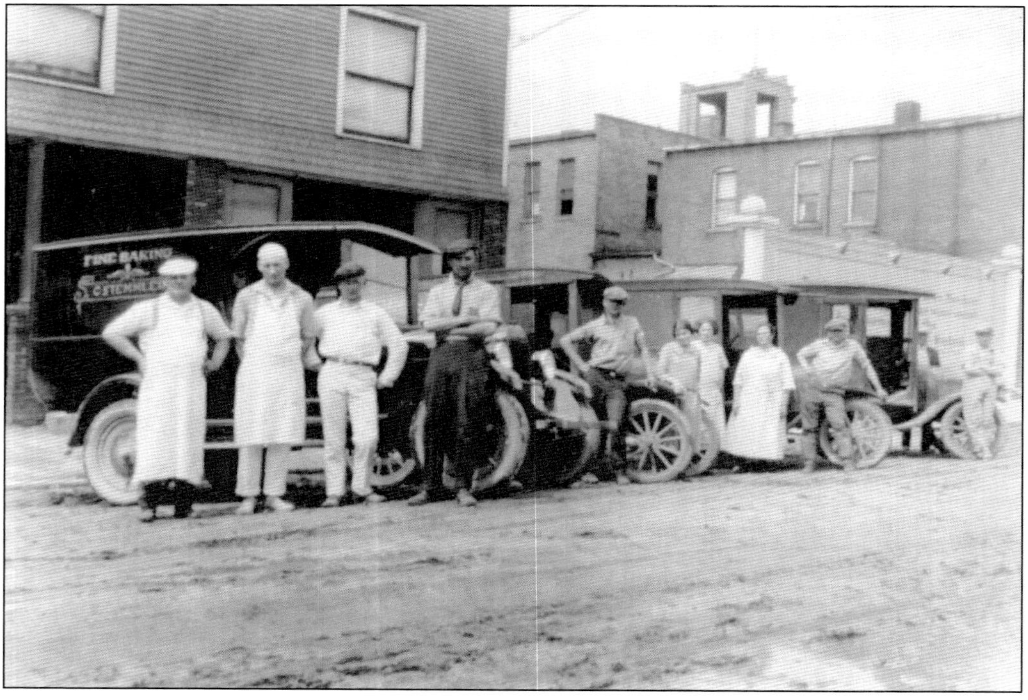

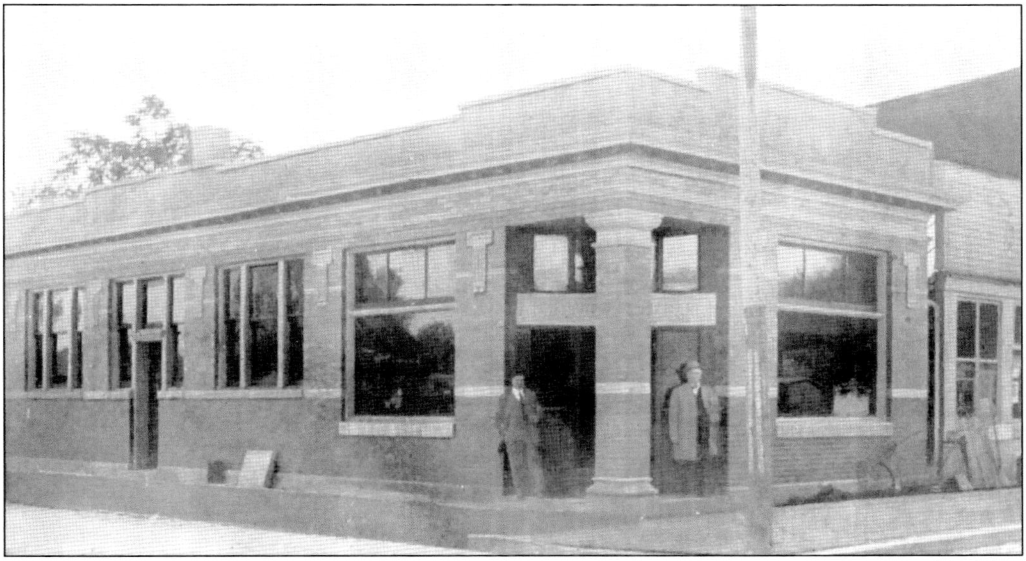

Before 1916, New Haven residents traveled to Fort Wayne for banking. A group of 200 stockholders put their resources together and founded the Peoples State Bank. In 1918, the bank moved into its newly constructed building on Broadway and Summit Streets. The bank closed in 1931, though in 1942 it reopened under the name of New Haven State Bank. In 1952, the business merged with Lincoln National Bank and Trust at 507 Broadway Street. (Todd Baron.)

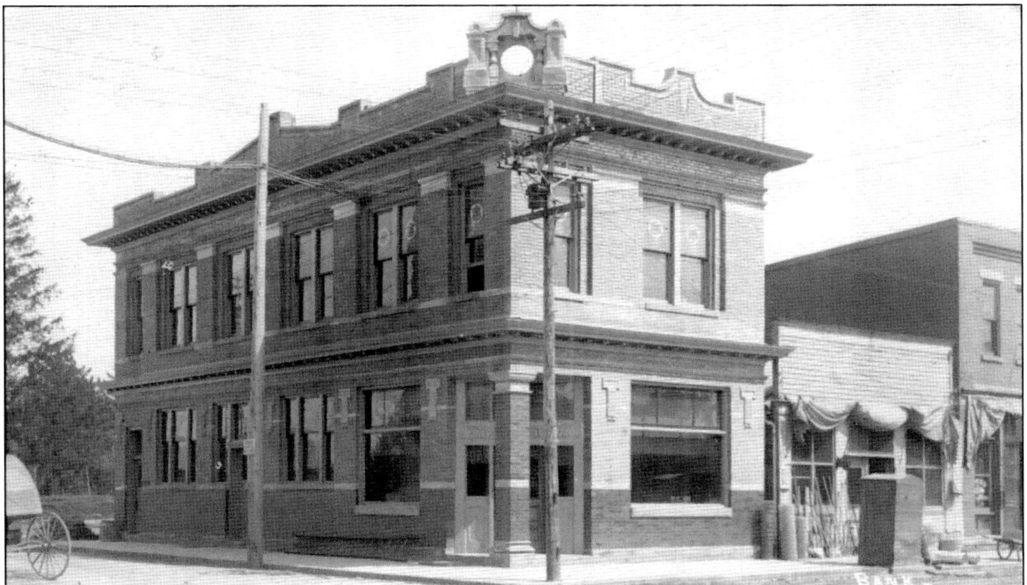

The New Haven Board of Trustees granted franchises to four telephone companies from 1896 to 1899. Telephone service began in 1901. The Home Telephone Company began "ringing bells" under the direction of D. J. Cable. The exchange was housed in the Null Building at 502 Broadway Street; later it moved to the added second floor of the New Haven State Bank building. Alex J. Merklein from Wausau, Wisconsin, installed a new clock at the corner of the building in the 1920s. (Todd Baron.)

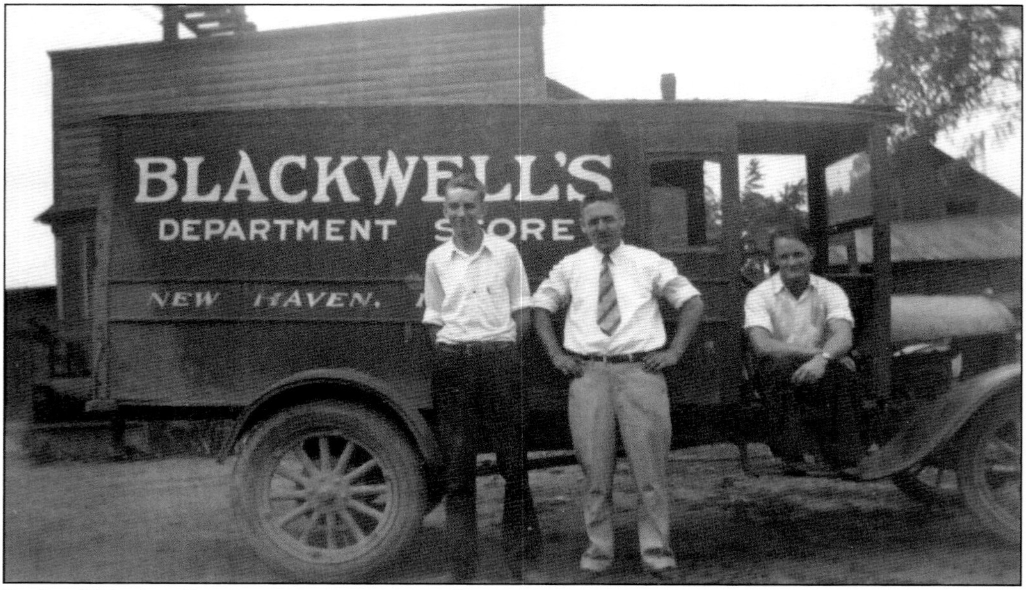

Richard Blackwell came to New Haven on business in 1908. In 1910, Blackwell and John Lomont purchased the store at 505 Broadway Street. Later Blackwell became the sole owner. It was a general department store that sold yard goods, sewing needles, work shoes, and overalls. On the grocery side, it sold sugar and flour, which were scooped out of barrels into bags. (Sue Asher Bradley and Lois Emenhiser, New Haven newspaper.)

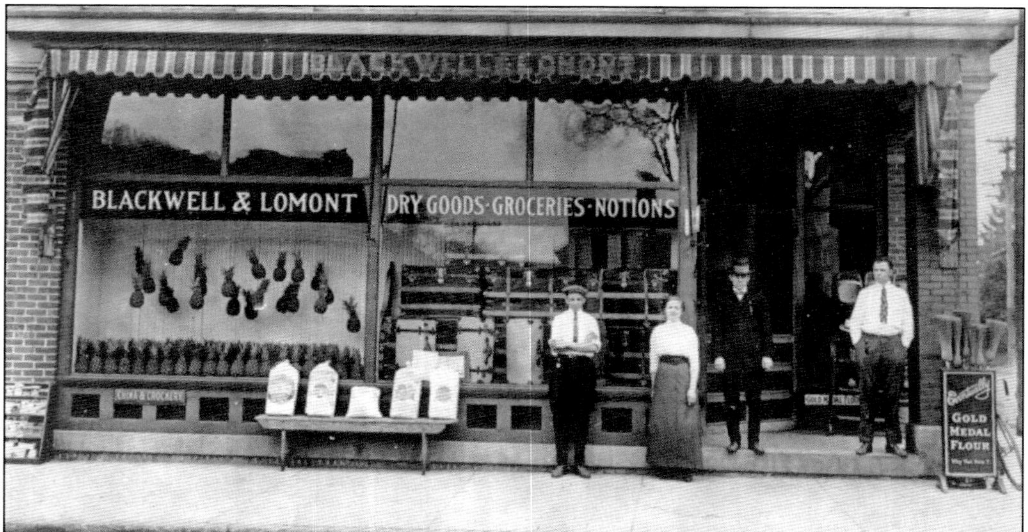

This photograph from 1915 or 1916 shows the historic department store known as the "Butter and Egg Store." In 1946, the dry goods store moved to the Meyer Building at 909 East Main Street. Soon Richard Blackwell's son Carroll became manager of the new furniture department. Richard Oliver Blackwell, older son of Richard Blackwell, continued to manage the grocery store. Richard Sr. died in 1968 and his widow lived on 810 West Main Street, in the family home. In 1973, the store at Broadway and Summit Streets sold when Richard Jr. retired. (Todd Baron and Lois Emenhiser, New Haven newspaper.)

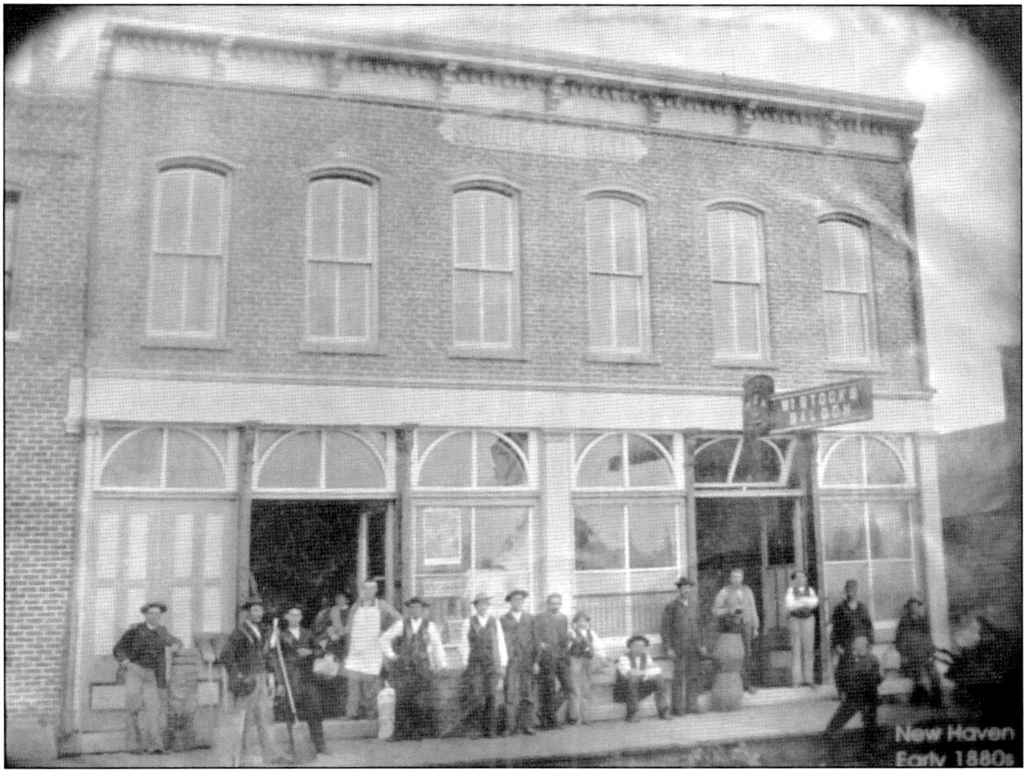

This building at 830 West Main Street is unrecognizable today. It was beautifully designed with half-moon windows, an old idea that has recycled in today's homes. The sign above the door reads "W. Stocks Saloon." The photograph above is dated 1918. Pictured at right is the same building at a later time. For many years, it was American Legion Post 330, but that group relocated west to Entrance Drive in New Haven. The Power House, a Christian group that created a safe place for teenagers after school, presently occupies the building. (Above, Dan White; right, Douglas Runyan.)

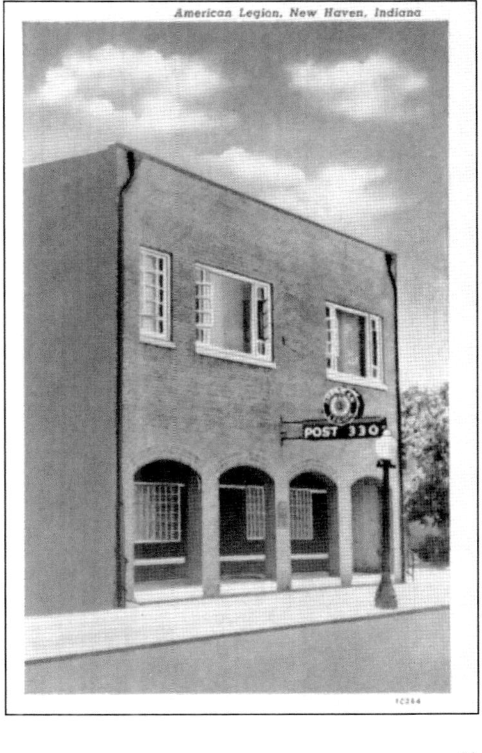

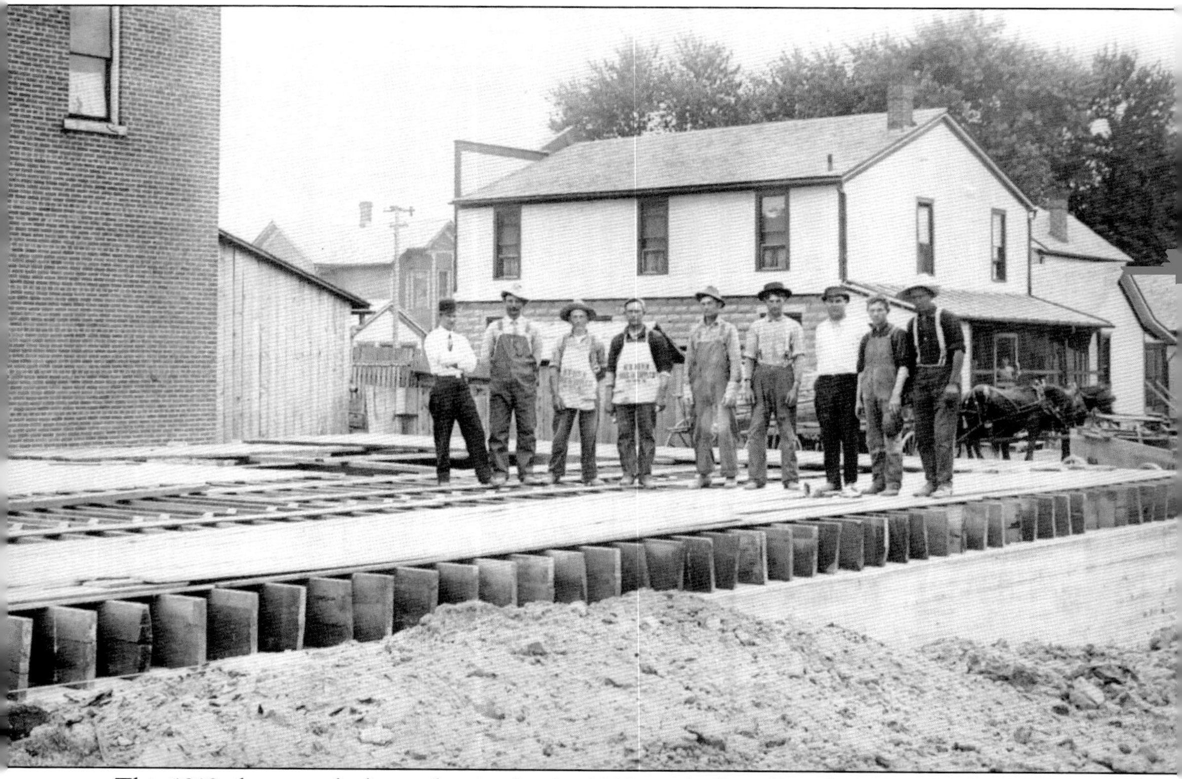

This 1912 photograph shows the site for the 1913 city hall on Broadway Street, the construction crew, and the New Haven Bakery on Main Street in the background. The fourth man from the left is August Werling. The city hall homecoming was celebrated on Labor Day of 1912. A celebration like none the city had ever seen before was planned by the volunteer fire department and included several political speakers; a huge dinner after the morning activities; and a variety of contests for adults and children, for which the merchants of Fort Wayne and New Haven donated over a hundred prizes. The most coveted contest was the "popular boy and girl" contest; the grand prize was a Shetland pony donated by Allen M. Hartzell. This homecoming was a great moneymaker, and the community raised $150 for the new city hall fund. The town board was comprised of R. E. Kaufman, Herman Grubb, and Will Schoenefeld; these men backed the firemen in their arrangements for the celebration. (Todd Baron.)

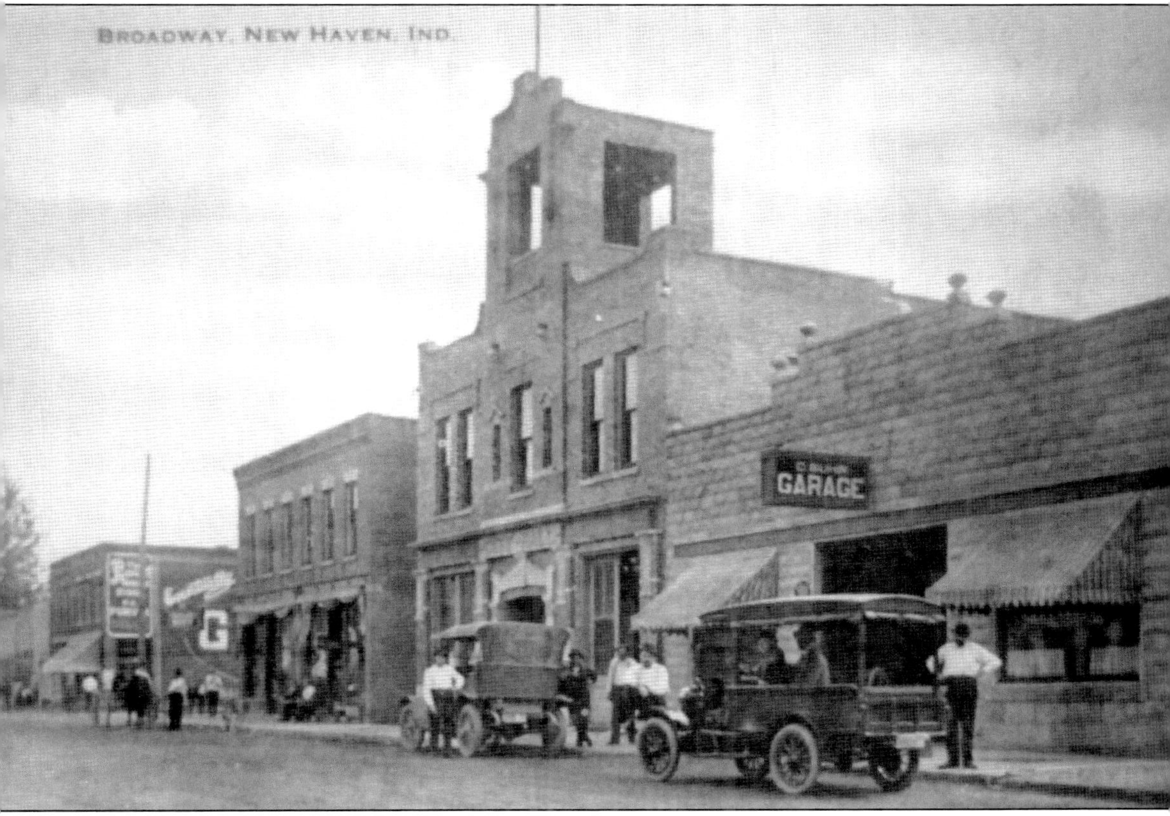

In the 1800s, the newly elected board of trustees met for one year in the Henry Burgess store. In 1881, a new town home was planned and 909 East Main Street was acquired. The building housed the fire equipment and boardroom, and also had an attached caboose. Blackwell's department store was located here in later years. In 1912, the old building was sold and the 1913 town hall was erected on the land once proudly occupied by the New Haven Flouring Mill. The new building boasted a second floor with an opry house, offices, and a boardroom. In the rear of the building, a basement entrance was installed that was large enough to house the fire equipment. The photograph above shows city hall after completion. The bell tower was removed some years later. Notice the autobus in front of C. Buhr Garage. Across the street on the corner is the Harry Purvis Drug Store. In 1920, the space to the left of city hall was built and housed a shoe store. C. Buhr Garage is currently Ruhls Furniture Store. (St. Louis Catholic Church, Jeff Hoffman, and Mark Paloni, "Old Timer" column.)

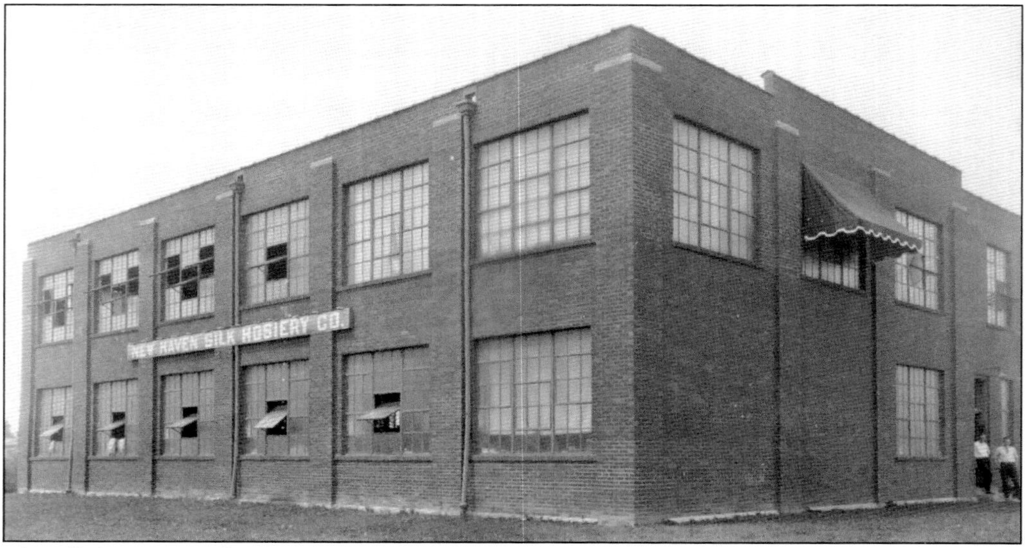

The silk knitting mills sat on State Road 14, between High and Broadway Streets; later the mills became Bennett's Clothing Factory. This photograph was taken in the 1920s. The building was removed, making space for a new city hall and police station in July 1999. Some citizens did not want to see the 1913 city hall sold for commercial use. The New Haven Area Heritage Association leased the building from the city and began restoring its interior. The association uses the boardroom for meetings. (Todd Baron.)

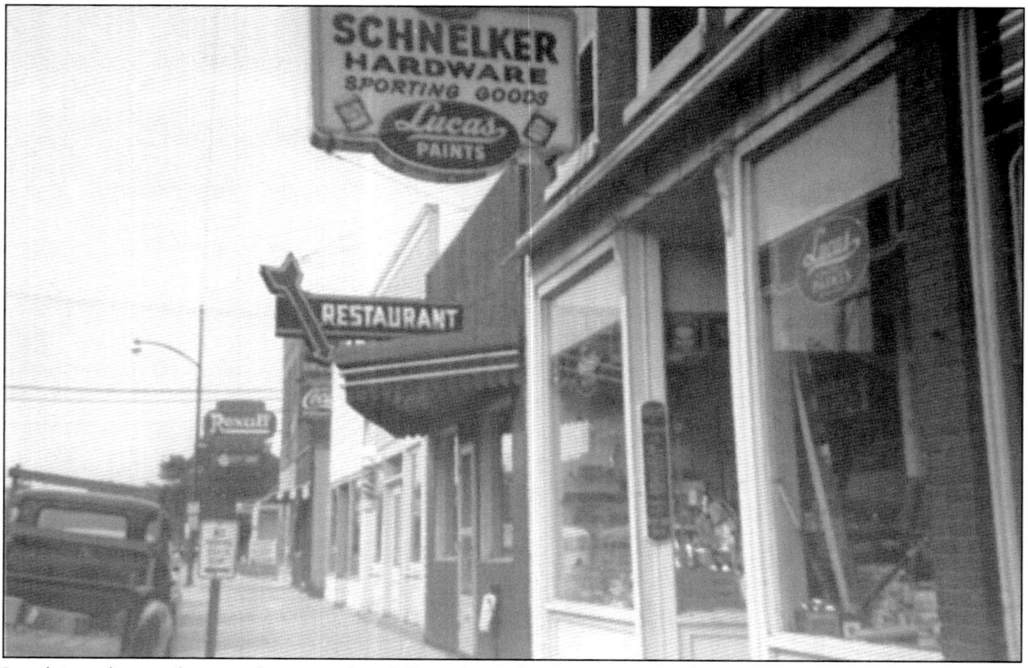

Looking down the southwest side of Broadway Street in 1941, this image shows several stores. Going down the street, Schnelker Hardware Sporting Goods is the nearest store, a restaurant occupies the next building, the next two stores are unidentified, and the next sign reads "Rexall, Charles Purvis Drug Store." (Bonnie Schnelker.)

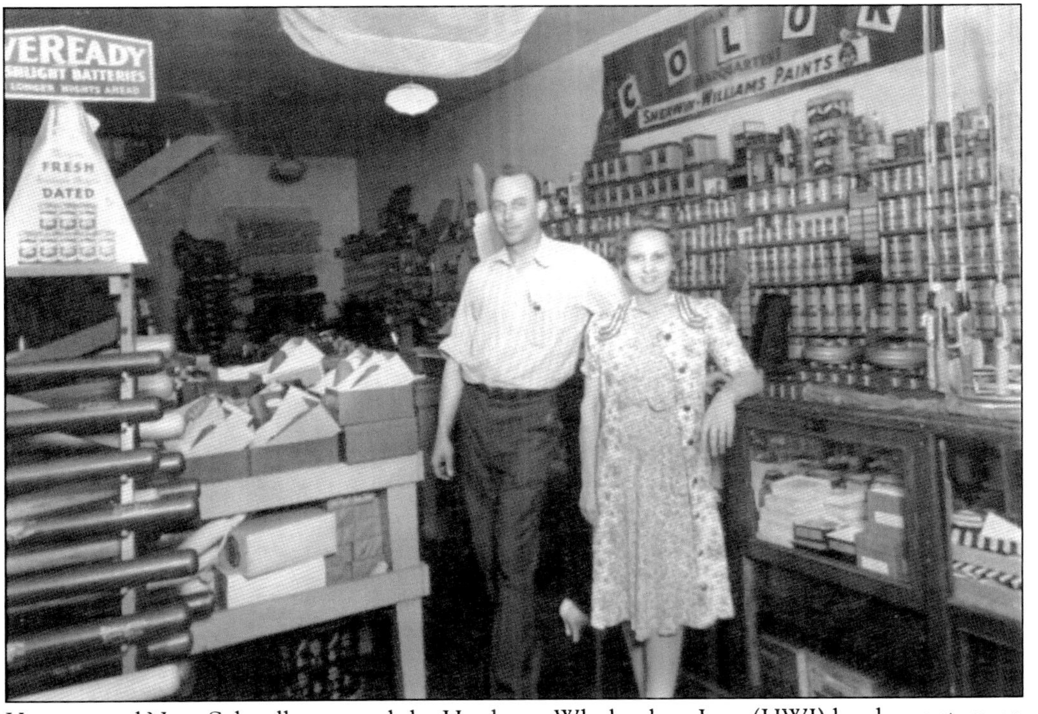

Herman and Nora Schnelker owned the Hardware Wholesalers, Inc., (HWI) hardware store on 504 Broadway. Herman was the seventh dealer to join HWI in 1941. It was the Dowling hardware store before the Schnelkers purchased it. (Bonnie Schnelker.)

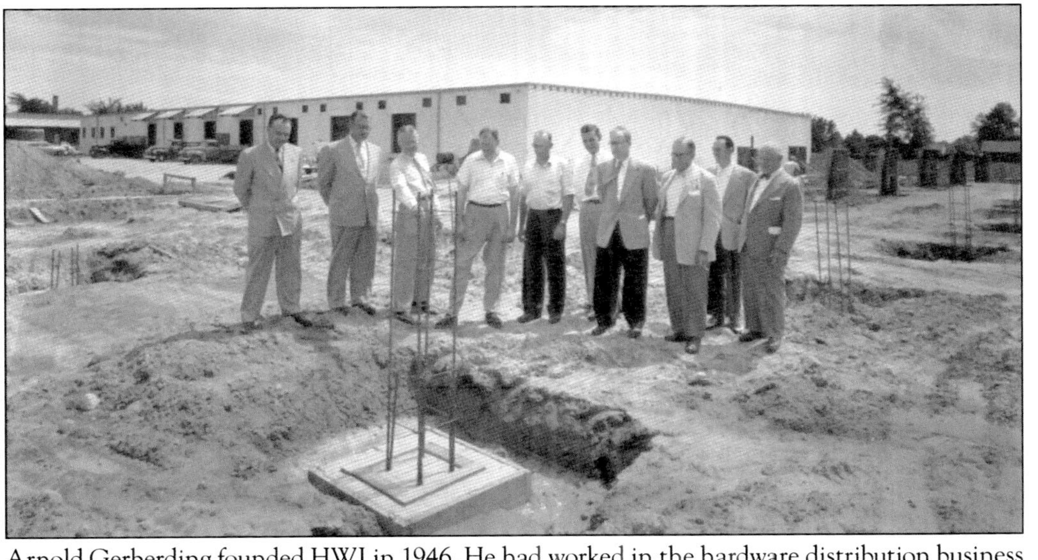

Arnold Gerberding founded HWI in 1946. He had worked in the hardware distribution business and was excited about the idea of a member-owned distribution center, which meant that only people who owned HWI businesses could own stock in the company. The idea was to help individual retailers compete with larger ones. Pictured here is the ground-breaking for the HWI Distribution Center. All are unidentified except the third man from the left, Arnold Gerberding, and the fifth man from the left, Herman Schnelker. (Bonnie Schnelker.)

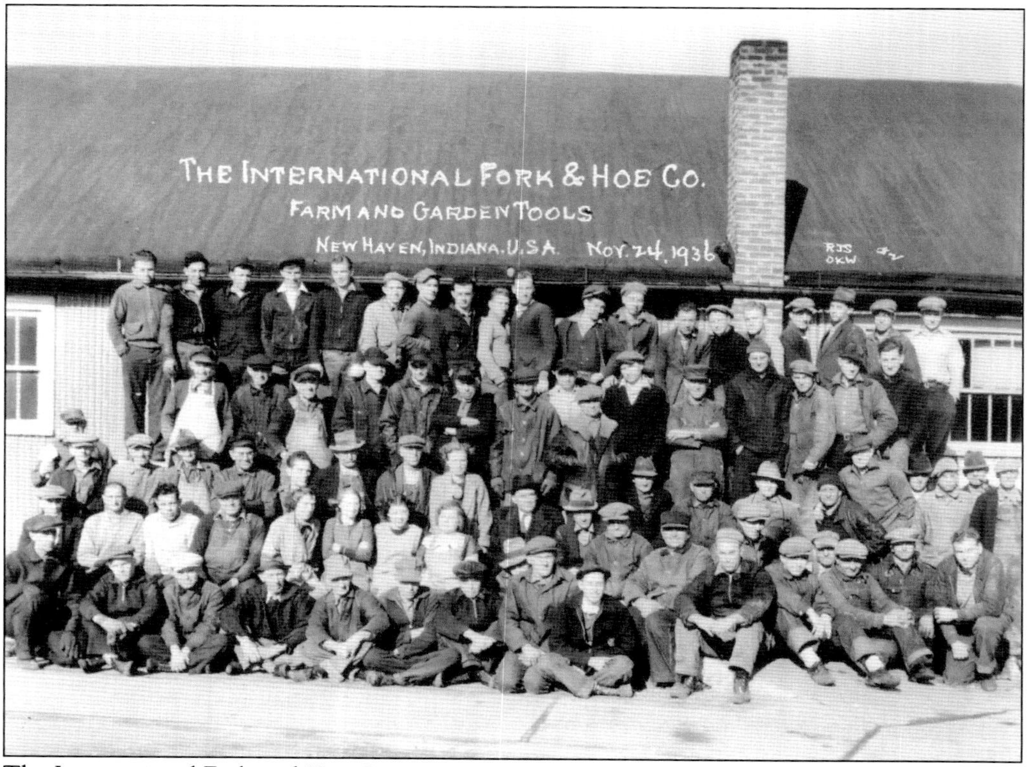

The International Fork and Hoe Company, a major provider of farm and garden tools, used raw wood from the area for machined handles for tool heads (purchased from other factories). By 1928, the company hired 17-year-old Margaret W. Greim, recommended by the International Business College, to run their office. The factory was located in east New Haven on Highway 14. By 1936, the number of employees more than doubled. In this photograph, Greim is pictured in the third row, eighth from left. Beside her is her boss, with a black hat and coat. (Warren Messman and Terry McDonald.)

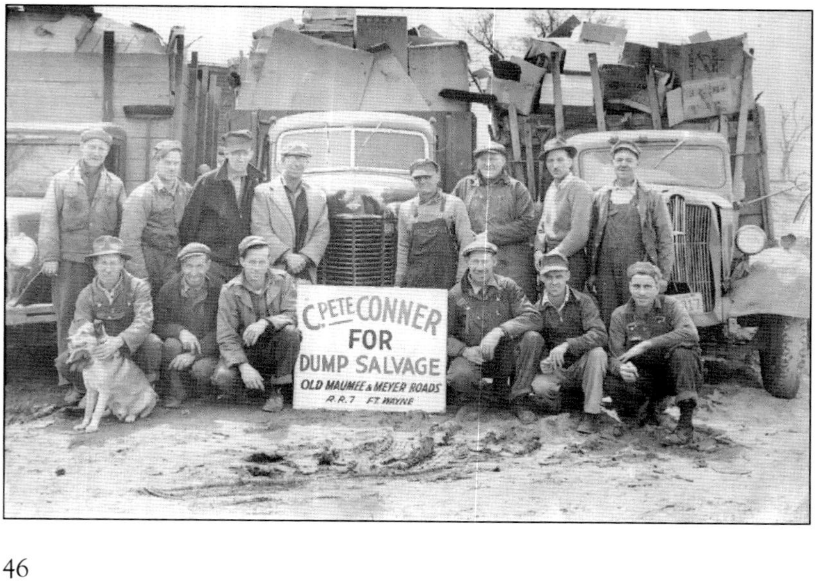

This photograph was taken at the edge of New Haven and Fort Wayne. The men are unidentified. They are posed in front of their trucks at C. Pete Conner for Dump Salvage located on Old Maumee and Meyer Roads. (Vivian Smith.)

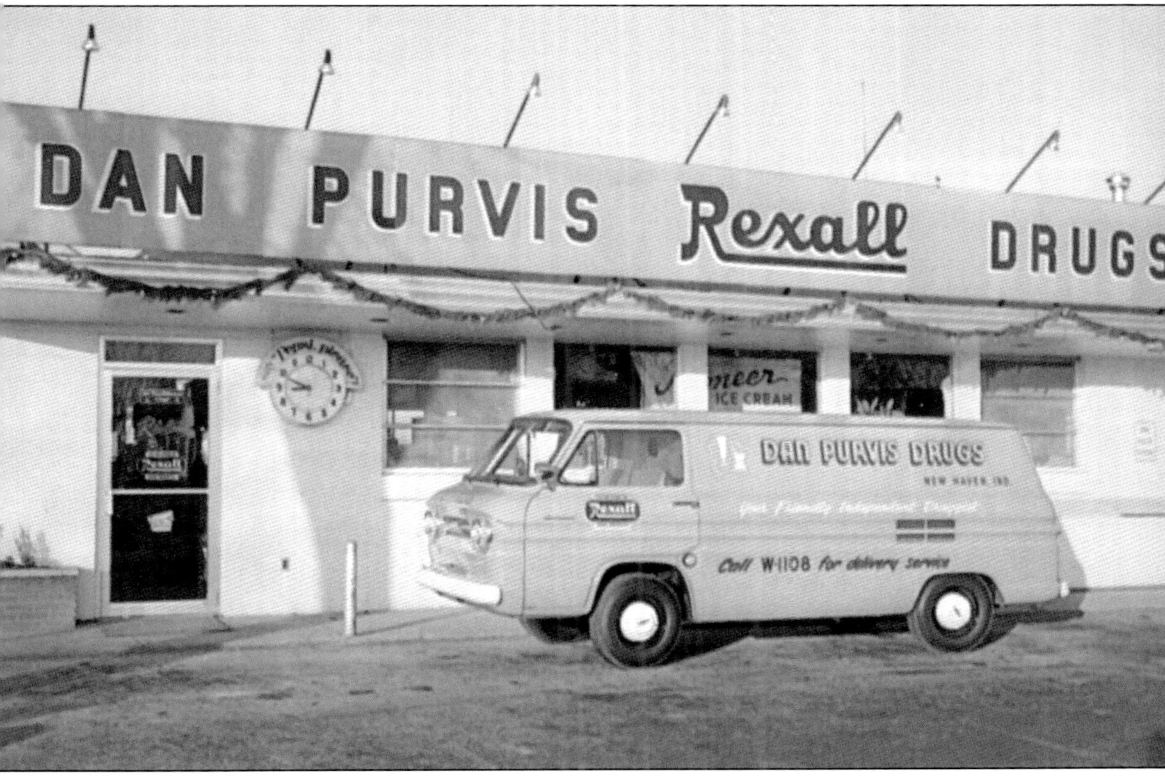

In 1913, Harry Purvis moved from Payne, Ohio, and established the first Purvis Drug Store at 502 Broadway Street. Since that humble beginning 96 years ago, the name has become synonymous with health care in the New Haven area. When Harry passed away, Dan Purvis was only 12 years old. Dan's mother, Dessie, was determined to not let go of the Purvis legacy. She hired non-family pharmacists to operate the store. Ten years later, Dan and his brother Charles took over the store, which by that time was located at 512 Broadway Street where T&D Printing is today. In 1955, two events took place—Dan bought out his brother Charles in the business and decided to build a second store at 725 Broadway Street. The property Dan purchased was across the street from New Haven High School, and the Marsh store was in the next block. The pharmacy occupation ran in the Purvis family—Dan's father, Harry; his four brothers; three uncles; two of Dan's brothers; Dan; and Dan's two sons, Dan Sr. and John, added their talents to the business. Dan sold the stores when the chain drugstores came to town. (Todd Baron and Rod King, *Fort Wayne News-Sentinel.*)

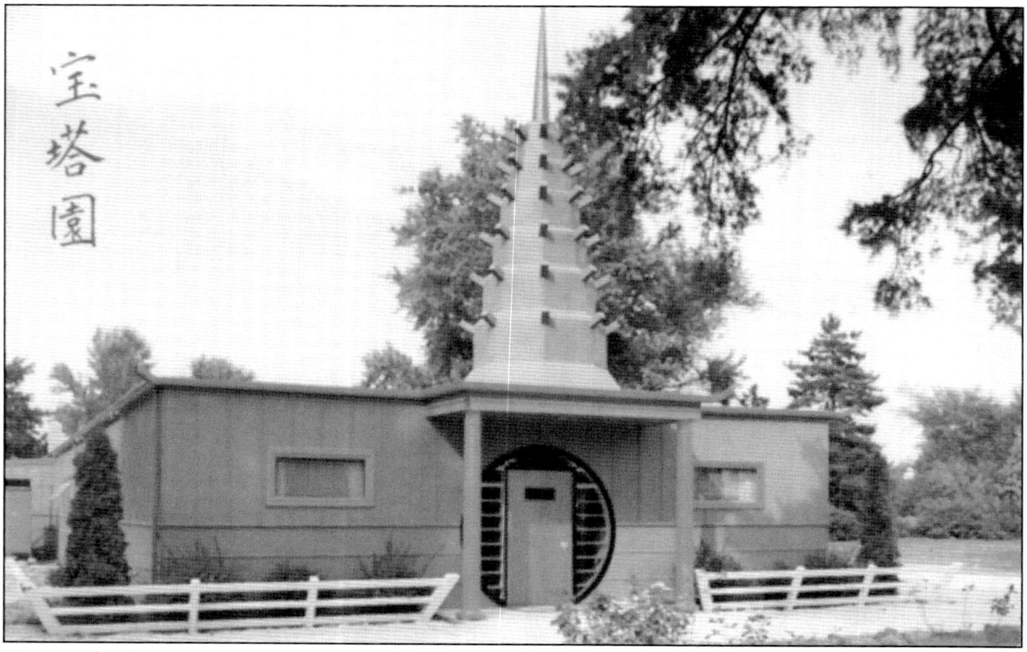

Here is the Pagoda Inn, photographed in 1955. It was located on Highways 14, 24, and 30, which merge just west of New Haven. The building was delightfully appointed and air-conditioned. Carry-out orders were offered and the telephone number was Eastbrook-4589. This was very progressive for the time and for New Haven. (Douglas Runyan.)

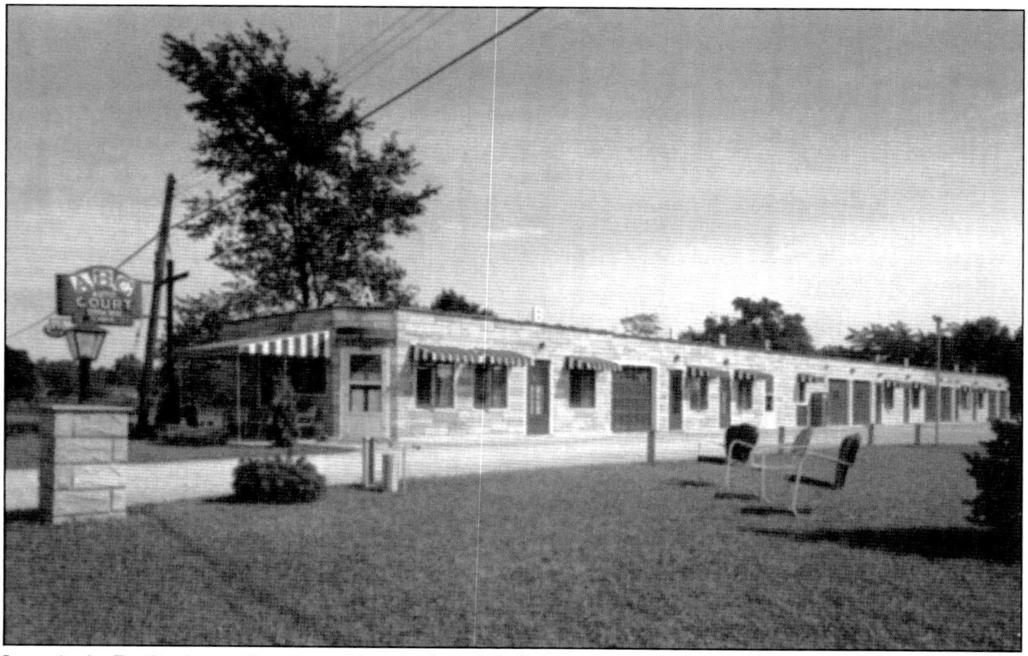

Long's A. B. C. Auto Court was located on Highways 14, 24, and 30. The business was known for advertising that it provided closed garages. Where would any overnight establishment offer garages today? The auto court also had steam heat and a nearby restaurant. (Douglas Runyan.)

Three

Streets and Public Services

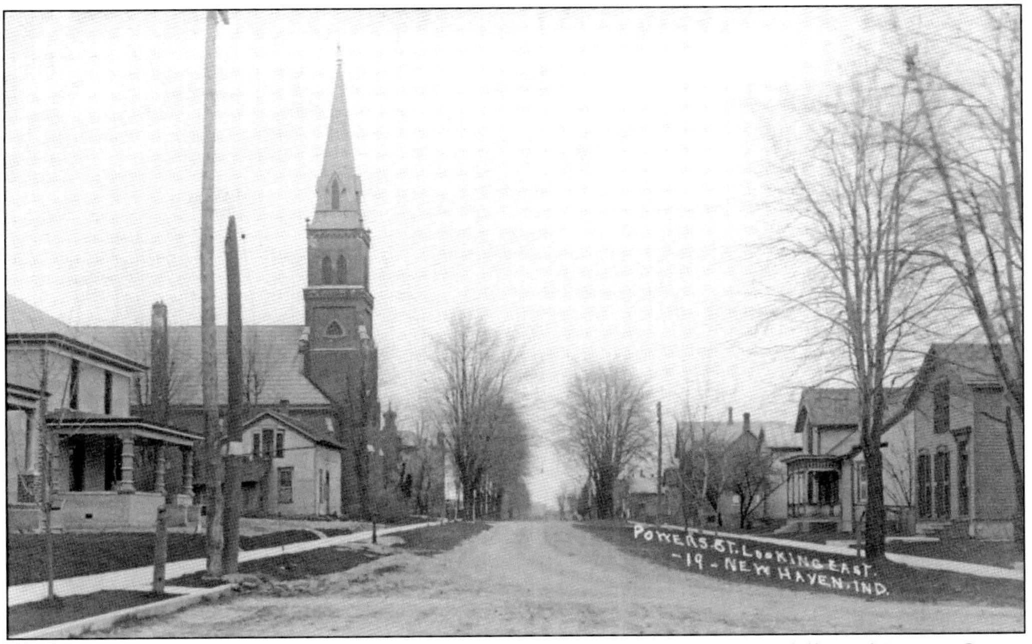

This image of Powers Street is looking east. Years later, U.S. Highway 24 followed Powers Street and Broadway Street through the middle of New Haven until the 469 bypass came about in the 1990s. In this photograph, the street is still a dirt road with concrete sidewalks. Some of the houses on the right are canal houses from the mid-1800s. On the left stands the proud St. Johns Catholic Church. It was erected in 1877 at the cost of $16,000. (Indiana Historical Society, 90390.)

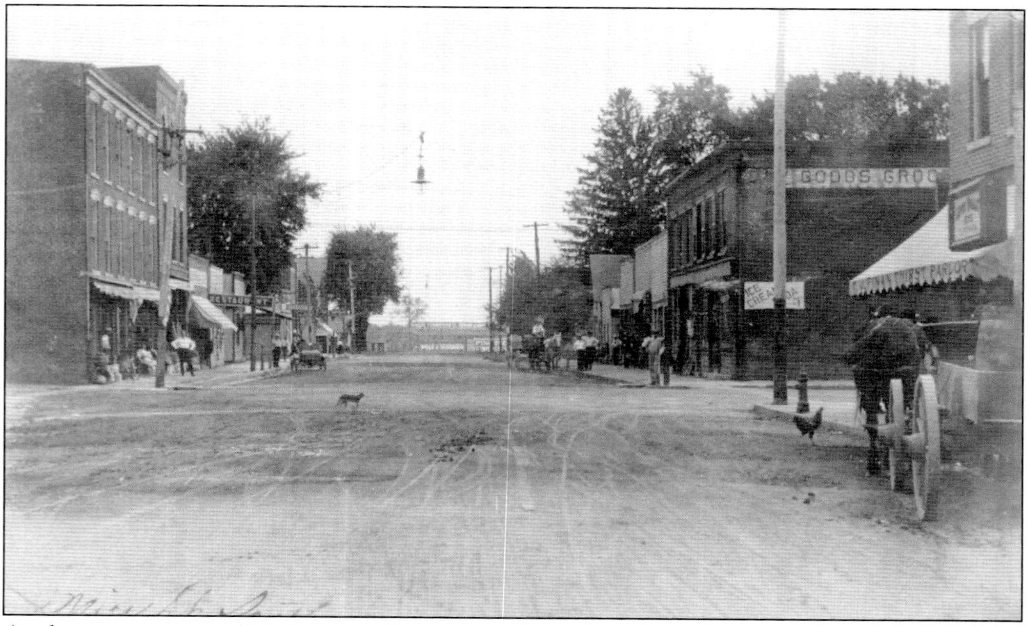

At the intersection of Main Street looking south on Broadway Street in 1912, the roads were dirt and the sidewalks were concrete with some curbs. At the south end of Broadway Street, a sign reads "Wolf & Dessauer." Looking right, the store on the far corner later become two stores. Today it is J&R Antique and Dolly Heaven. The next four stores are the original wood-framed buildings, three of which still stand. Across the street are two brick buildings, which today are the Trion and the Edward Jones office. The next building is wooden and later became Lincoln Bank. The 1913 photograph below is taken from Main and Broadway Streets, looking west down Main Street. In 1881, a brick town well was dug at the intersection of Main and Broadway Streets. Looking down Main Street, on the right, is New Haven Bakery. (Both, Todd Baron.)

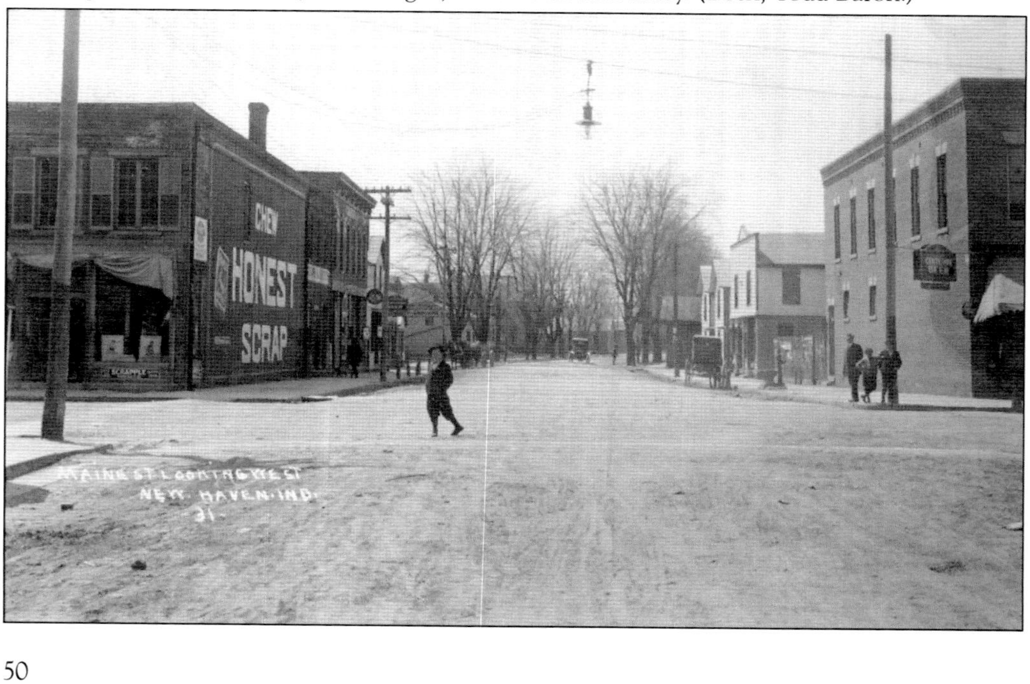

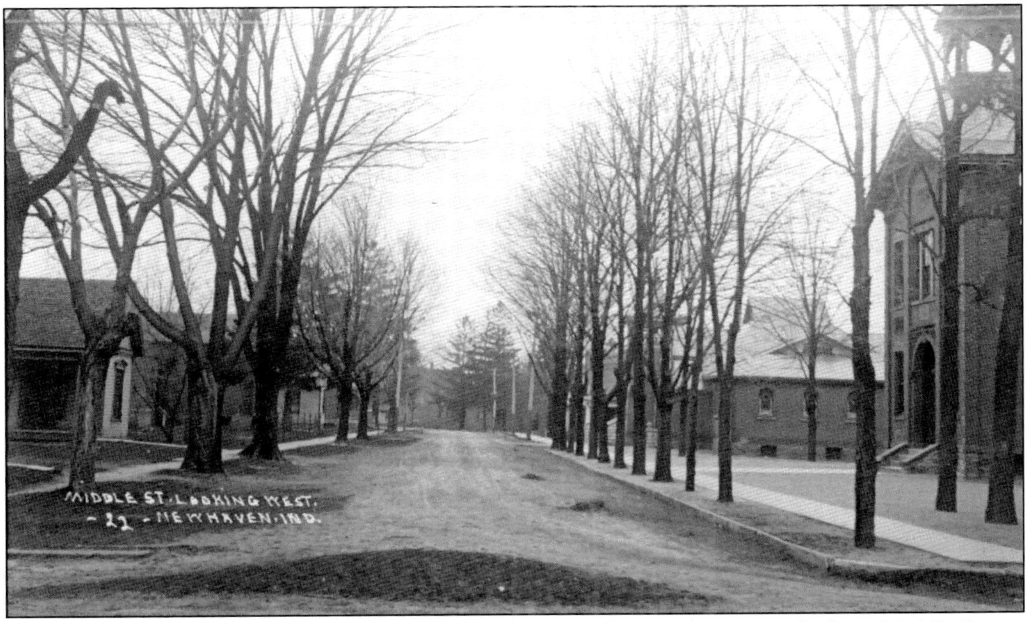

This image of Middle Street is looking west, if one is standing at the east end where Middle Street ends at Eben Street. The streets are still dirt but the sidewalks are made of concrete and the right side has curbs. The New Haven School is on the immediate right. A two-room schoolhouse was erected in 1858. After incorporation in 1866, it became a town school and two more rooms were added. In 1885, this building was removed and a brick structure was erected. Later the town purchased a lot to the east and four additional rooms were added. At this time, it became a township school. The photograph below shows Middle Street looking to the east. Two churches were located on this street. They were the Methodist Episcopal and the Methodist Protestant churches. They consolidated in the 1940s and built the beautiful New Haven Methodist Church on Lincoln Highway West, which was dedicated in 1955. (Both, Todd Baron.)

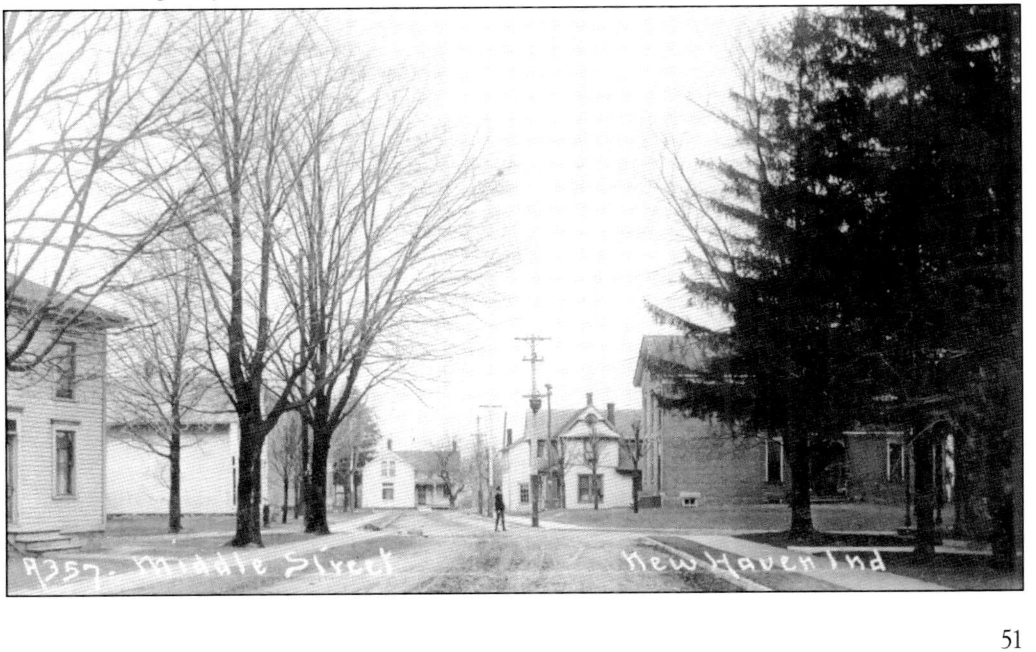

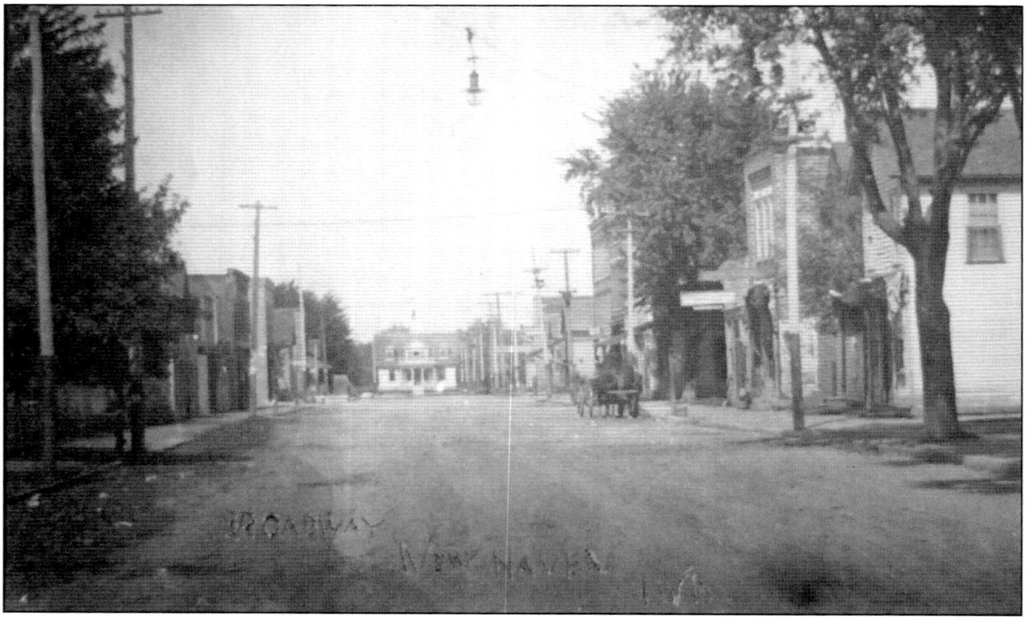

Dr. Gustave Brudi's house was at the north end of Broadway Street. In later years, his house was removed and Broadway Street extended to the edge of town and became Landin Road. The bridge on Rufus Street closed, and a new four-lane bridge replaced it on Landin Road. The streetlights in the photograph above were lowered at night and raised in the morning. The building on the far right is the old post office on Middle Street. (St. Louis Catholic Church and Jeff Hoffman.)

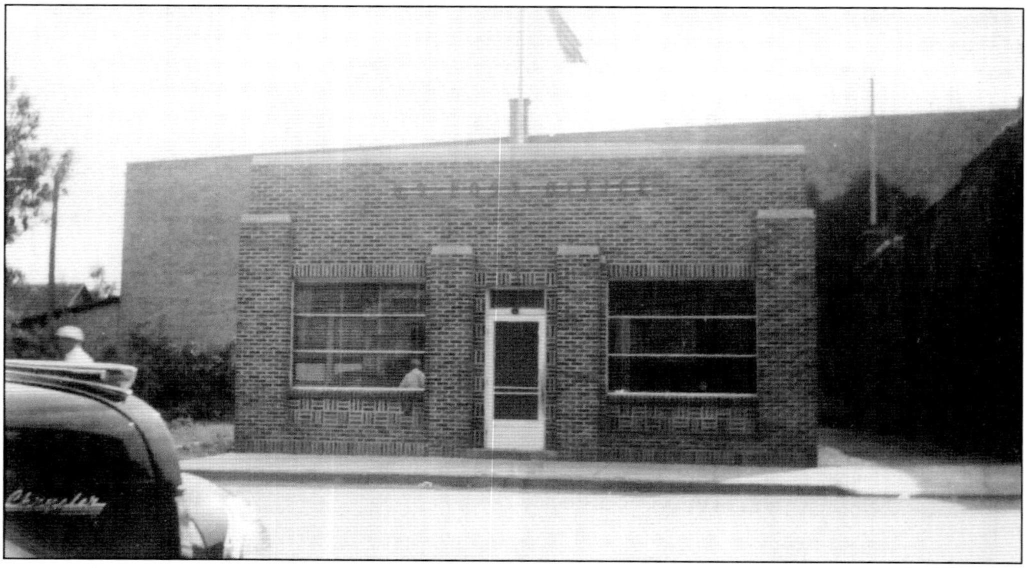

Designed by Robert Burns, the new post office was constructed according to plans and specifications set out by the federal government and was privately owned and leased by the government for postal purposes. The building was 30 feet by 40 feet; it had one story and a basement. The mailboxes were of lock design to accommodate patrons before and after closing hours. The 47-year-old post office at Middle and Broadway Streets, designed by Robert Burns, was removed. (Brooks Construction.)

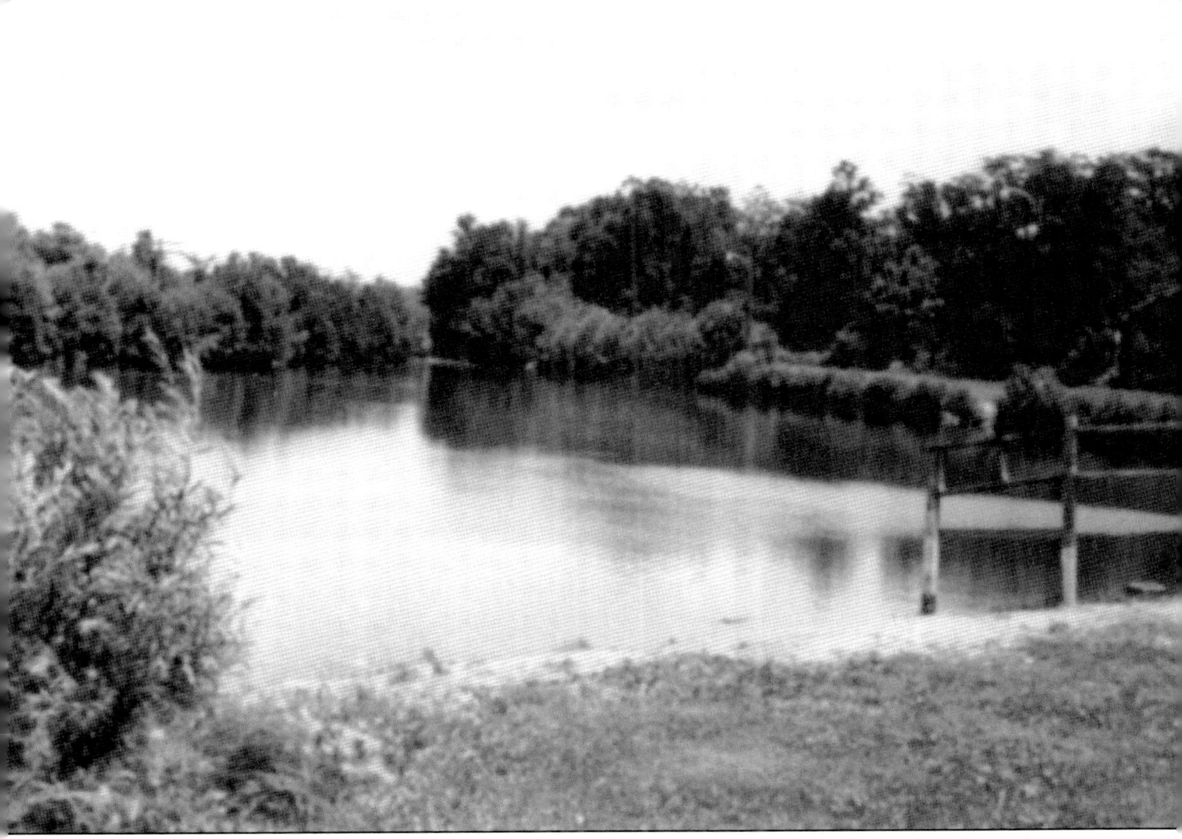

Looking at tranquil Moser Park, it is hard to imagine this was the scene of three railroad accidents over a period of 40 years. The New Haven Park and Playground Association started in 1950 with its main funding sources being Canal Days and donations. Some of the first members were Richard Van Kirk, Joe Isenbarger, Homer Harper, and John Edwards. The New Haven Park Board organized in 1955, and its first meeting was held February 9, 1956. The first board members were Dr. G. I. Lake, Cecil Andorfer, John Whitelock, and Fred Lahrman. The first year's budget was $1,000. In 1957, they became the New Haven-Adams Township Parks Department. When unincorporated Adams Township was included, Scott Armstrong was appointed as township representative. The park board consisted of four members appointed by the mayor of New Haven—two Republicans and two Democrats—along with one Adams Township resident who was appointed by a county judge. (New Haven Park Department.)

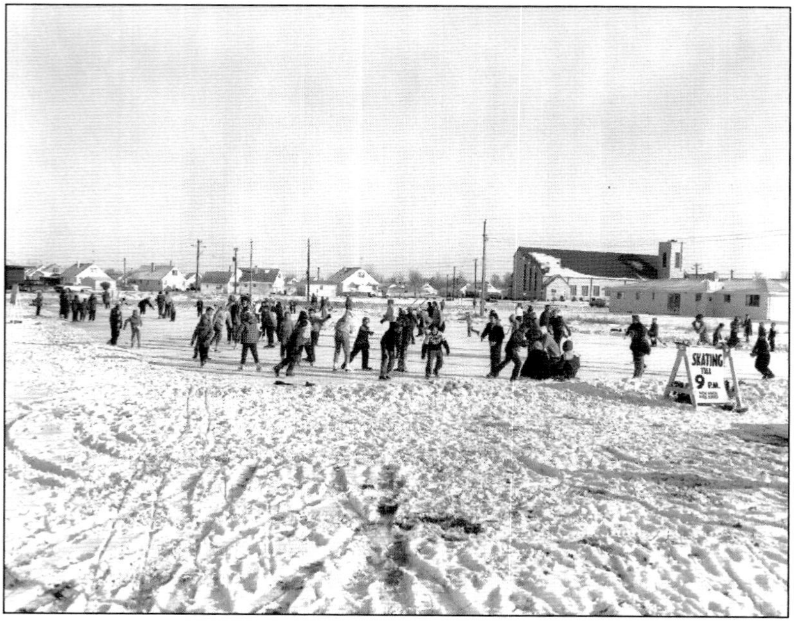

This 1950s photograph is of the skating pond located at the corner of Green Street and Highway 14. The Fifth Third Bank and Doug Runyan's office stand at this corner in 2010. Emanuel Lutheran Church is in the background. The sign reads "Skating until 9 p.m. New Haven Park Board." (Douglas Runyan.)

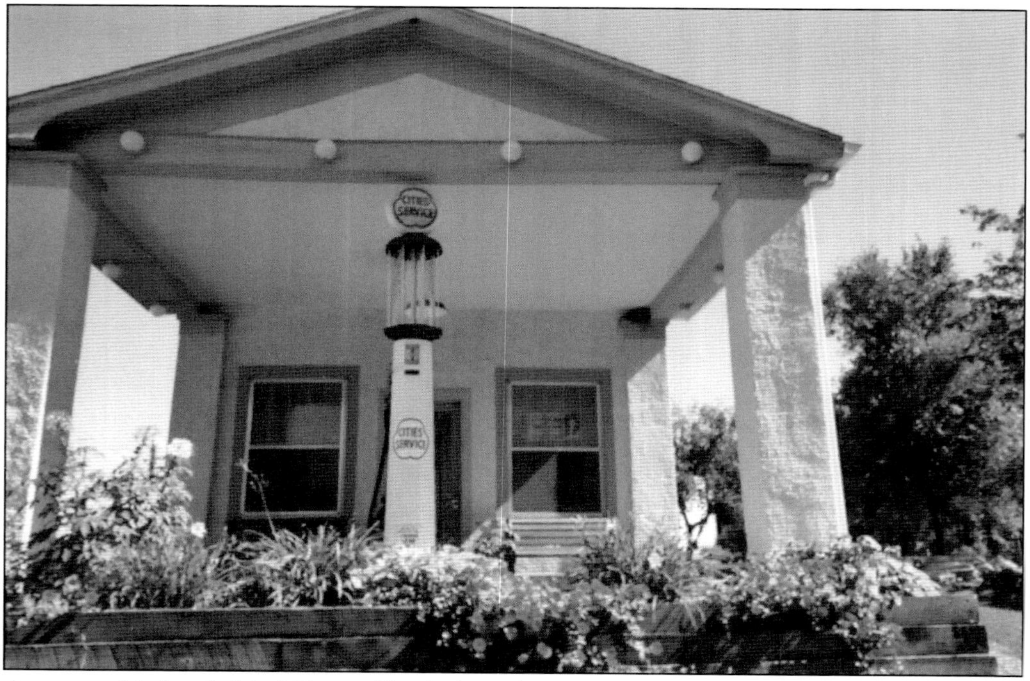

A summer kitchen behind George Hazelet's residence was converted to a gas station in 1917. He then moved the building from behind the residence to the street. The residence and station sat on North Rufus Street, which was the main road into New Haven from the north. On rainy days, the station was a community gathering place until it closed in 1958. In the 1990s, the gas station was moved to Stemmler Parkway in Havenhurst Park. The park department restored the original facade. (New Haven Park Department.)

In the 1970s, Carrel Knee trained teenagers to be swimmers' aids. In 1931, the Town of New Haven opened the first swimming pool at the site of the city water tower. The pool had concrete walls and a gravel floor. At that time, overflowing the pool with clean water, which would displace the dirty water that was already in the pool, was how they cleaned the pool instead of using chemicals. In 1940, it was closed for health reasons. (New Haven Park Department.)

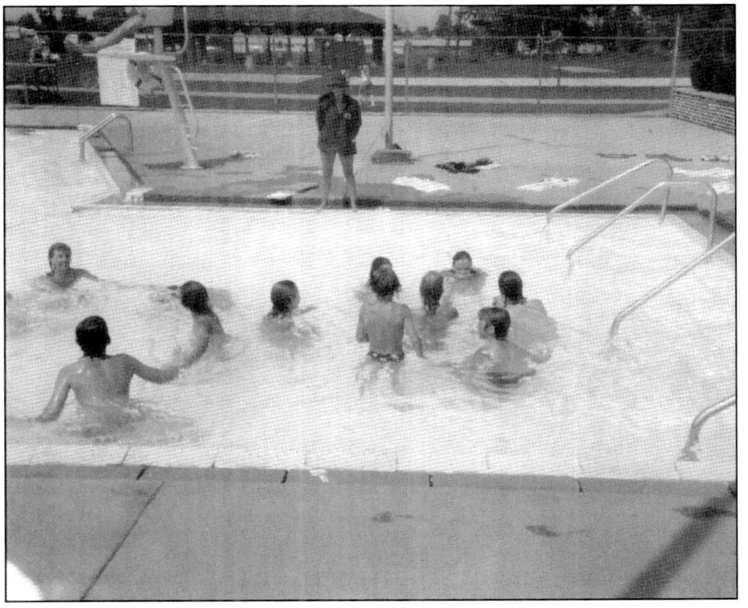

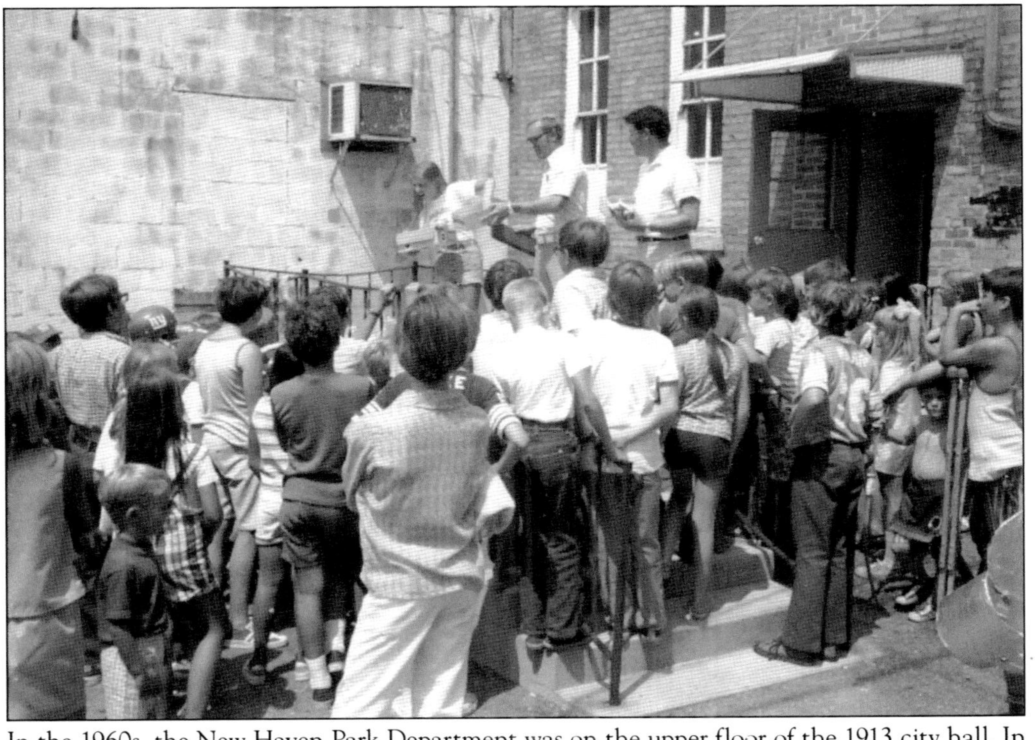

In the 1960s, the New Haven Park Department was on the upper floor of the 1913 city hall. In the photograph above people have lined up to register for classes. The park department opened two swimming pools, one in Meadowbrook in 1961 and the second was Jury Pool in 1969. Moser Memorial Park was developed into a tennis, basketball, and baseball park with a beautiful pond. The New Haven Park Department board purchased the building on 1125 Hartzell Street for offices and public classrooms in 1982. (New Haven Park Department.)

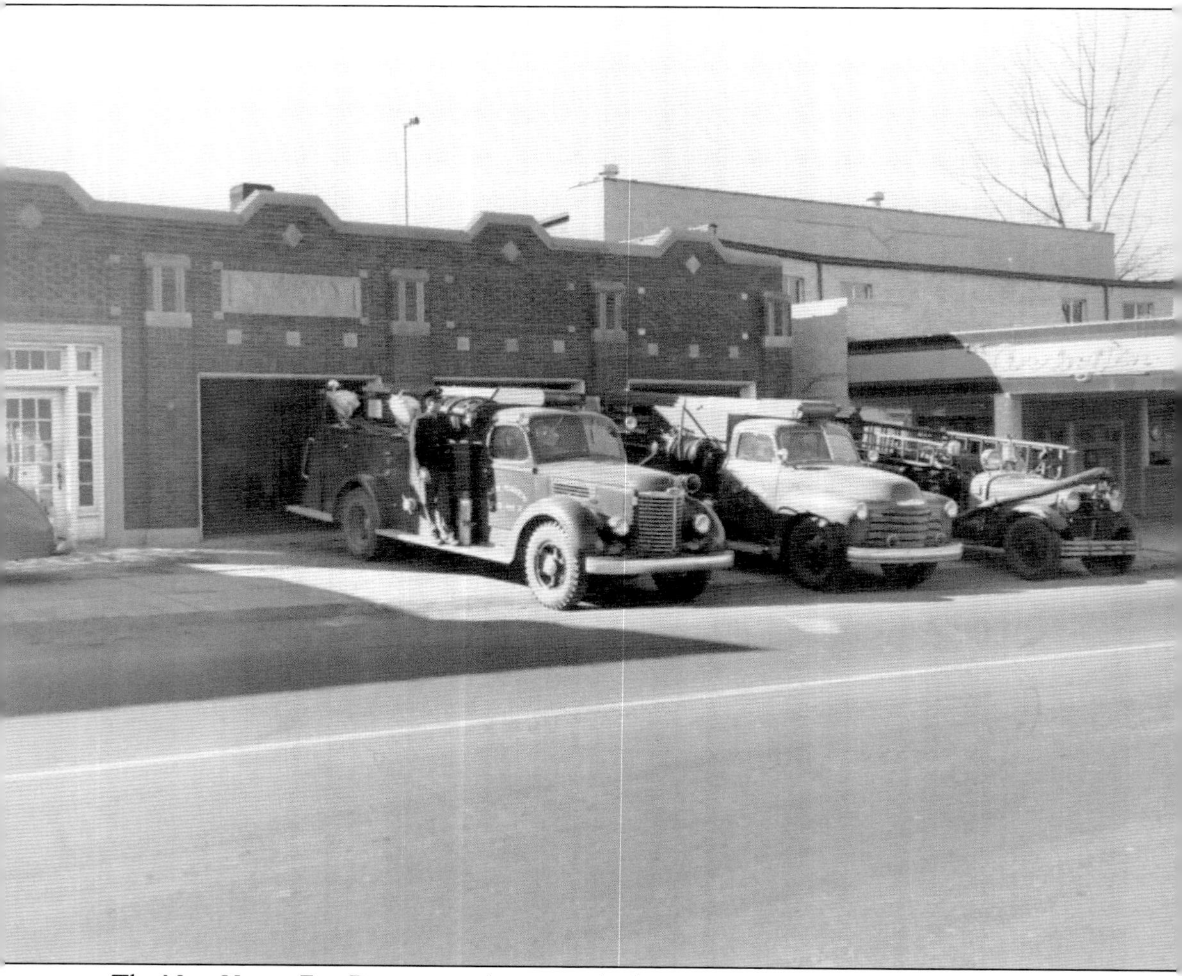

The New Haven Fire Department began in the late 1800s. It was located on Broadway Street. In those days, horses pulled the fire equipment and water was pumped from tankers by hand. Because it had not rained for some time, on October 9, 1871, trustees appointed eight men to patrol the railroad and town each night until it did rain. The men worked for nine nights and were paid $13.50, or $1.50 per night if they worked less than nine. Six men patrolled the railroad and two patrolled the main streets. On December 4, 1884, fire chief J. Brudi's report read as follows, "Gentlemen, I herewith present my annual report as follows: The engine is not in good working order (as the plunger had not been packed.) There is about 450 feet of good hose that can be used. Two axes, two wrenches, and spanners I can account for. Hammer and oil cans area missing. Very respectfully, Joseph Brudi, chief." On March 4, 1885, the fire company disbanded and wished to sell the fire bell. On January 5, 1887, Brudi was requested to put the fire engine in proper shape for use and reinstate the fire company. (Marie Mehring and the *1966 New Haven Centennial History* book.)

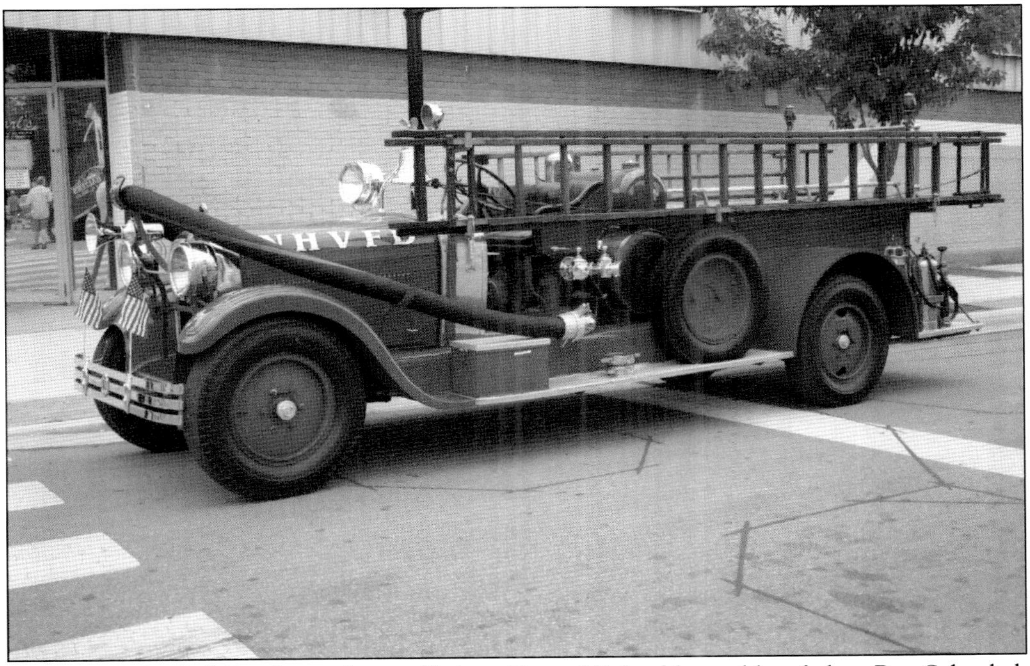

Marylen (Schuckel) Pemberton's grandfather, Conrad Schuckle, and her father, Ray Schuckel, worked for the fire department. Conrad was employed from 1900 to 1925. He maintained the horses and the fire equipment. In 1925, the department purchased a 1925 Studebaker fire engine (seen above), which is still shown on special occasions. Because he could not drive, Conrad resigned. Ray was a volunteer from 1944 until 1970. (Photograph by Stevia Webster; Jim Pemberton.)

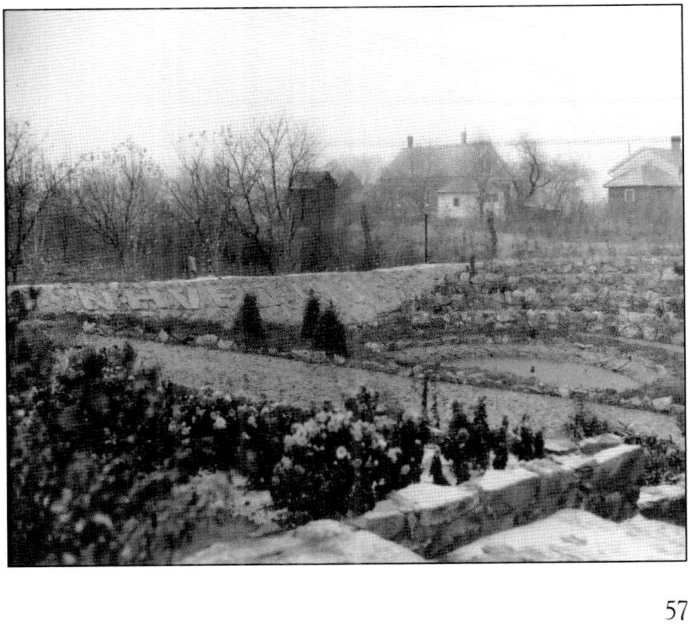

In 1937, the fire department installed a beautiful sunken garden in the bed of the Wabash and Erie Canal, which was located behind the fire station. The plantings included shrubs, flowers, walkways, and a pond. The letters NHVFD (New Haven Volunteer Fire Department) and the year 1937 were printed on the dam. The water tankers were filled with water from the pond. In 1957, the garden was removed so a concrete parking lot could be installed. (Jim Pemberton.)

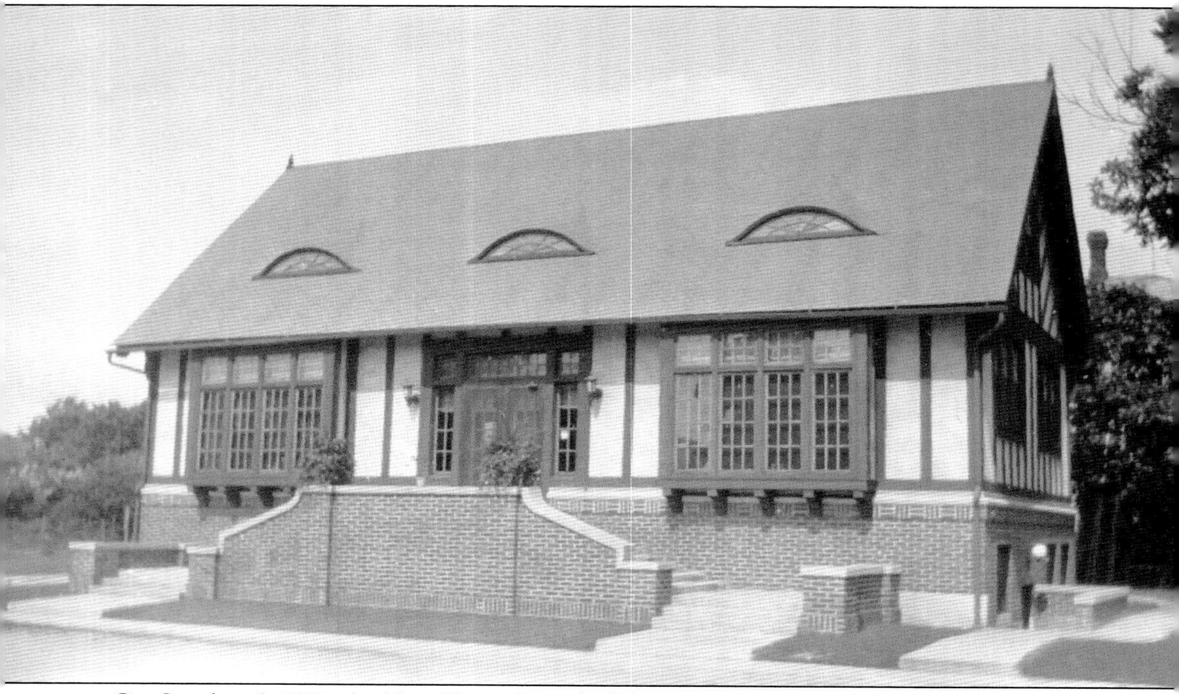

On October 5, 1921, the New Haven Board of Trustees granted permission to install a branch of the public library in town hall for as long as the city did not need the room. Mrs. Lepper was the first librarian. On January 2, 1924, under the direction of F. A. Blaising, the board of trustees purchased land from William Federspiel and he was paid by 12 civic-minded men. The library was built at 435 Ann Street and opened on October 1, 1925. It was designed in the British half-timber and English Tudor styles. In 1982, the library was remodeled and the basement was converted from storage rooms to public restrooms, new offices, and a meeting room. In 1990, this same building was enlarged and made handicap accessible. In 2000, a beautiful new library was built at Green Street and Dawkins Road. The number of volumes in the first library was 600; in 2000, the number of volumes grew to 17,000. (Bob Vonderau and the *1966 New Haven Centennial History* book.)

Four

Celebrations, Churches, and Schools

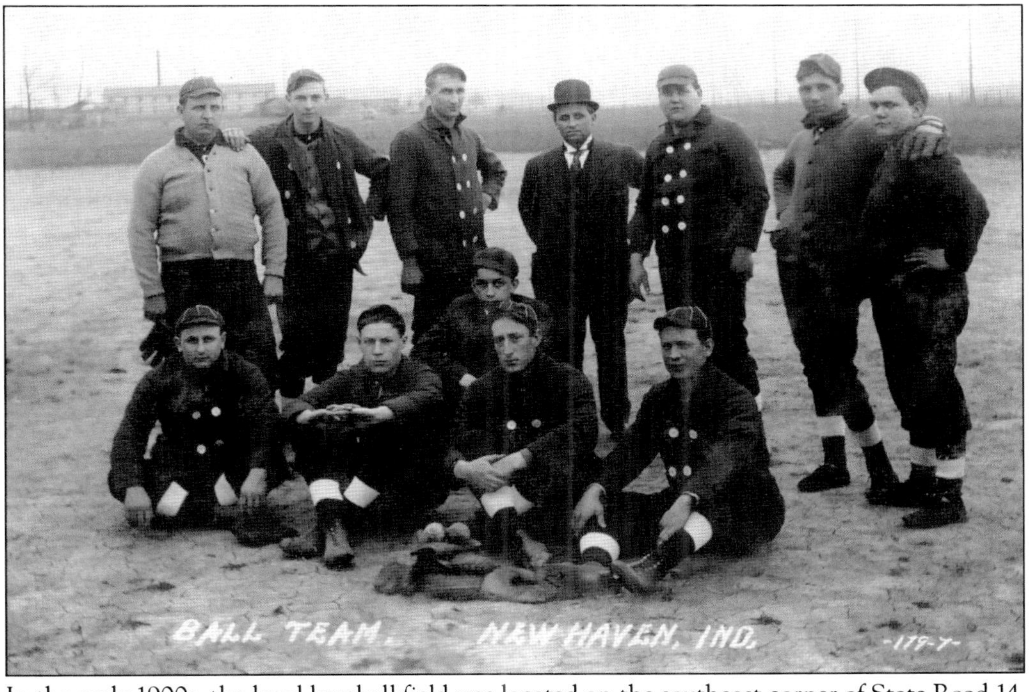

In the early 1900s, the local baseball field was located on the southeast corner of State Road 14, also called Dawkins Road, and Broadway Street. This was the original site of the first baseball diamond in New Haven. Baseball was the most popular sport at that time and was the first sport to be organized in town. Later this corner became a commercial location so a second ball field was moved north of Hartzell Street, on the east side of Broadway Street, south of the railroad tracks. These players are unidentified. (Todd Baron.)

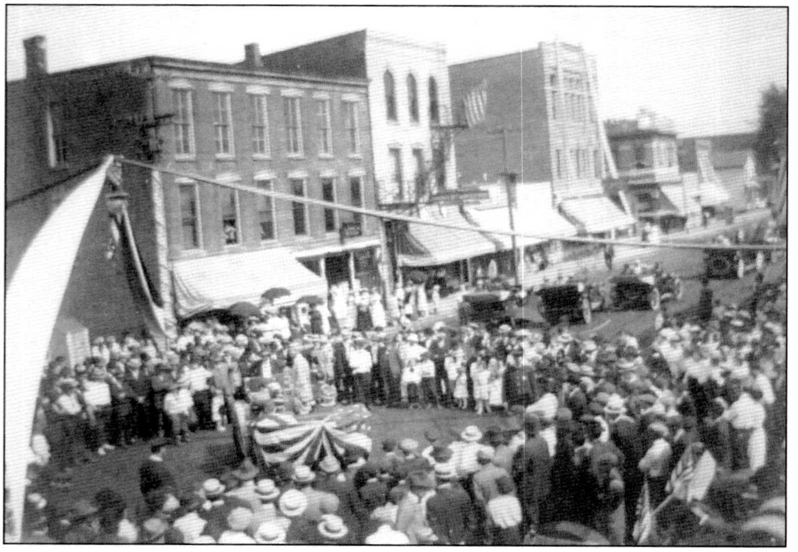

This 1900s patriotic parade was held downtown at Main and Broadway Streets. The town celebrated festivals downtown every year, forerunners to the Canal Days of today. (St. Louis Catholic Church and Jeff Hoffman.)

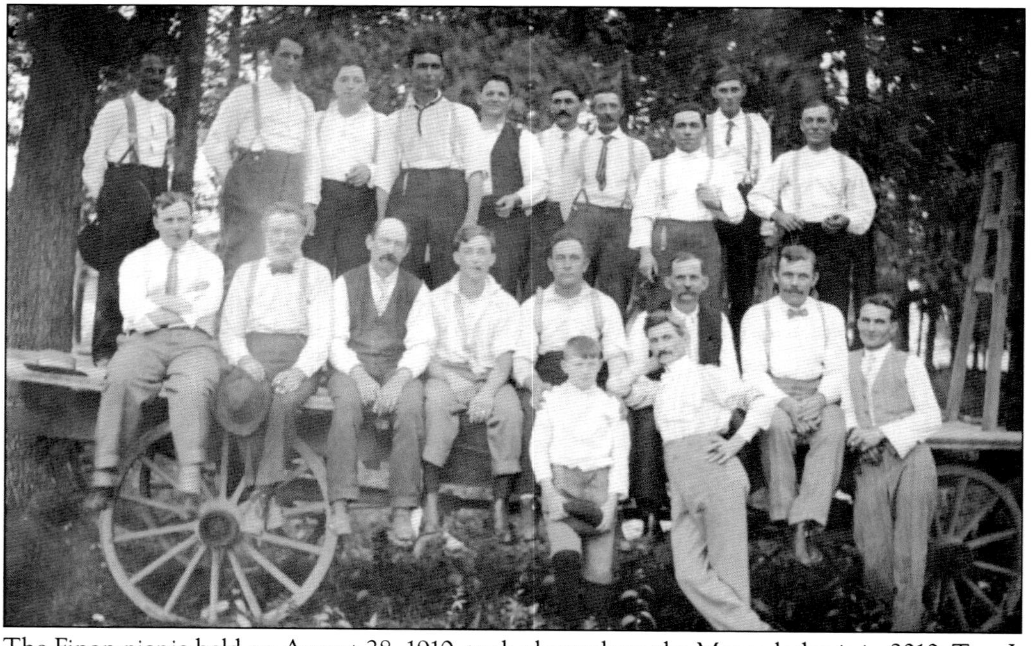

The Finan picnic held on August 28, 1910, took place where the Moose lodge is in 2010. Tom J. Finan owned the Finan Thirst Parlor. Pictured are (first row, from left to right) an unidentified boy and Lawrence Kleinrichert; (second and third row, in no particular order) Kit Hanna, Cap Ankenbruck, Jake Landin, Bern Mack, Joseph Buctman, William Schoenefeld, Sam Stock, Cooney Schuckel, Alfred Bowers, John Daily, August Meyers, Lee Gustison, Ed Kallmeyer, Anthony Welling, Charles Schnitker, Ed Welling, August Hanefeld, and Bud Roy. (Todd Baron.)

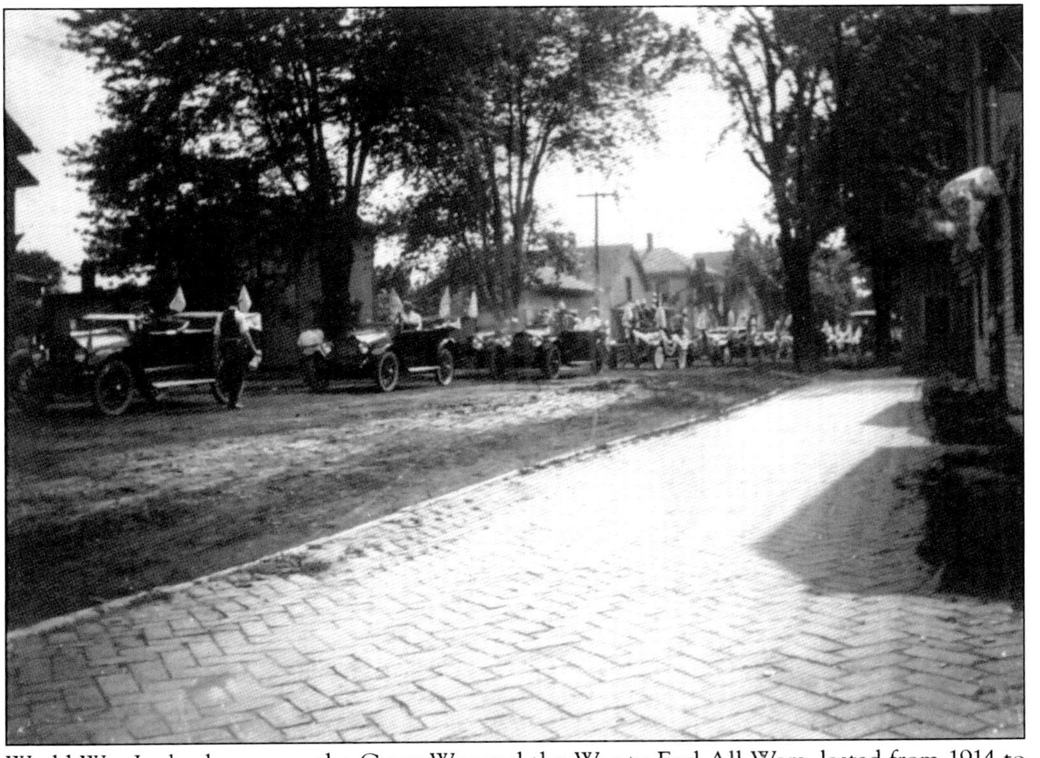

World War I, also known as the Great War and the War to End All Wars, lasted from 1914 to 1918. These photographs were taken in the years after the war and show celebrations honoring local World War I veterans. A grand parade of cars decorated with patriotic themes lined up one behind the other and drove down the streets of New Haven. In the photograph below, the gentleman at the left is Joe Kallmeyer. (Both, Todd Baron.)

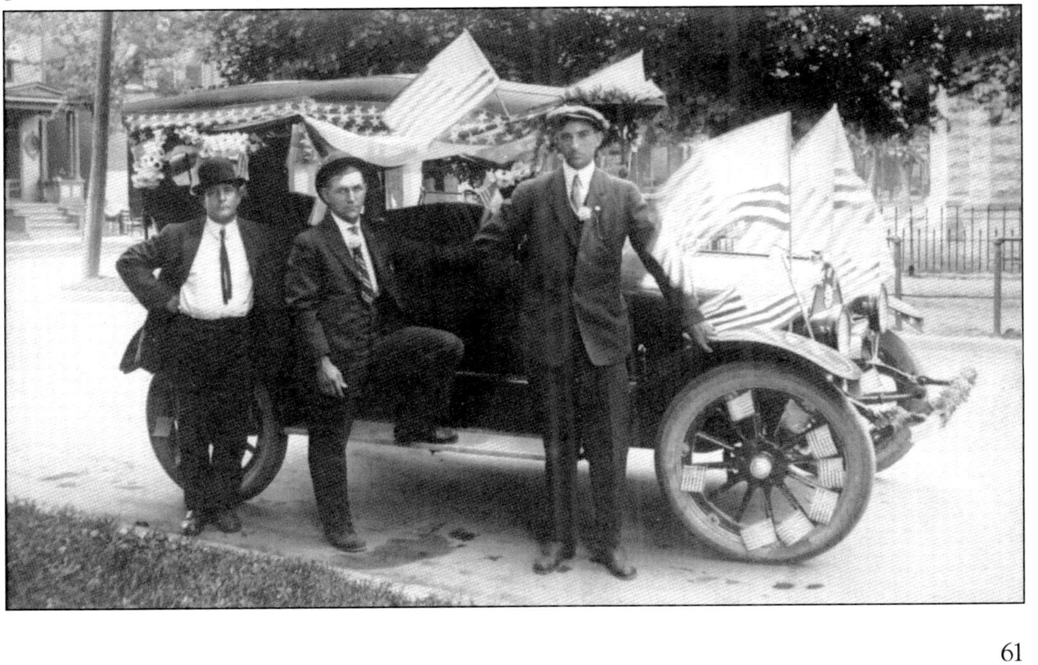

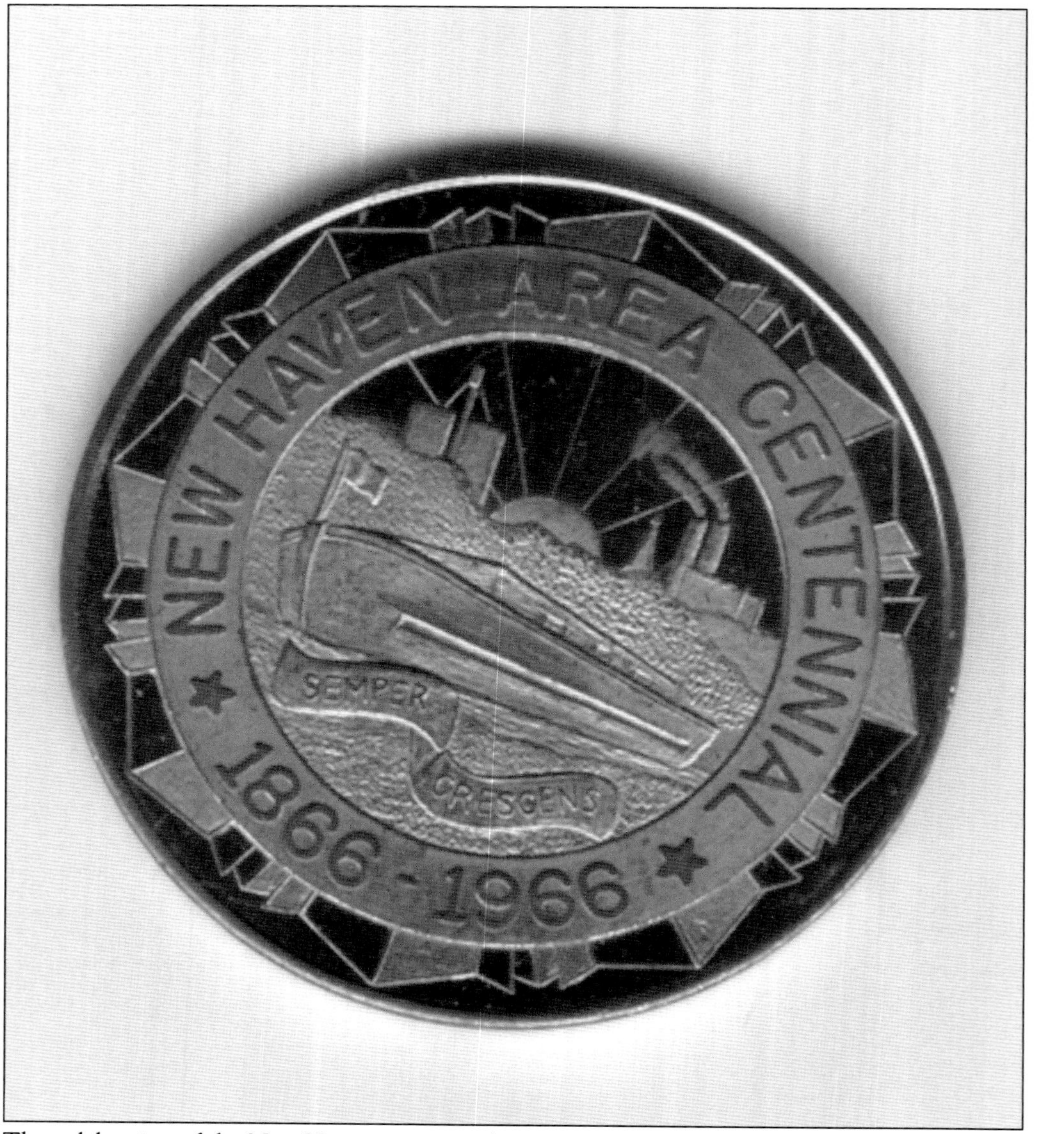

The celebration of the New Haven centennial in 1966 marked the 100th birthday of the town's incorporation. It was in existence many years before 1866, but not as a voting town. The centennial celebration started on Sunday with a series of religious day programs, including open houses at all New Haven churches and an old-fashioned potluck picnic at Schnelker Park, followed by a religious music concert at John H. Young Field. The celebration schedule included the registration of New Haven old-timers, an aquatic program, a daylong industrial exhibit at Central Lutheran Church, youth day play activities at John H. Young Field, an agricultural exhibit at John H. Young Field, an old-fashioned dress contest, and a gigantic seven-division parade through the town on Saturday. The highlight of the weeklong observance was the 90-minute historical spectacular *Launch CXL 111*, in which a cast of 300 area residents portrayed northern Indiana's history from the days of the opening of the wilderness by French traders to the present. The centennial celebration ended the following Saturday night with a "modern times" record hop at Schnelker Park. (Lynn Shaw and John McDowell, *Fort Wayne News-Sentinel*)

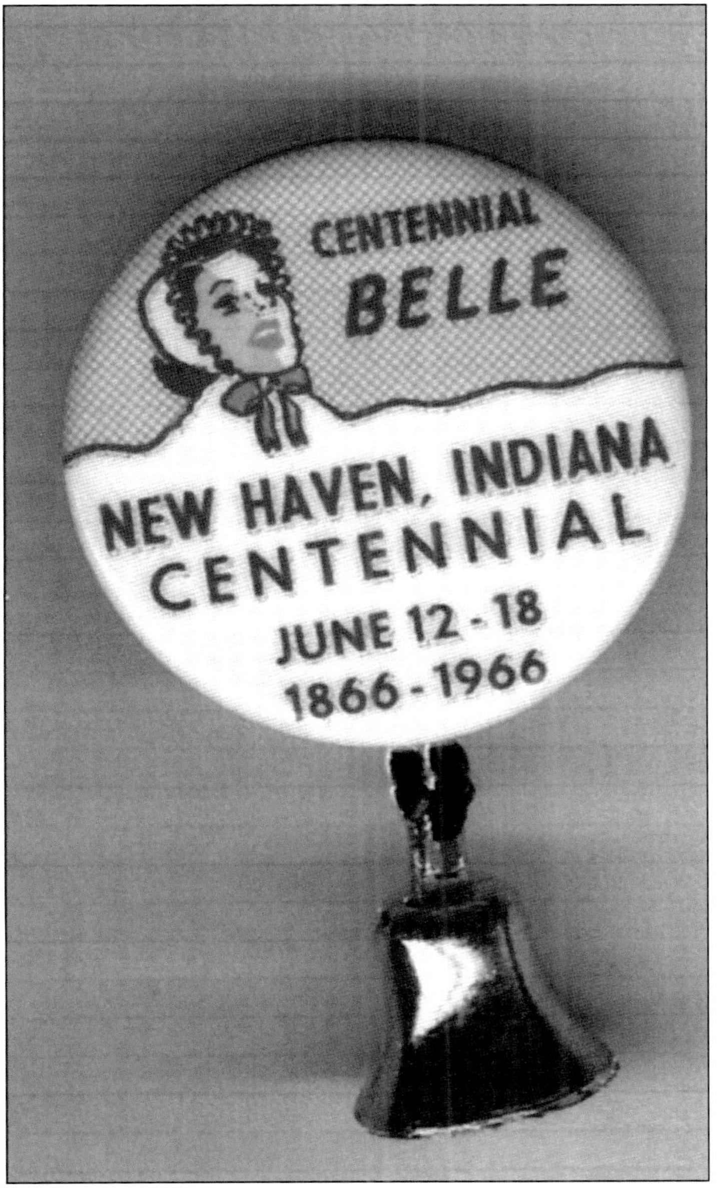

The historical show was presented each evening and closed Saturday, June 18, at the New Haven High School's John H. Young stadium, where a special stage that was 290 feet long and 80 feet deep had been constructed. Under the direction of Robert Shelfow, a veteran motion picture and television director, the show depicted events of the French and Indian War, the campaigns of Gen. Mad Anthony Wayne, the building and operation of the old Erie Canal, the development of the railroads, and the Civil War days to present day. Authentic costumes and settings were designed for the pageant, and props like horses, cattle, wagons, and old-time automobiles and bikes heightened the realism of the performance. Each show concluded with a fireworks display. The cast was assisted by a 100-voice choir and narrators who told the story portrayed by the actors on the huge stage. Carl Nicholas, the New Haven High School choral director, was chairman of the historical committee. (Ornel Kitchen and John McDowell.)

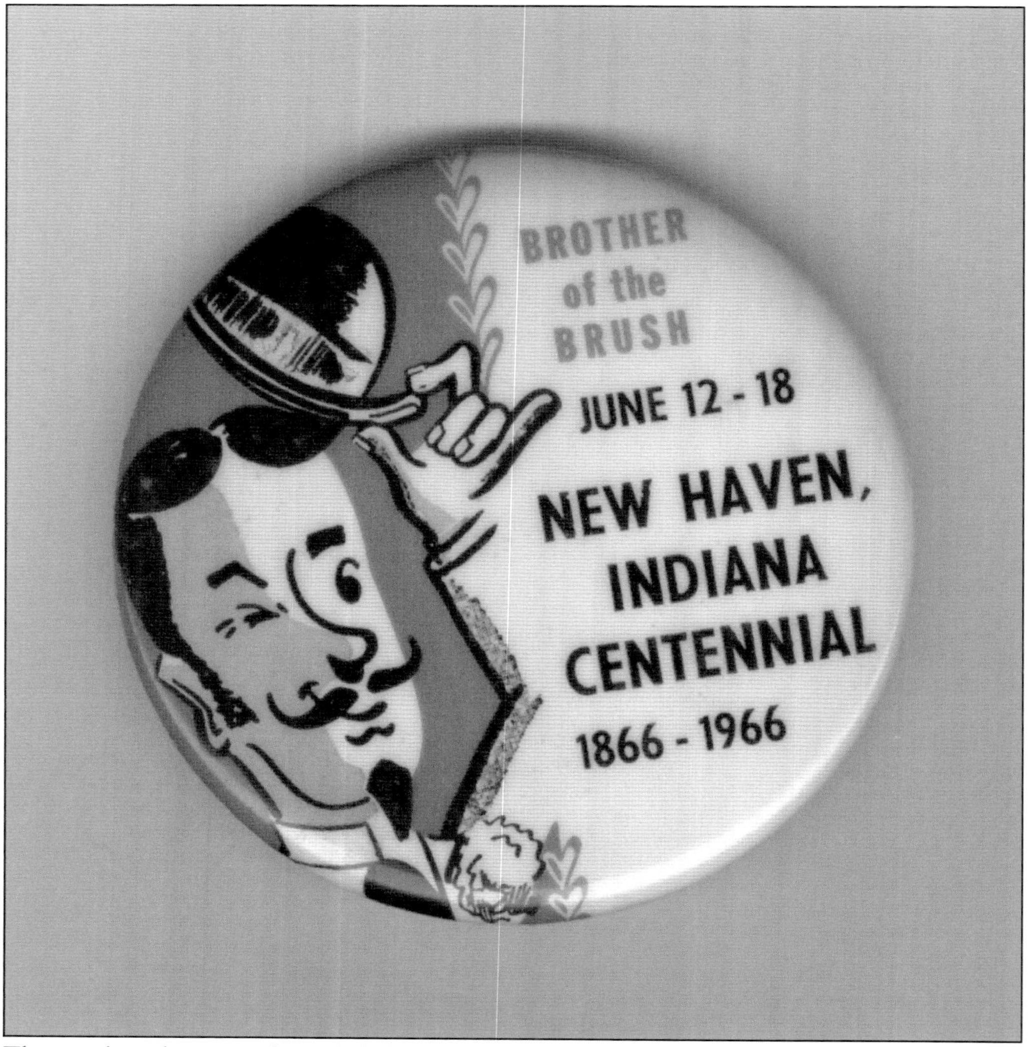

The two-hour-long parade included floats, oxen teams, wagons, buggies, antique automobiles and bicycles, veterans organizations, fire and police units, and a large number of area bands. The parade started at the end of Park Avenue, near the Lutheran school, and proceeded to Broadway Street, north to Rose Avenue, and east to a conclusion at Seward Street—a 1.5-mile route. Other centennial celebration events were an amusement arcade, an all-star Little League game, concerts by the New Haven High School Band, a beard-judging contest at John H. Young Field, a ladies golf tournament, and a muzzleloader rifle match. New Haven's Lana Shaw, a member of the internationally known Serendipity Singers, came with the group to the event, where they entertained the crowd with their songs. Col. Harland Sanders of the Kentucky Fried Chicken Company, in cooperation with the Pancake House in New Haven, presented an award to the man with a beard that most resembles the Colonel Sanders beard. (Ornel Kitchen and John McDowell.)

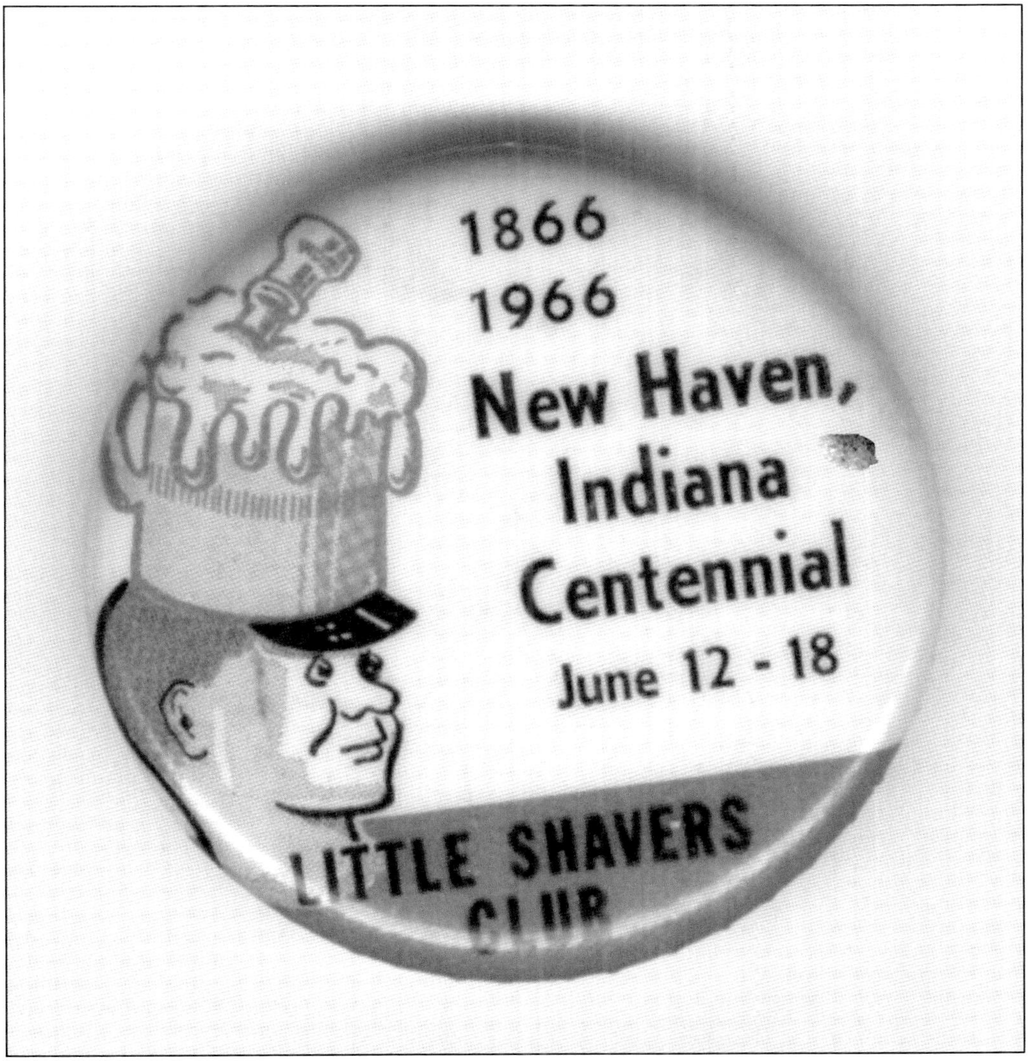

More than a thousand men sprouted whiskers in observance of the town's centennial celebration. Dick Hamman's beard was a veritable monument of distinction. It took him exactly six months and five days to grow his crop of whiskers. On the night after the judging it took barber Lynn Shaw 11 minutes and 43 seconds to shave off the champion's blue-ribbon beard. Hamman was among nearly 300 New Haven men who competed in the town's beard-judging contest. It was a wondrous celebration for such a small town. Women and daughters walked around with old-fashioned long gowns and bonnets or fancy hats. In contrast, parachutists came out of the sky and landed in a nearby field. (Lynn Shaw and John McDowell.)

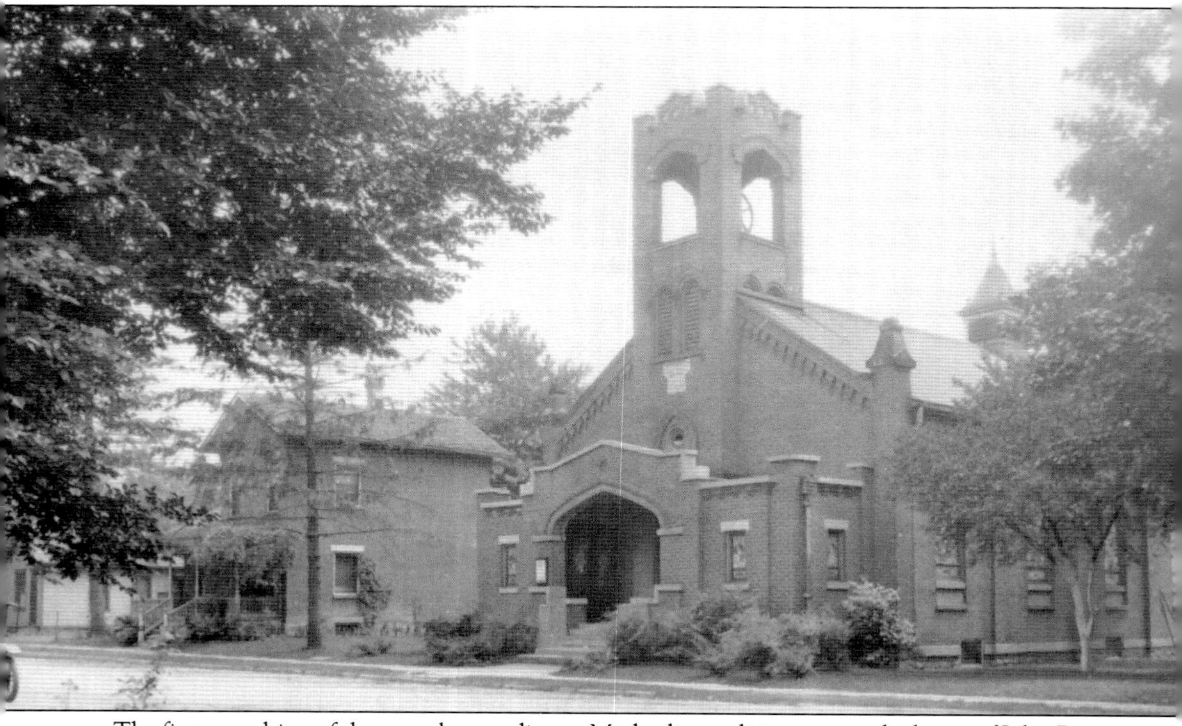

The first preaching of the gospel, according to Methodist tradition, was at the home of John Rogers. Rev. David Pattee preached in 1838 in Jefferson Township in the log schoolhouse of the settlement. They eventually came to Adams Township, joined the New Haven Church, and worshipped in the Methodist Protestants old frame church until 1866. Henry Burgess erected a brick structure on Middle Street, pictured here, that was dedicated in 1867. In 1939, the Methodist Episcopal Church and the Methodist Protestant Church merged and became the Methodist Church. On June 1, 1942, the name became New Haven Methodist Church and the congregation purchased land at 630 Lincoln Highway West. A new Indiana limestone church was built and dedicated on December 1955. (Todd Baron.)

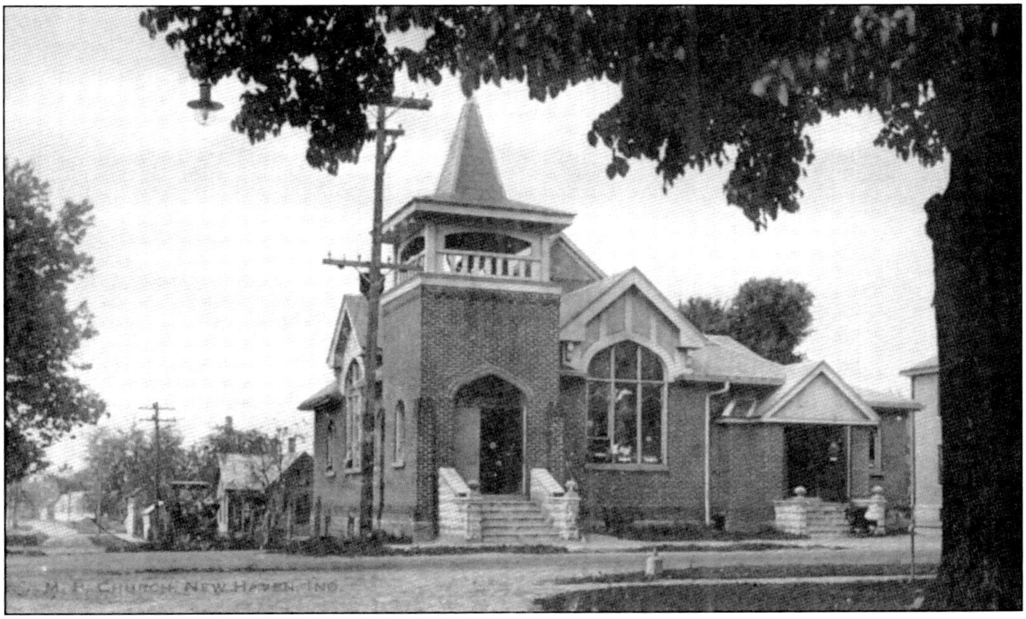

The earliest records of the Methodist Protestant organization, effected about 1838, show that the congregation was under the ministry of Rev. Edward Hickland. The first Methodist building was erected from 1847 to 1858. Near the turn of the century, the frame building was sold to Dr. Null, who moved it to the canal bed along Broadway Street, which is the present site of the fire station. On the same site on Middle Street, this new brick building was dedicated in 1902. The photograph below shows the parsonage of the Methodist Protestant Church. It was located on Middle Street but through the years has been removed. (Both, Douglas Runyan,)

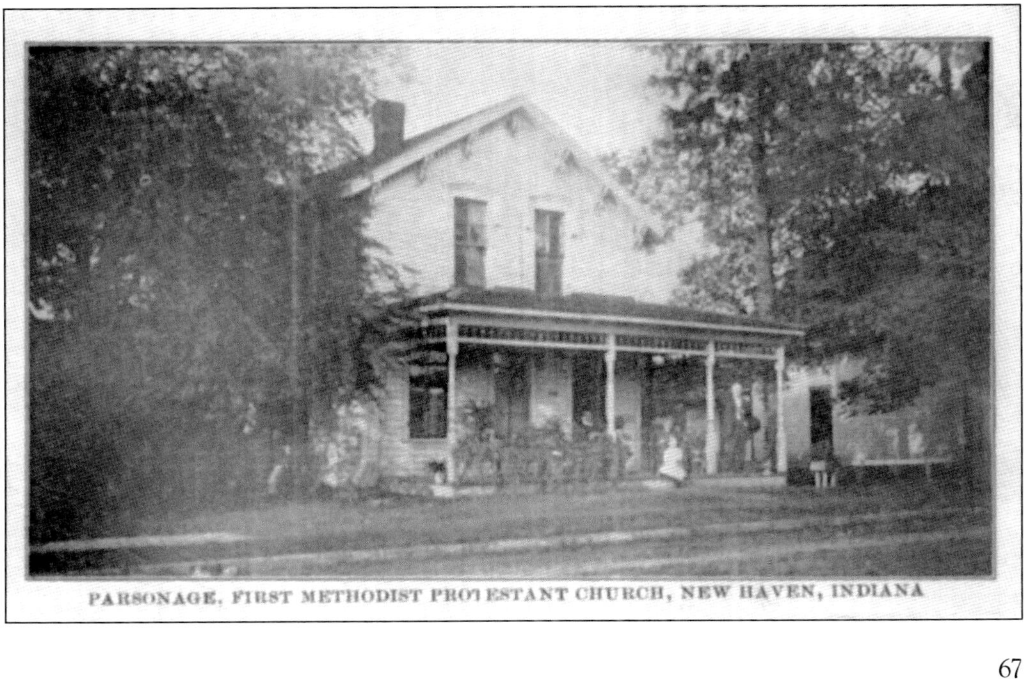

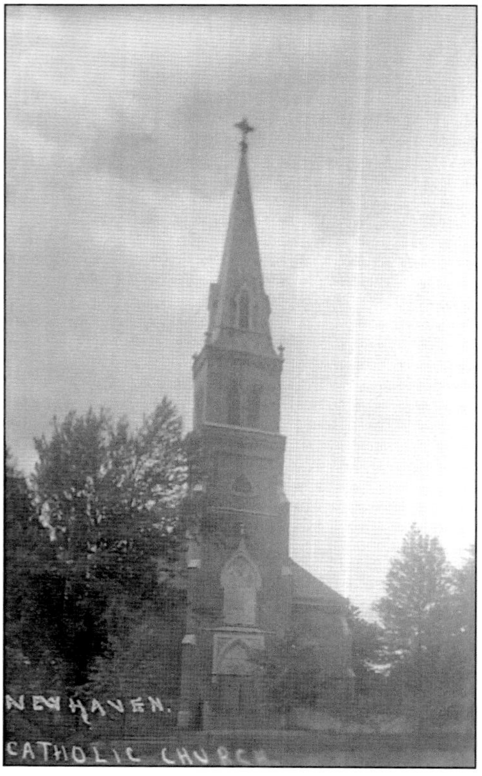

St. John the Baptist Catholic Church originated with Fr. Alexius Botti holding monthly services alternately at the home of Nicholas Schuckman on 757 Main Street and a dry goods store owned by the Messrs. Bueter and Schnelker (now Trion Restaurant). A brick church was erected in 1859 at a cost of $4,000 and was used until 1876. Under the direction of Father Wiedau, a new church was erected at the cost of $16,000 and dedicated on November 11, 1877. (Douglas Runyan and St. John Baptist Catholic Church.)

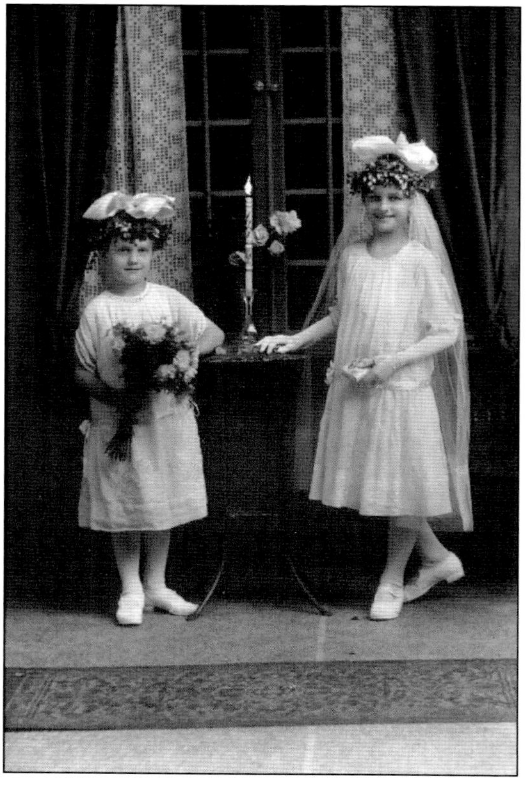

In 1922, Florence Ehinger, right, celebrated her First Communion at the St. John the Baptist Catholic Church. Her sister Clara stands beside her. On Palm Sunday 1954, there was a fire. Construction of a new church was considered. It was not until 1975 that the new church was dedicated. (Helen Smith.)

The first Catholic school opened in 1864 at 1008 Powers Street. In 1872, a 40-foot-by-56-foot brick school building was constructed at a cost of $8,000. The sisters of St. Agnes took charge of the school in 1873. Ground was broken for the 85-foot-by-145-foot school on May 19, 1949. A second floor was added in 1957. The present convent was built in 1949 at a cost of $60,000. (Todd Baron and St. John Baptist Catholic Church.)

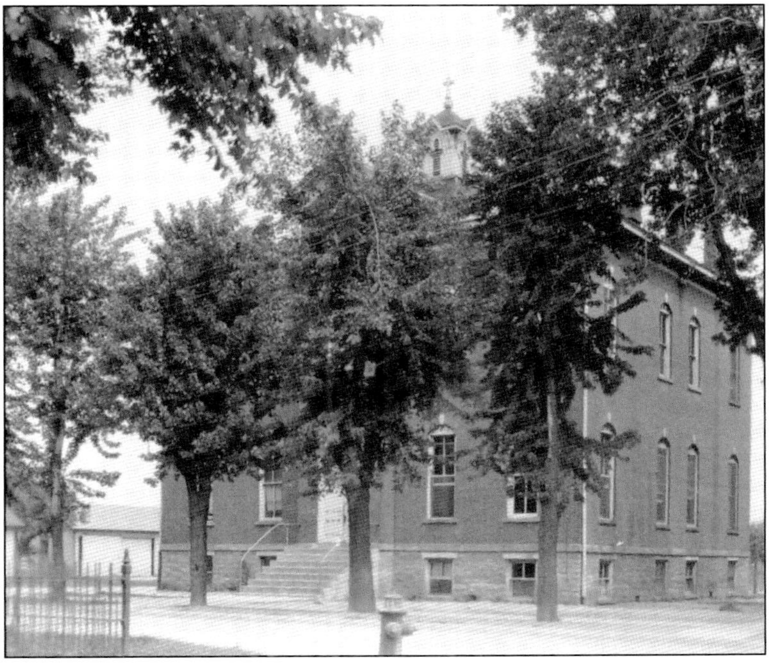

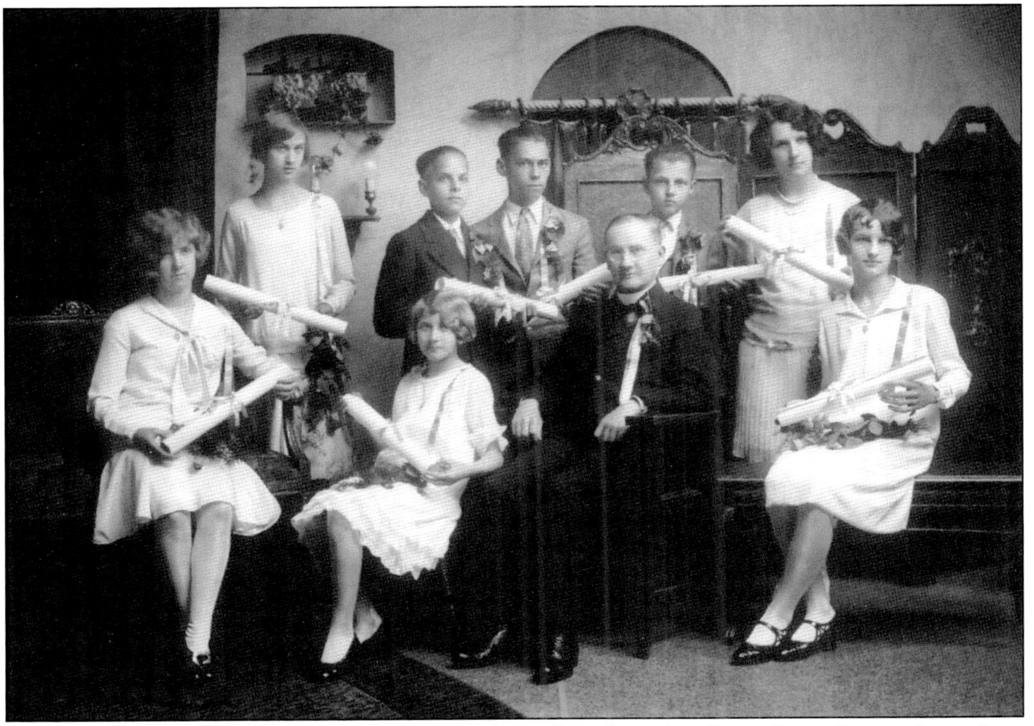

The 1928, St. John the Baptist Catholic High School graduated eight students. Pictured are, from left to right, (first row) Magdlein Marcotte, Mary Krominaker, Friar Faust, and Florence Ehinger; (second row) Helen Schnelker, Wilfred Becker, Maurice Pranger, Harold Schnelker, and Hilda Urbine. (Helen Smith.)

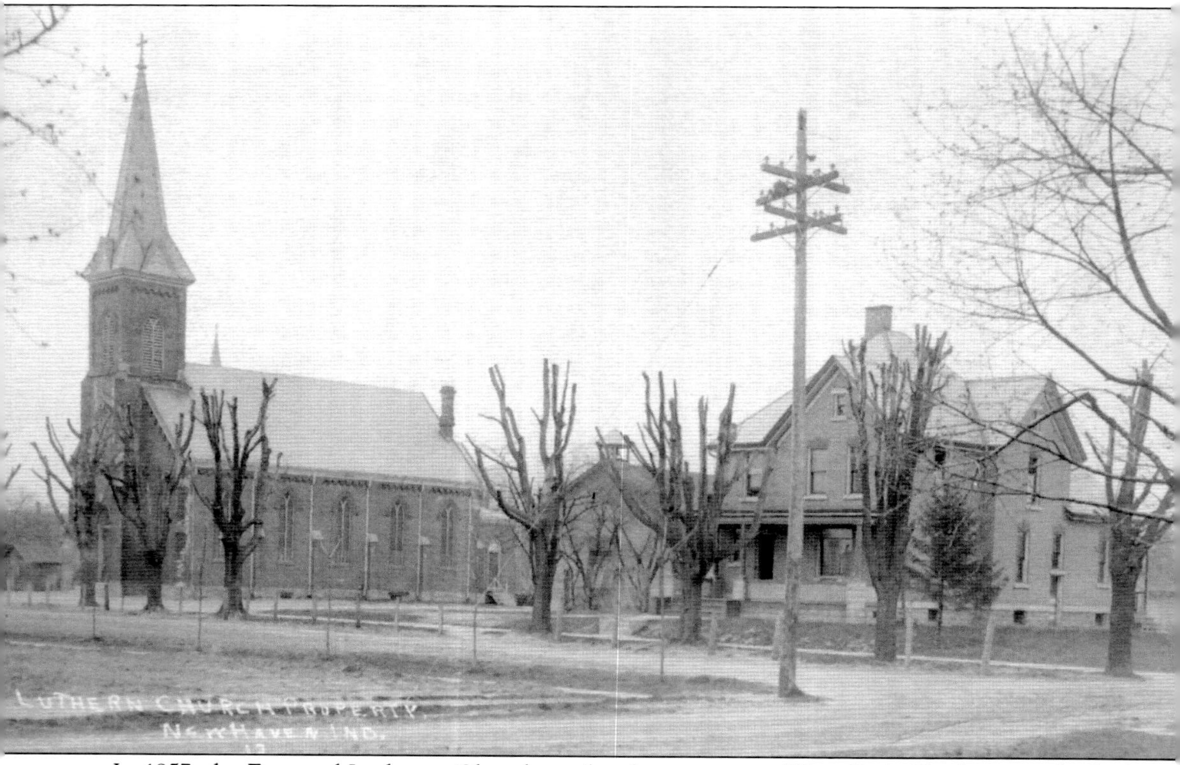

In 1857, the Emanuel Lutheran Church, under the pastorate of Rev. F. A. Herzberger, who had assumed the pastorate at Soest in Marion Township, Allen County, announced a meeting to take place in the shop of wagon-maker George Foerster. As a result of this meeting, a congregation was organized in 1858. The home of Fred Linneman at 811 Main Street was a temporary place for services. In 1859, August Lallow received a contract to construct the frame church and was paid $175 for his labor. Henry Burgess and his wife, Catherine, donated the building site of two lots. During 1881, the brick church was built on Bell Avenue. In 1908, a nine-room parsonage was constructed and in 1915 a two-room school was built on the same property. This photograph was taken around 1900. Looking closely, the old church can be seen between the newer church and the parsonage. In 1960, a new church was built and dedicated on 800 Green Street. Not long after, the Central Lutheran School was added. (Todd Baron and Rita Wissman.)

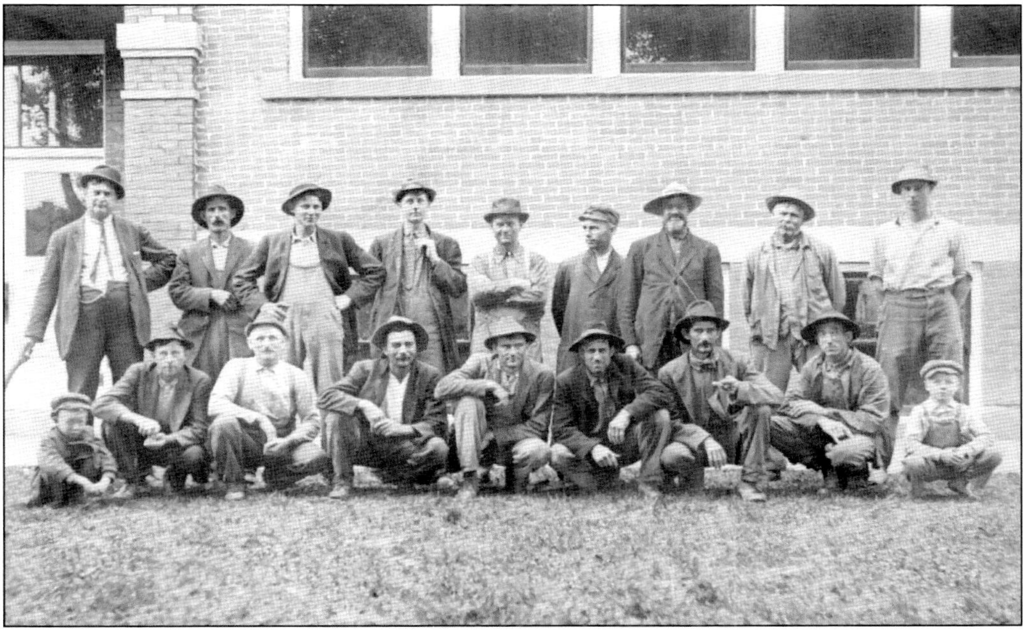

This photograph was taken around 1914. The construction crew built the Emanuel Lutheran School, located on Bell Avenue, at a cost of $9,655. It went through grade six. August Werling is in the second row, fourth from the left. (Todd Baron.)

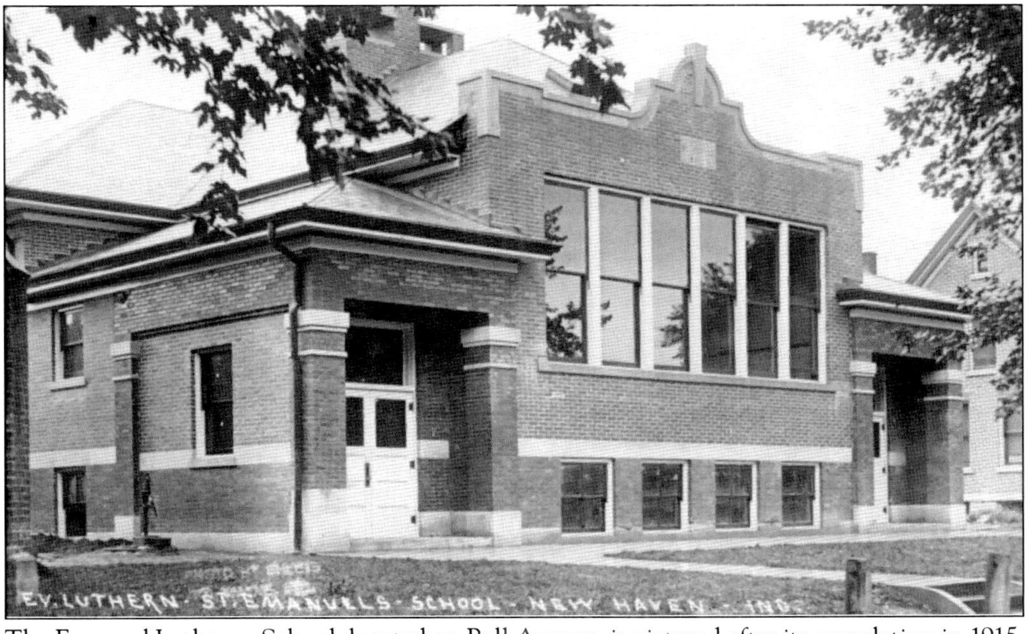

The Emanuel Lutheran School, located on Bell Avenue, is pictured after its completion in 1915. In 1949, the Emanuel, St. Paul, and Martini congregations adopted a plan to build a consolidated school, which was dedicated in 1952. Property was purchased at 800 Green Street, next to the new school, for the purpose of erecting a new church building, which was dedicated in 1960. (Todd Baron.)

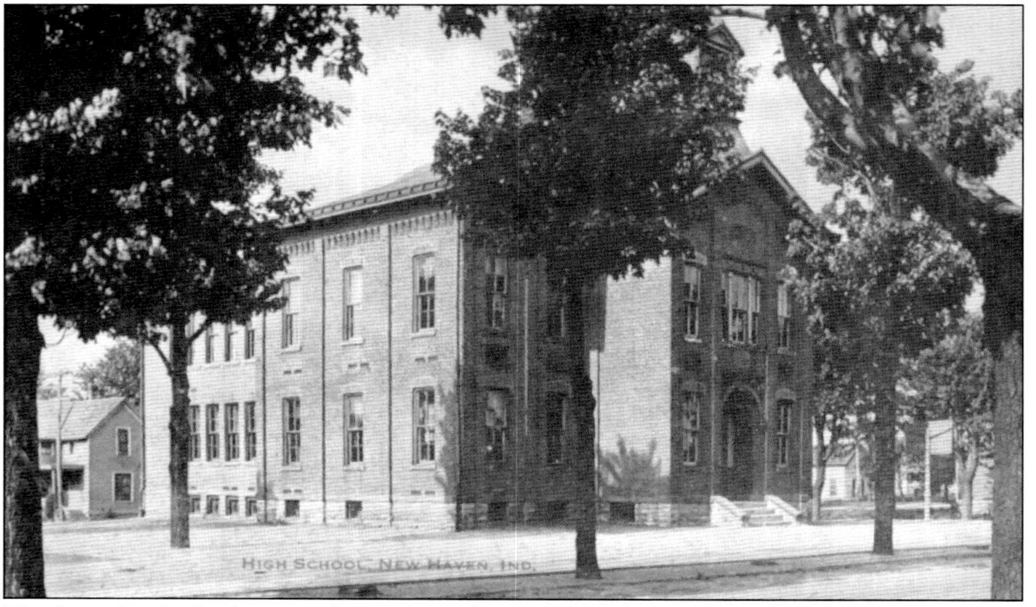

The first school, a log house with puncheon floors and windows of greased, glazed paper, was built in 1829 on Absalom Holcomb's property between Parrot Road and U.S. Highway 30. In 1868, a public school opened on 707 Main Street. A brick high school, pictured here, was built in 1885 at the end of Middle Street. Students attended three years there but went to other schools for their final year. In 1911, all grades were included. The first yearbook, *The Ultimatum*, was printed in 1916 with 10 students graduating. (Todd Baron.)

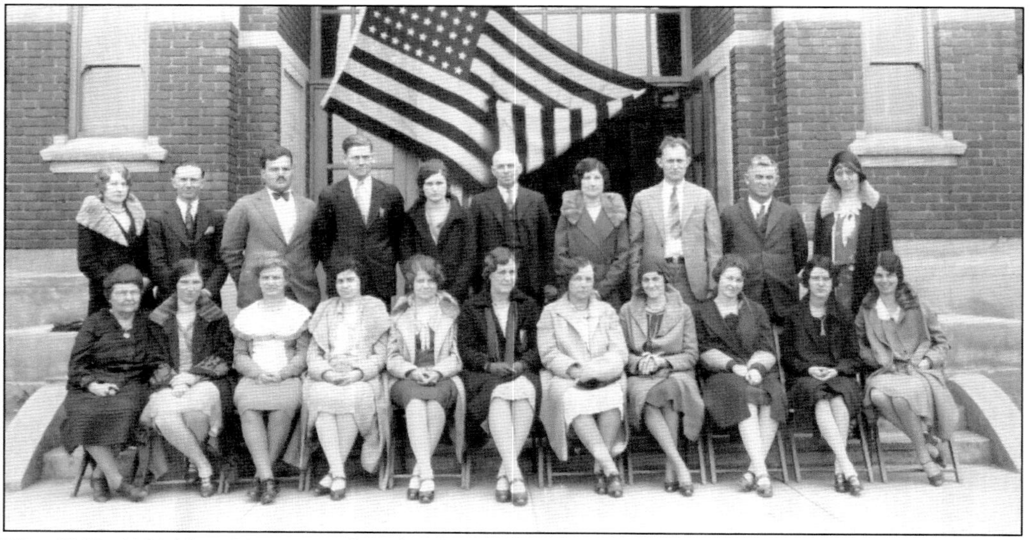

The 1929–1930 New Haven High School faculty included, from left to right, (first row) Maude Caps, Florence Harris, Olive Lenhart, Mary Kenny, Lola Parish, Naomi McFadden, Evelyn Walter, Geraldine Guild, Lenora Simon, Harriet Daniels, and Harriet Lake; (second row) Mabel Hutker, Earl Marshall, John Young, Arthur Parr, Doris Speaker, Fred Pranger, unidentified, Ben Clem, unidentified, and Merrie McClellan. (Sue Asher Bradley.)

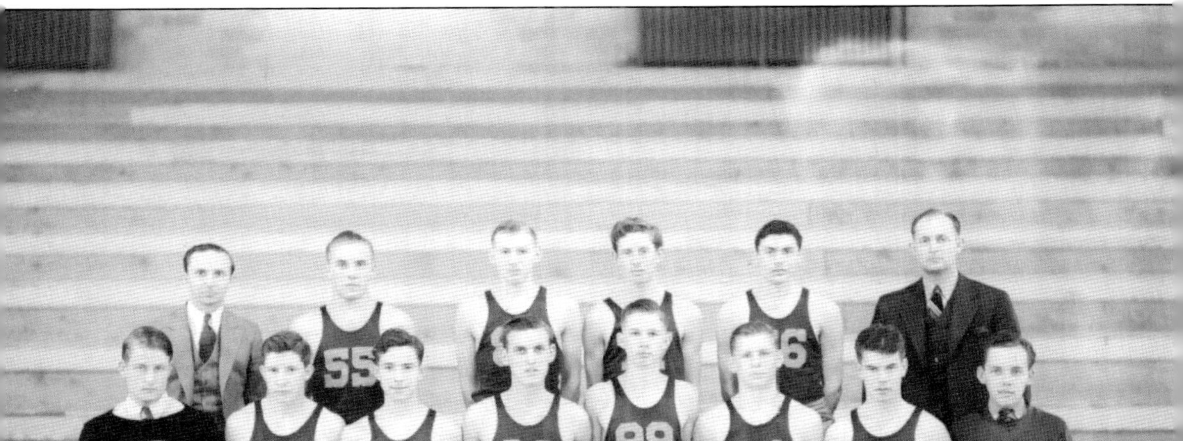

The New Haven High School basketball team of 1936–1937 was the first to use the new gymnasium. Following a bloody basketball game played on the gravel school yard in 1913, the school principal learned that the upper floor of the Meyer building, home of Blackwell's Department Store on Main Street, was vacant. Rent was $2 per game, and admission was 10¢ per game. An average game drew a crowd of 50 to 60 people who had to wear coats because the room was not heated. Players were often injured when they plowed into the radiators, but they wore their scars as badges of honor. The team then moved their games to the upstairs of the building on Main Street that is now used by the Power House. This room was smaller with low ceilings, and players had to bounce the ball off the ceiling into the basket. The state inspector ruled the building unsafe, so the team moved to the Cream of Rice building, which stood where Hartzell Street runs into Green Street. Later the inspector also ruled it unsafe. A new gymnasium and cafeteria were built in 1936. (Todd Baron.)

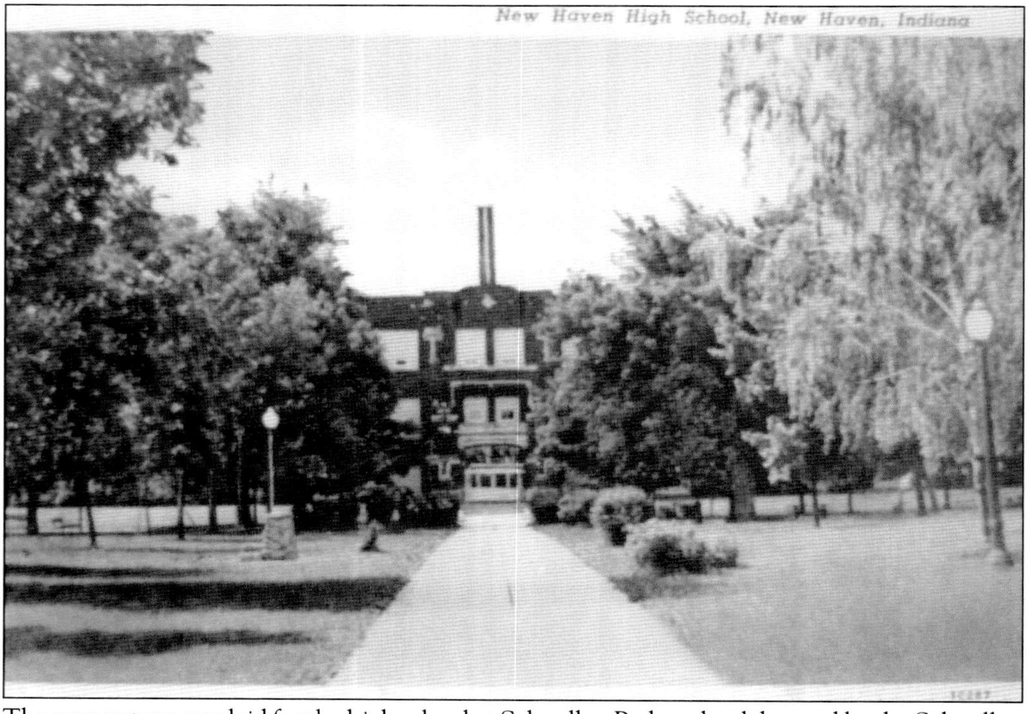

The cornerstone was laid for the high school at Schnelker Park on land donated by the Schnelker family in 1922. The building was finished in 1923. Twenty-one students graduated in the spring of 1924. In 1936, a gymnasium and cafeteria were completed and were in use until the 1970s when a new high school was built on 1300 Green Road. The first graduating class had 250 students. (St. Louis Catholic Church and Jeff Hoffman.)

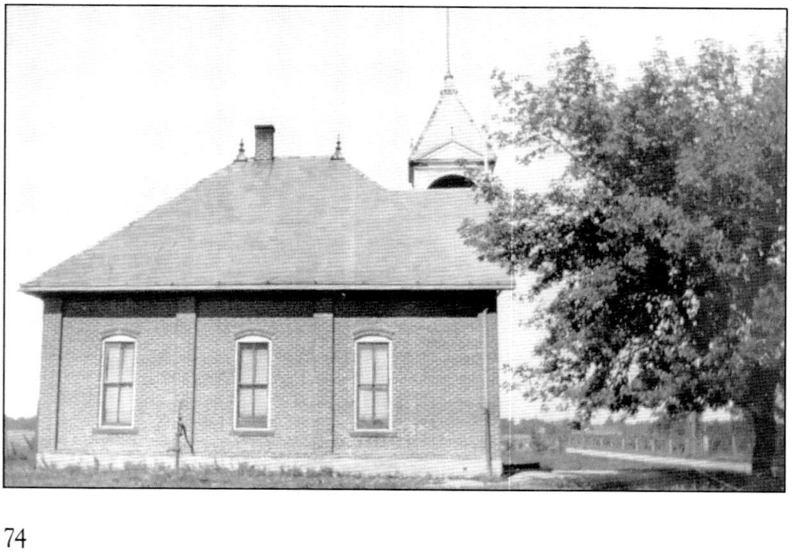

Adams Township School No. 11 was located on Tillman Road, 1 mile east of Minnich Road. The year it was built is unknown, as is the school's name. It closed in 1930 and was the last standing school in Adams Township. (Deborah Eidson.)

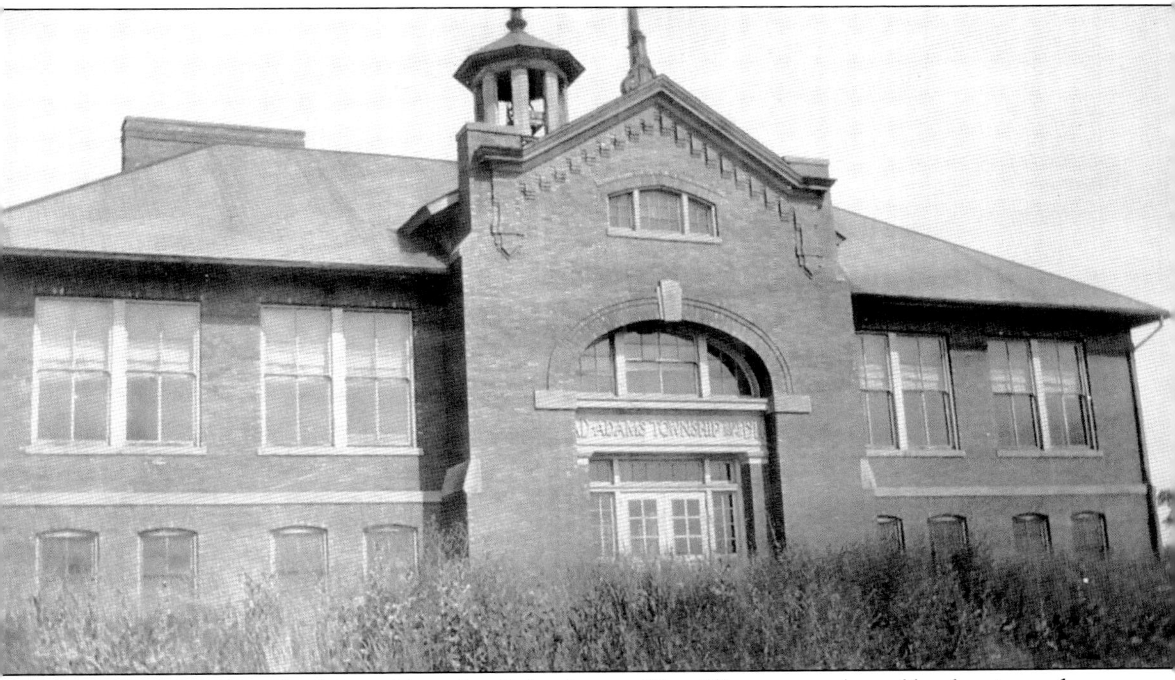

From 1880s to 1920s, the Adams Township School east of Fort Wayne was adopted by the city and called the Adams School, later named Wayne Haven because it was located on the border of Fort Wayne and New Haven. The school accommodated grade-schoolers and a full high school course. Curriculum included domestic science and an agricultural course. Children traveled from all over the township by automobiles, interurban train, and other means to get to school. In 1916, fifty-four students attended the high school; nine graduated. Architect Henry Meyers, of Fort Wayne, designed the most advanced school plans. The exact location of this building is not known, but it may have been in the Sunnymeade area. (Deborah Eidson and Allen County Library.)

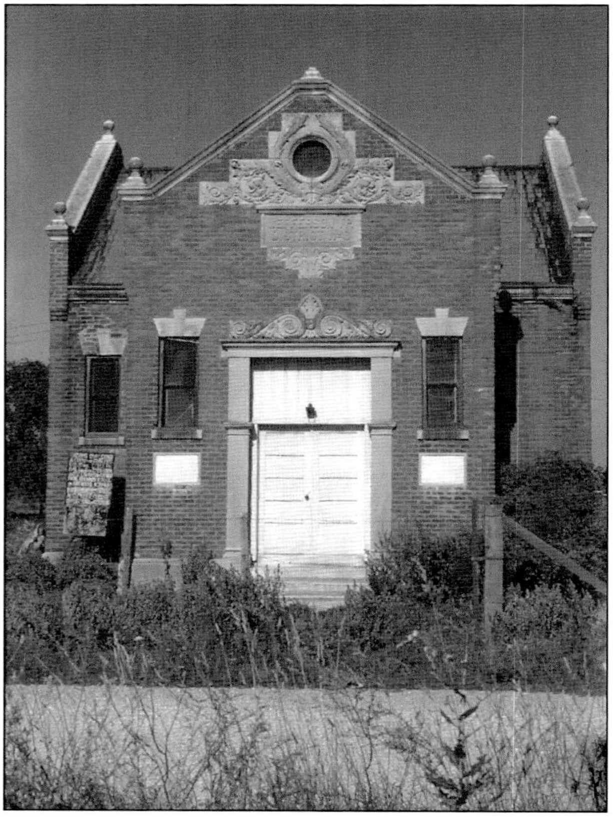

Jefferson Township School No. 6, Helmick School, was located at Doyle Road and Lincoln Highway. It was built in 1906 and closed in 1921—the last school to close in Jefferson Township. The building is not standing today. (Deborah Eidson.)

Jefferson Township School No. 5, Center School, was located on Lincoln Highway in Besancon and was built in 1892. It closed in 1939. The building still stands close to St. Louis Catholic Church. (Deborah Eidson.)

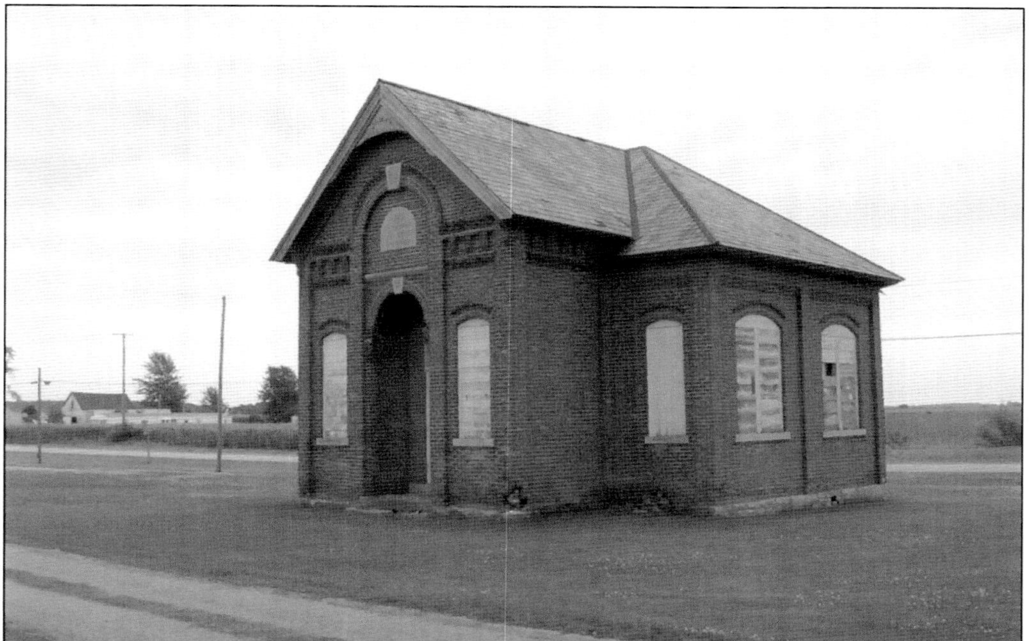

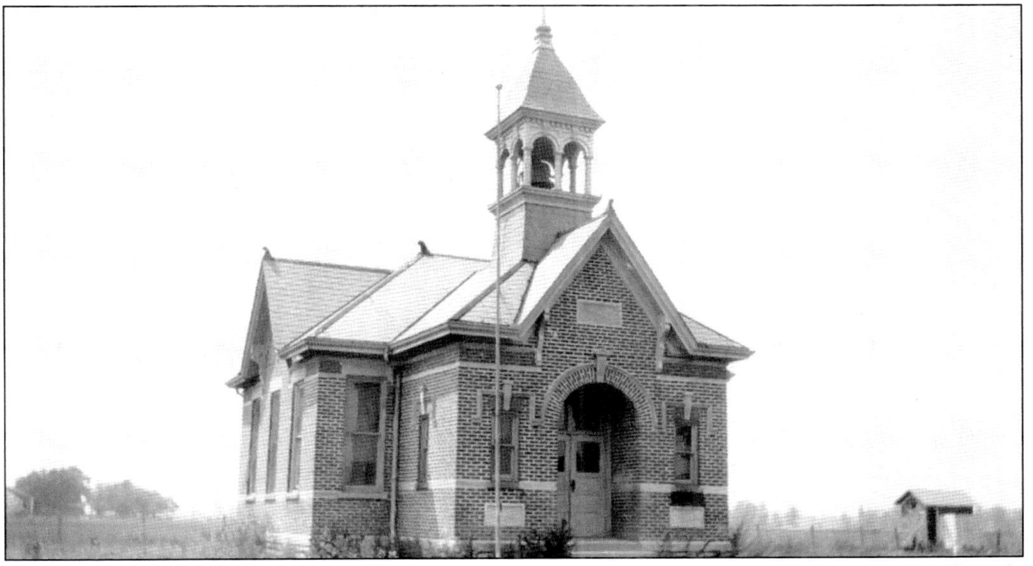

Jefferson Township School No. 1, Whitney School, was located at the northeast corner of Doyle and Edgerton Roads. Built in 1890, it closed in 1938. The building still stands today. In 1907, the teacher was Mrs. Creighton Linden Butler. Students included Clem Henry, Ervin Bandelier, Gladys Bandelier McFadden, Ruth Main and Hilda Barrow Henderson, Felicien Henry, Mae Heine, Ethel Bandelier, Albert Heine, Harold Bandelier, Emma Heine, Clara Werling Heine, Christ Ulmer, and Laura Barrow Emke. (Deborah Eidson.)

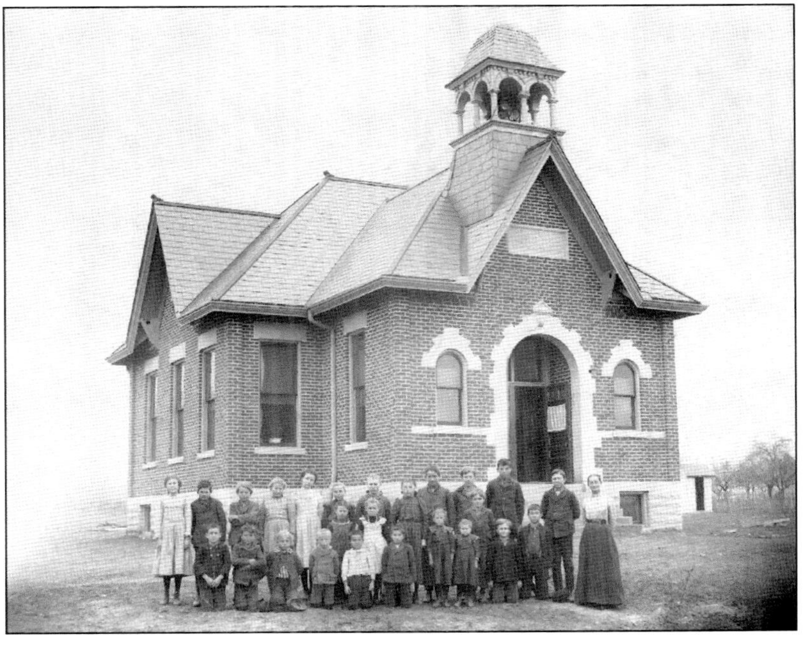

St. Joseph Township School No. 6, Vonderau School, was located at the corner of St. Joe Center and Wheelock Roads. The school was built in 1891 and closed in 1936. (Deborah Eidson.)

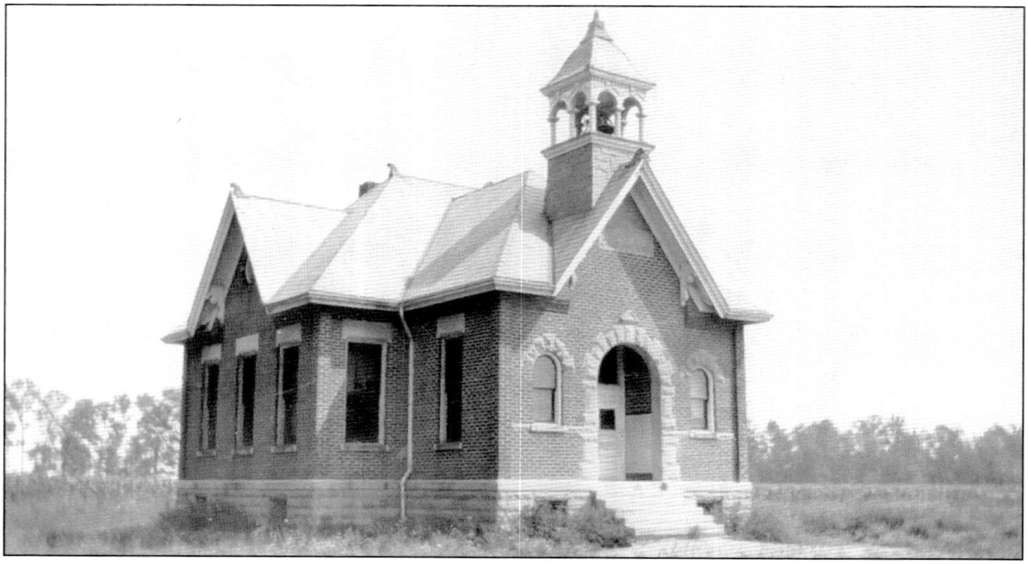

St. Joseph Township School No. 7, Burchardt School, was located at the corner of Parent and Landin Roads. It was built in 1898 and closed in 1936. The building is now in use as a residence. The bell tower is gone, but the building looks very much the same, with no additions or changes to the front entrance. (Both, Deborah Eidson.)

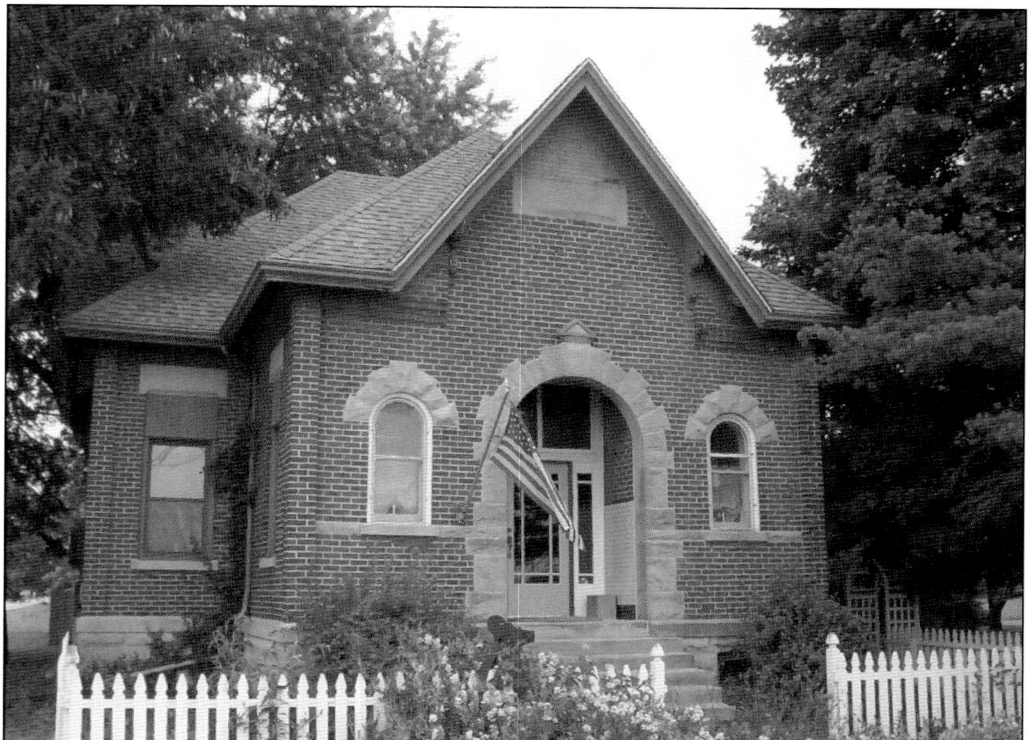

Five

Historical Residences and Local Citizens

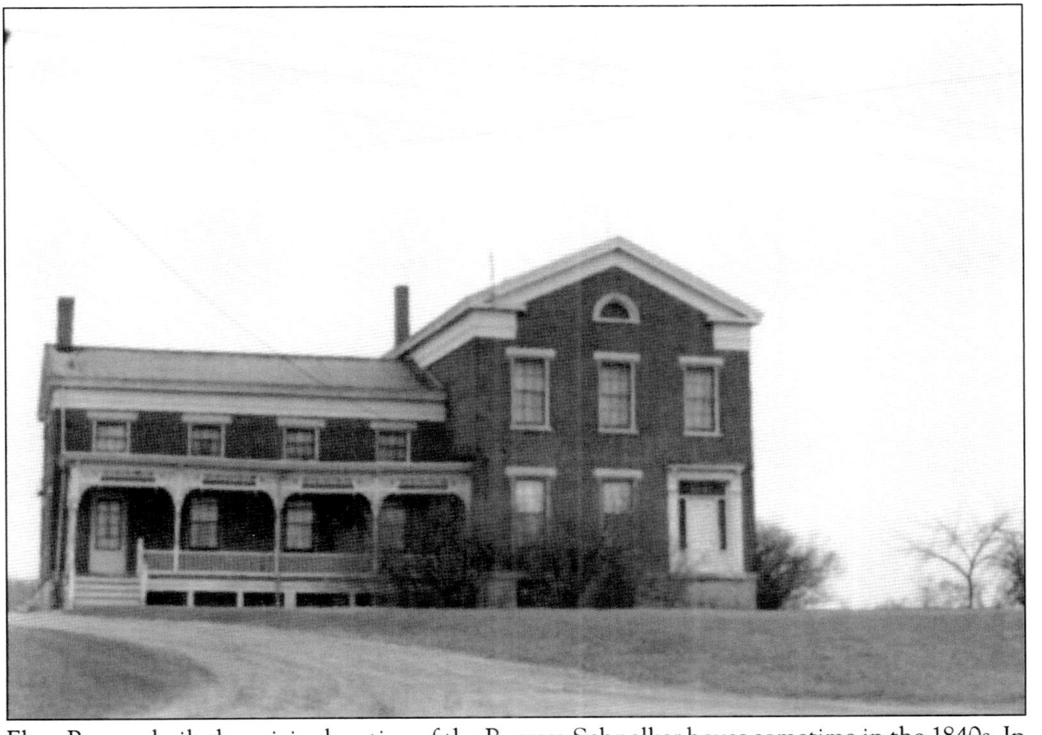

Eben Burgess built the original section of the Burgess-Schnelker house sometime in the 1840s. In 1852, he built an addition, including a country ballroom on the third floor. The entire house was erected using native redbrick from the creek behind the house. In 1880, the Burgesses sold the farm to the Schnelker family and moved to Kansas. The Schnelkers lived there for about 100 years. The home was demolished in the 1980s. (Dan White and *Fort Wayne News-Sentinel*, 1979.)

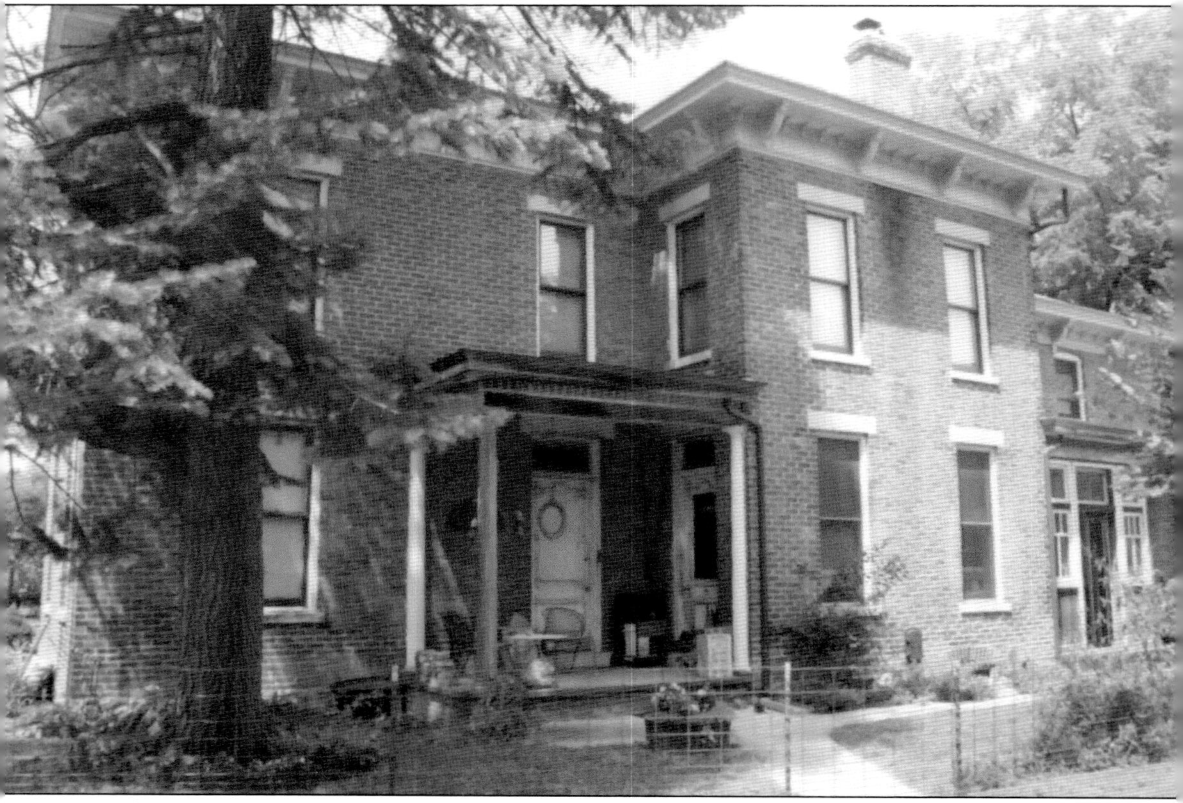

Alison Adams purchased the Thimlar farm at 549 Rose Avenue in 1987. Robert Burns wrote that it was part of the farmland settled by his great-grandfather, Jesse Adams, in Adams Township in 1823. Jesse Adams came downstream to homestead the area that would be New Haven. After he sold the farm in 1837 and moved inland to Jefferson Township, several owners had the place up until the Civil War. The Thimlar family purchased the farm after the war and built an Italianate-style brick house on Rose Avenue (then Thimlar Road) in the 1870s. There were four rooms downstairs and four rooms upstairs. It was progressive to have built-in closets in three bedrooms. It also boasted front and back stairs. The house and farm were abandoned 10 years before Alison Adams purchased the property. (Alison Adams and Stevia Webster.)

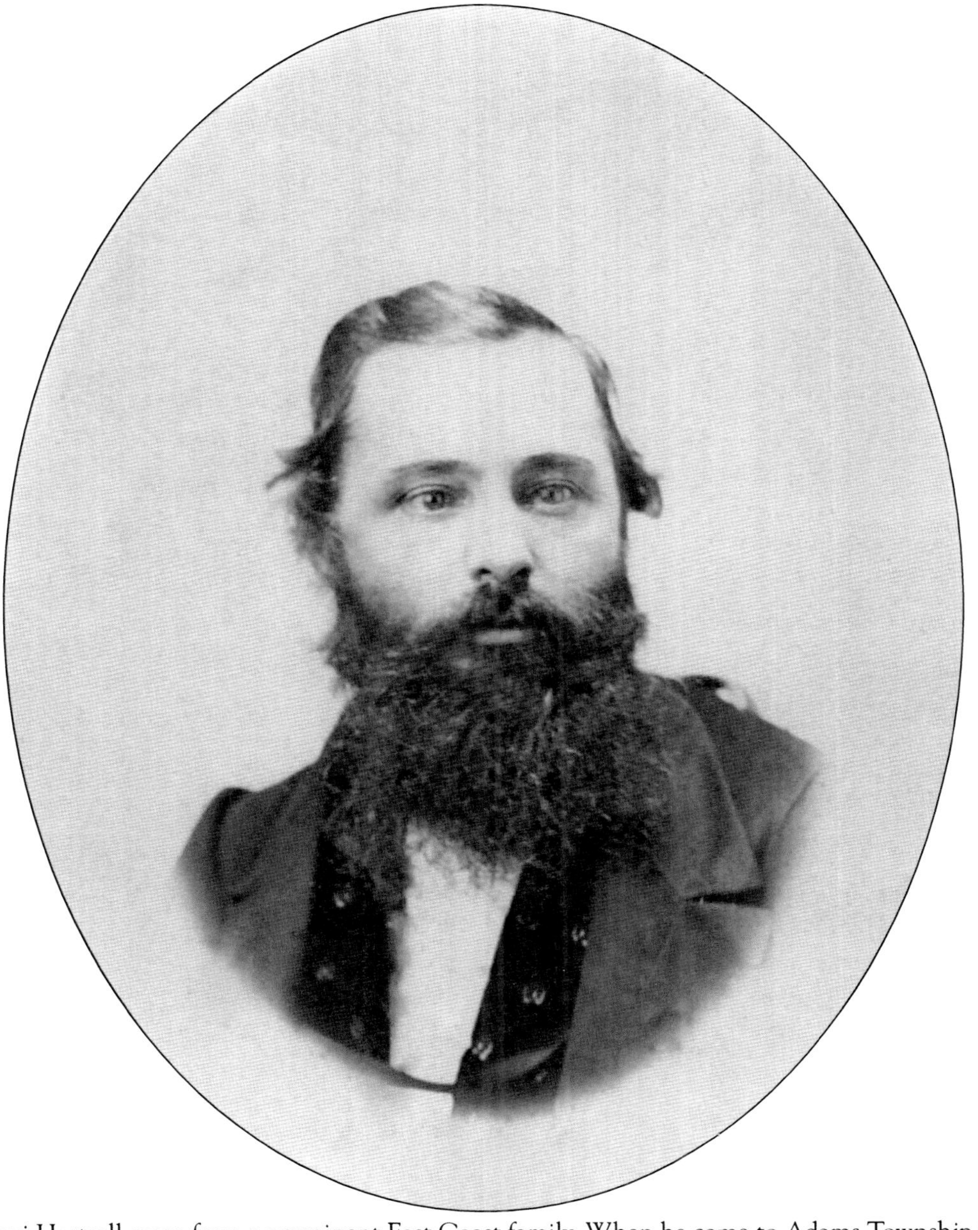

Levi Hartzell came from a prominent East Coast family. When he came to Adams Township in 1833, Levi purchased more than 400 acres on Hartzell Road. He was instrumental in helping start the first gristmill and constructing the Wabash and Erie Canal by securing timber for docks. He was also an enrolling officer in the Union ranks of the Civil War. His son John, who is pictured above, was born in 1851 and worked on the farm while he trained in the common schools. He married in 1876 and moved to an adjoining farm of 300 acres. He worked the land for dairying and raised livestock, Shropshire sheep, Poland swine, horses, and cattle. He had a very successful dairy, delivering about 100 gallons of milk daily. He was a staunch Republican but never sought office. He and his wife, Minnie, had two daughters, Naomi Olive and Iola Ethel. (Sue Luther and Allen County Library.)

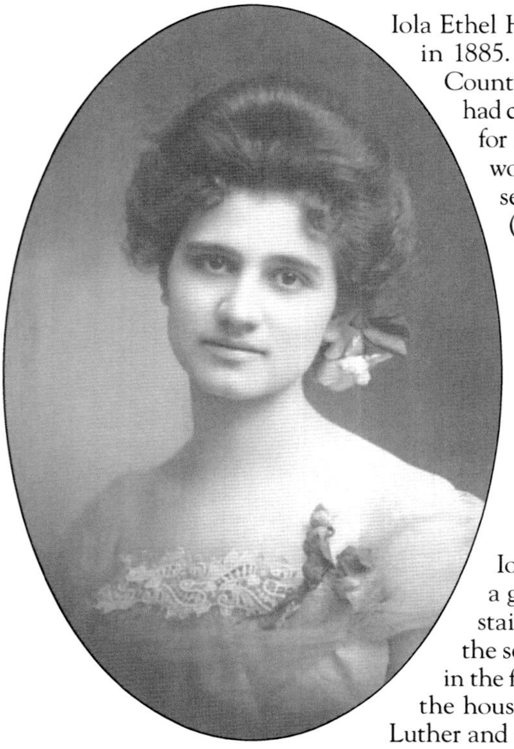

Iola Ethel Hartzell was born to John and Minnie Hartzell in 1885. She came from a prominent family in Allen County. She married a Mr. Keller, though they never had children. Iola was later married to William Moeller for 17 years. Described as a tall, slender, well-dressed woman, Iola announced the introduction of social security on the radio. She died at age 90 in 1975. (Sue Luther and Allen County Library.)

Iola made her home at 707 West Main Street in a grand Victorian house, still standing, with front stairs used by the family and back stairs that lead to the servants' quarters. The property boasted a gazebo in the front yard and a carriage house in the back. Before the house was built, a school sat on the property. (Sue Luther and Allen County Library.)

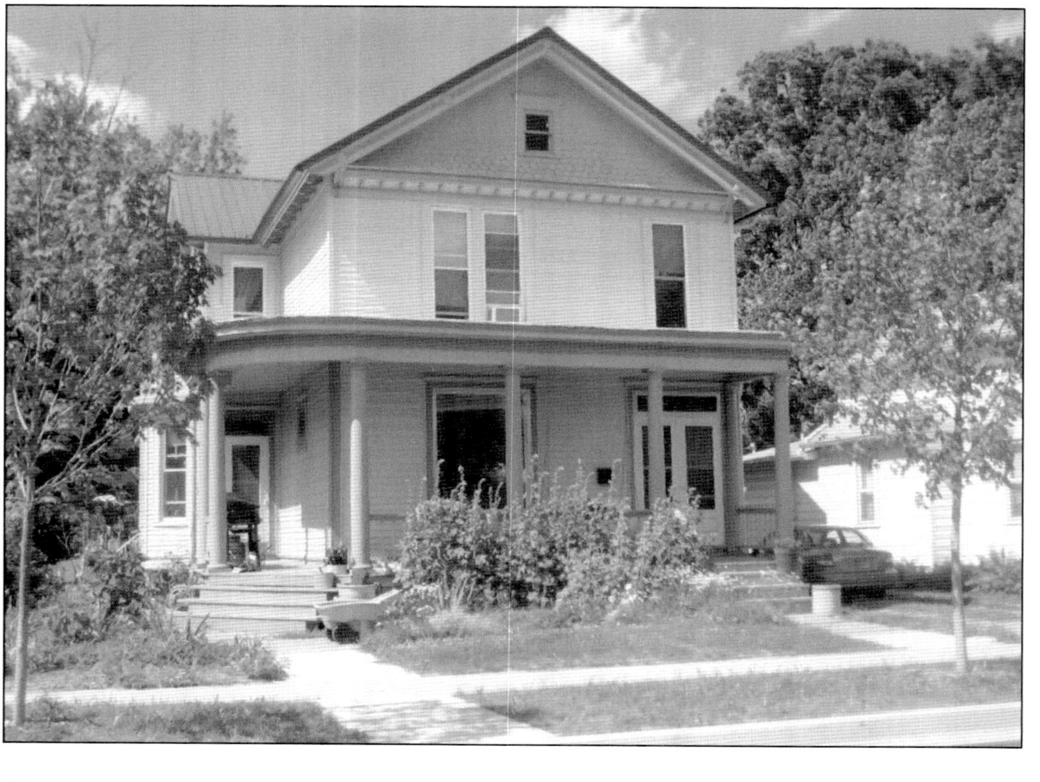

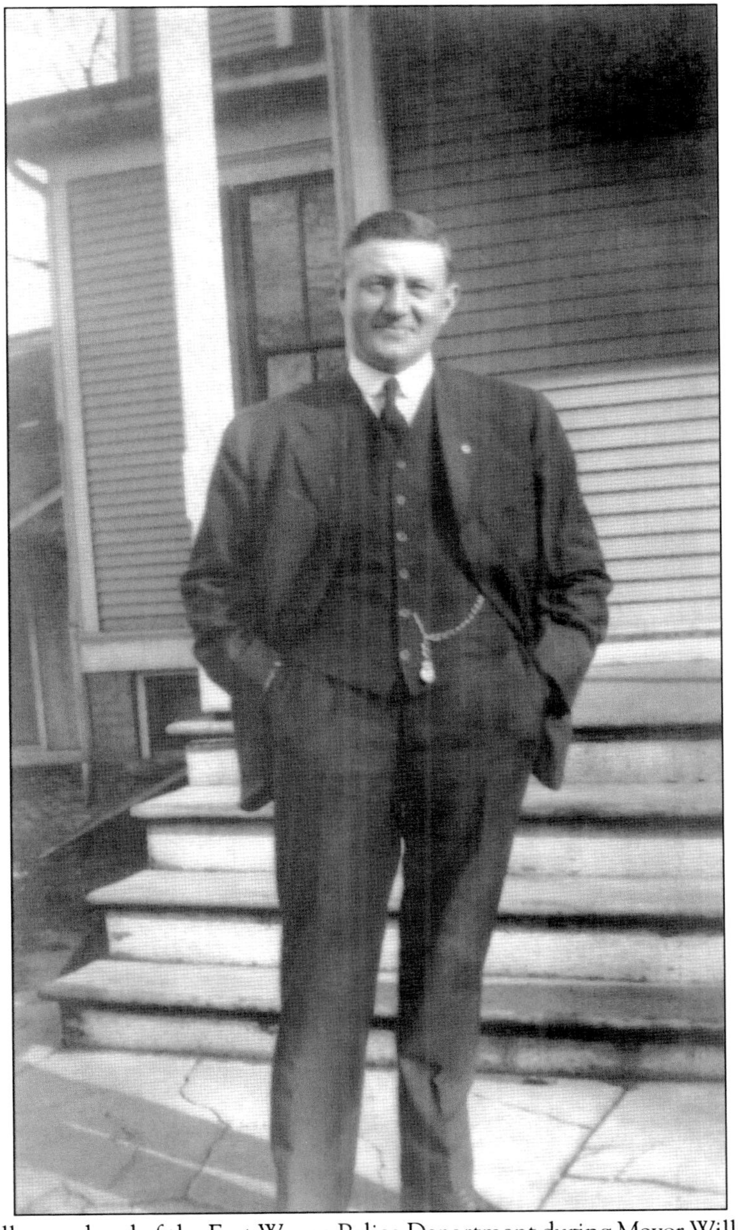

William Moeller was head of the Fort Wayne Police Department during Mayor William J. Hosey's term. After 14 years as police chief, Moeller worked as an investigator for the Indiana State Highway Department. A machinist by trade, Moeller had worked in the Pennsylvania railroad shops for many years. He was prominent in the machinists union and served as a delegate to state and national conventions. A follower of boxing, he officiated important matches. When his health began to deteriorate, Moeller left his residence in Fort Wayne for a farm south of New Haven on Hartzell Road, where he raised cattle. Later he moved to New Haven. He operated a filling station on the site of the old interurban train station. He died at 61 and was buried at the Independent Order of Odd Fellows cemetery on Hartzell Road, beside Iola Hartzell Moeller. (Sue Luther and Allen County Library.)

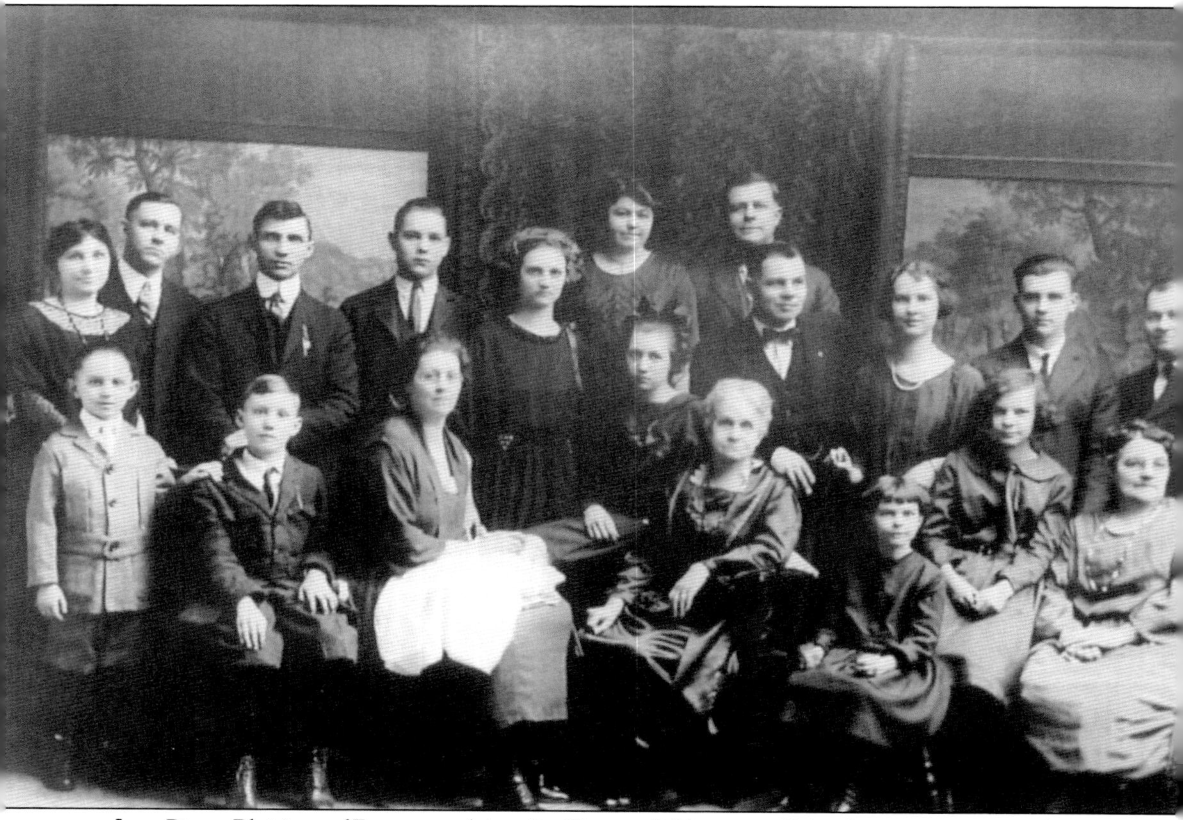

Jean Pierre Blaising, of France, and Amelia (Frossard) Blaising, of New Jersey, were married in 1874. This family photograph, taken in 1920, shows, from left to right, (first row) Robert Blaising, son of Louis Blaising; Paul Federspiel, son of Teresa (Blaising) Federspiel; Teresa (Blaising) Federspiel, daughter of Jean and Amelia; Mildred Federspiel, daughter of Teresa (Blaising) Federspiel; Ameliel Blaising, wife of Jean Pierre Blaising; Sellma Blaising, daughter of Henry Blaising; Doris Blaising, daughter of Victor Blaising; and Maude (Dawkens) Blaising, wife of Felix Blaising; (second row) Mamie (Berz) Blaising, wife of Louis Blaising; Louis Isidore Blaising, son of Jean and Amelia; Robert Blaising, son of Louis Blaising; Harold Federspiel, son of Teresa (Blaising) Federspiel; E. Kenneth Federspiel, son of Teresa (Blaising) Federspiel; Vivian Federspiel, daughter of Teresa (Blaising) Federspiel; Chloe Blaising, wife of Henry Blaising; Henry Victor Blaising, son of Jean and Amelia; Stephen Blaising, son of Jean and Amelia; Nellie May Blaising, daughter of Felix Blaising; and Mellville Blaising, son of Felix Blaising. (Katie Day.)

John August Blaising was born in France and moved to New Haven upon arriving in the United States. He was employed by the Nickel Plate Railroad as a section foreman on the interurban train. Blaising, seated, and Mary Magdalina Rupple, standing at the far left, were married in June 1899 at St. Mary's Catholic Church in Fort Wayne. John Rupple, brother of the bride, was the best man. Teresa Blaising, cousin of the groom, was the maid of honor. Teresa married John Federspiel in October 1902. (Katie Day.)

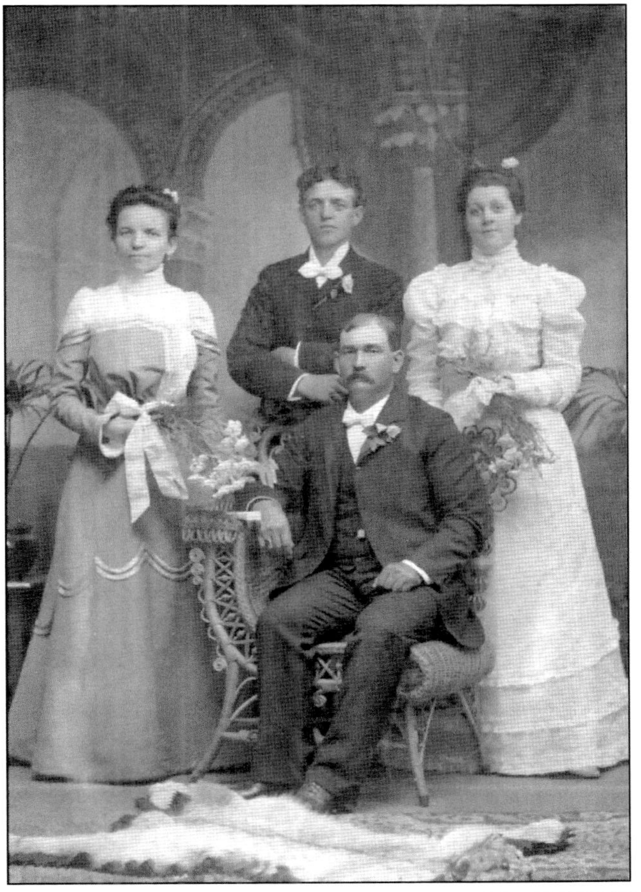

August Blaising worked as a section foreman on the interurban train sometime between 1910 and the 1920s. This photograph shows August, also called "Gus," pictured here on the far right, standing. The other men are unidentified. (Katie Day.)

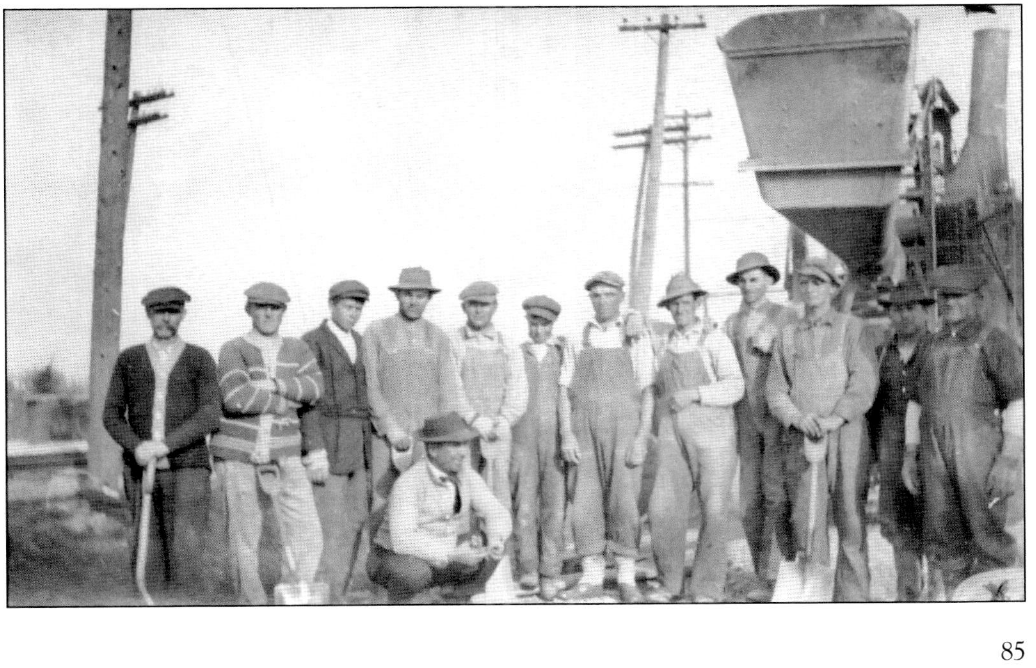

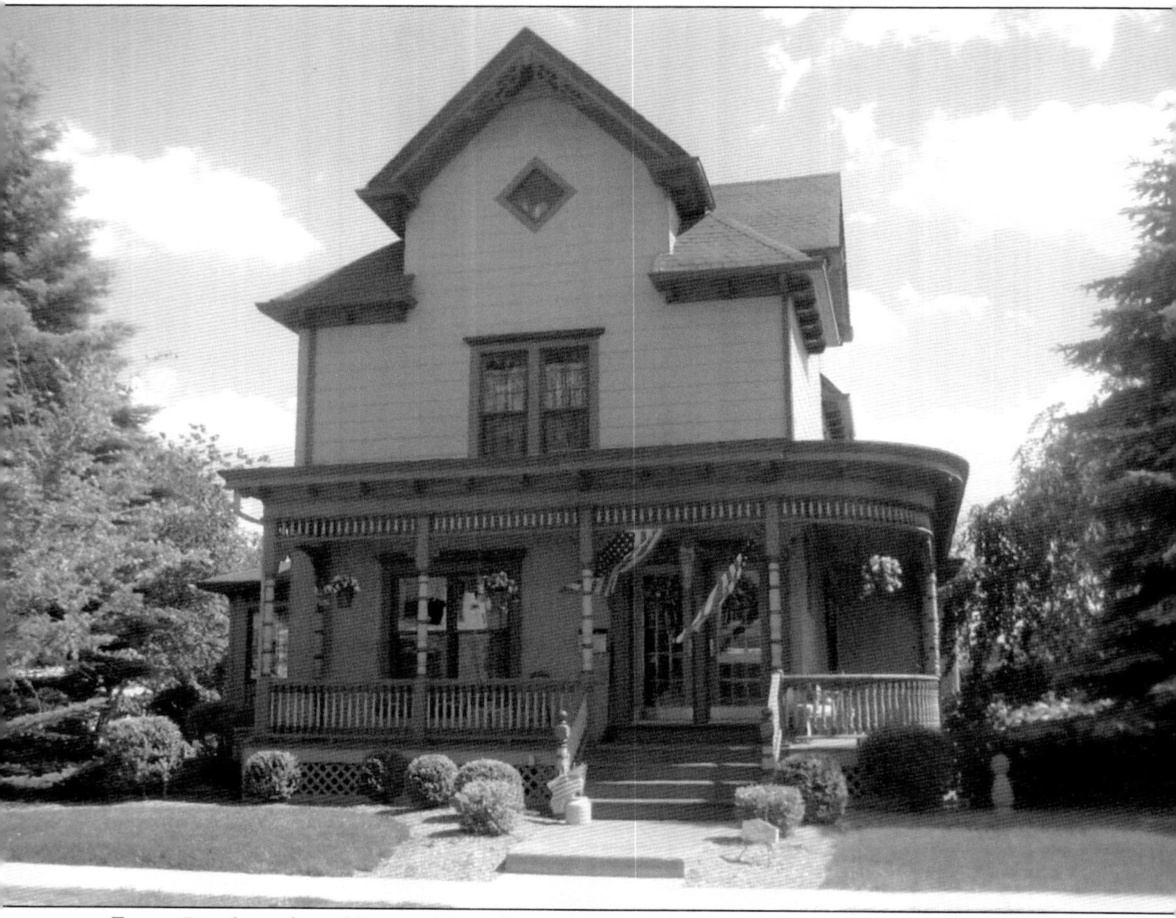

Emma Pond purchased lots on Main Street in 1888. She was married to Olen Pond, and the Ponds lived in their large Victorian house for many years. Olen, who served in World War I, worked in Chicago and was home only on weekends. During the week, Emma walked wherever she wanted to go, and many memories and stories are shared about her frugal ways. After her husband died in 1937, Emma willed her property and personal items to the bishop of the Fort Wayne diocese of Fort Wayne. The property, known as "Pond Haven," was to be used as a home for retired priests. Ultimately, the home was not eligible for the uses stipulated, and the properties were sold and the monies used toward Catholic education. Emma later honored her patriot husband by commissioning master sculptor Frederick C. Hubbard to create a large female statue standing on a tall column, and she donated the Olen J. Pond memorial to Memorial Park in Fort Wayne. Emma lived on the property until her death in 1942. (Dan White.)

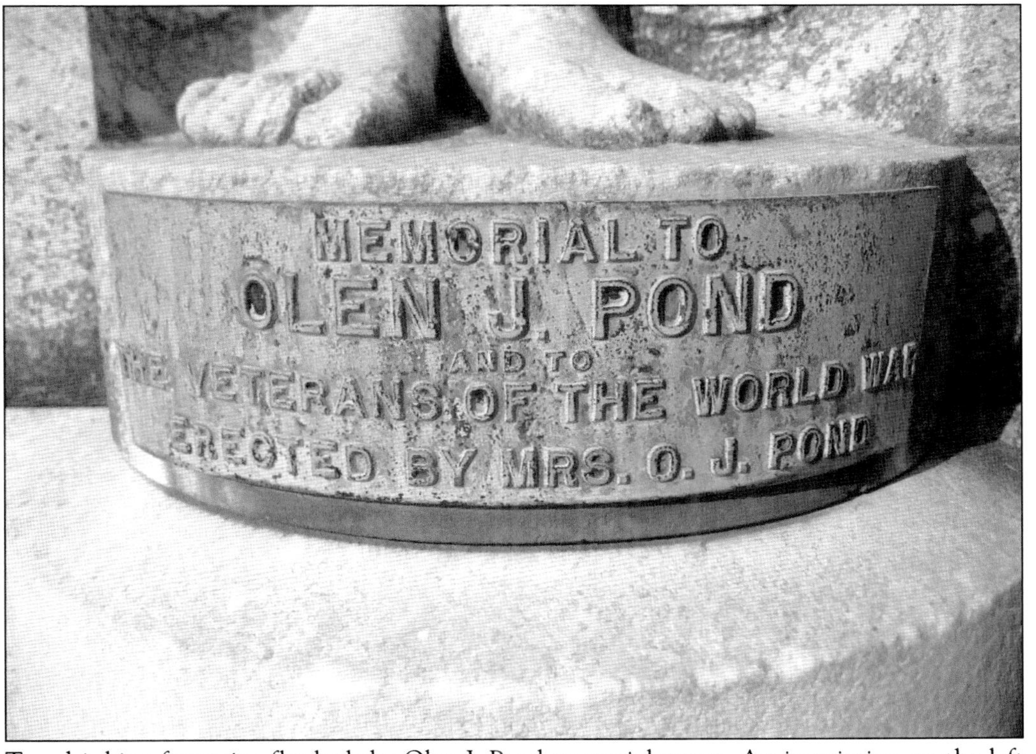

Two drinking fountains flanked the Olen J. Pond memorial statue. An inscription on the left front of the sculpture's base reads: "Memorial to Olen J. Pond and to the Veterans of the World War. Erected by Mrs. O. J. Pond." Once, a local family was at Franke Park for a reunion, and they rented the smaller building by the pond. They were surprised to see a plaque above the fireplace that read, "Emma and O. J. Pond," hence the nickname "Pond Pavilion." (Zenda Snyder Bateman; Dan White.)

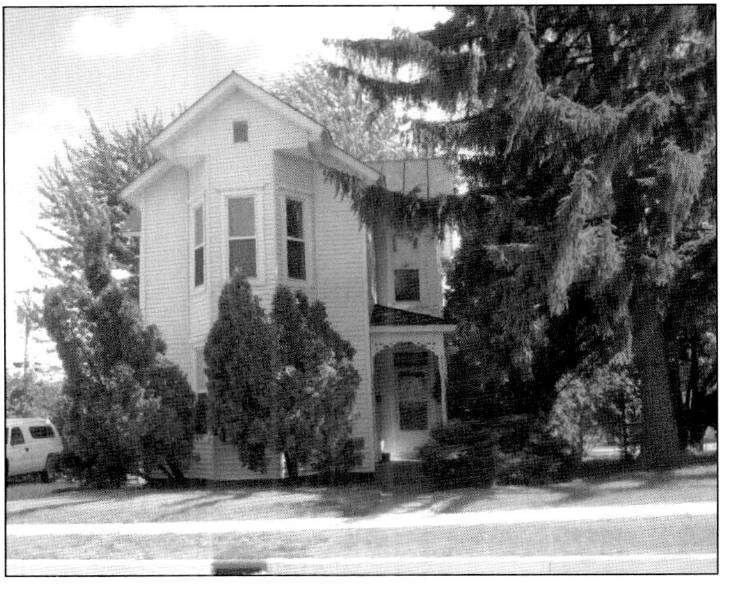

This beautiful Victorian home was built in the 1890s at 820 West Main Street. It is on the south side of the street, the first home as one travels from downtown. (Stevia Webster.)

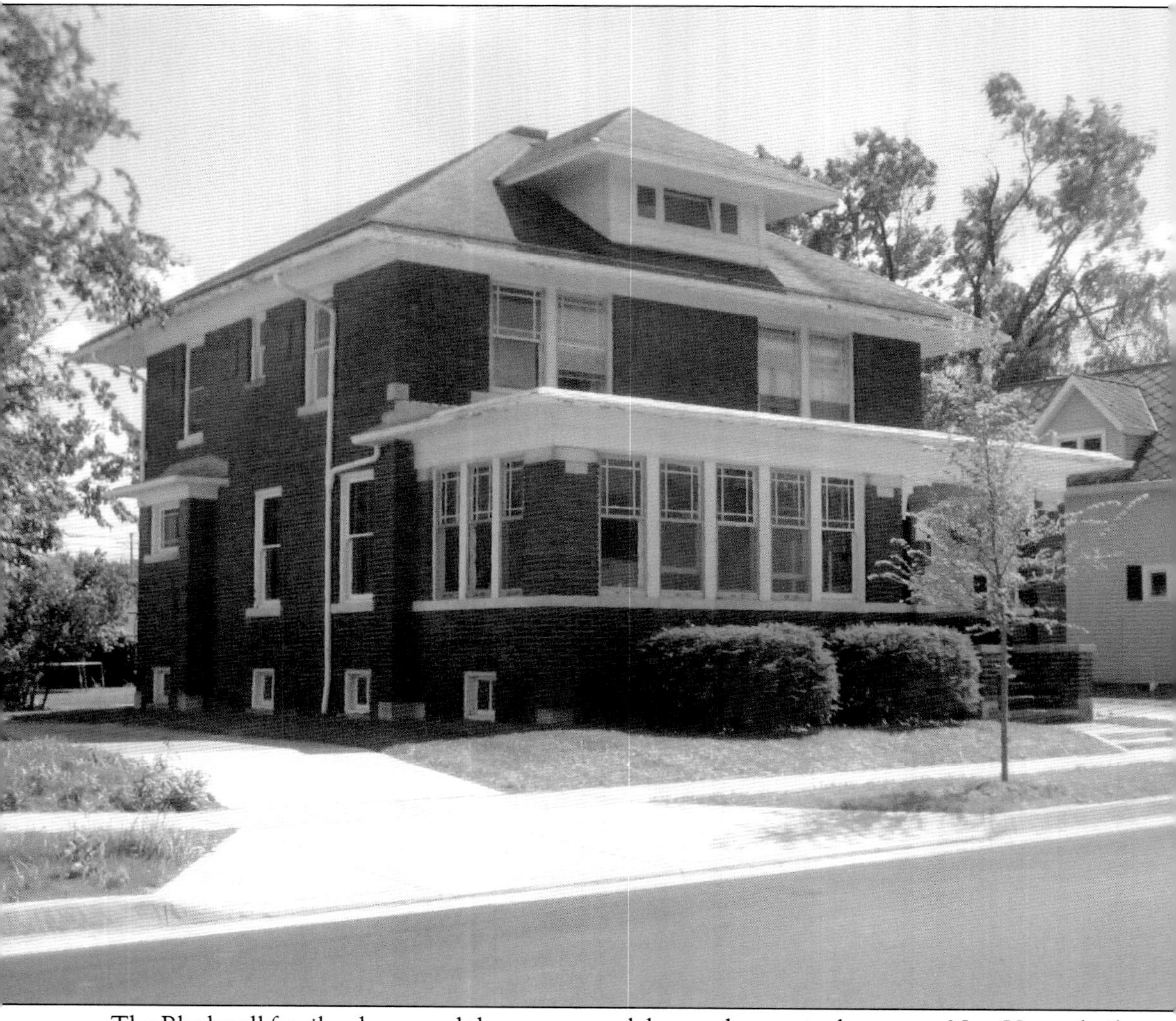

The Blackwell family who owned the grocery and dry goods store in downtown New Haven built this home in the early 1900s at 810 Main Street. While their house was being constructed, they lived in the house next door at 802 Main Street, seen to the right of the Blackwell house above. This house is one of five original homes constructed on Main Street. Richard Blackwell and his wife, Georgia, had seven children, Richard, Carroll, Charlie, Sharon, Patricia, Marilyn, and another child whose name is not known. Charlie served in World War I. While on leave, he died in a train accident at the crossing north of New Haven. Carroll operated the department store, and Richard Jr. was the owner of the grocery store until it closed. Richard Sr. died early in life, before retirement age, and Richard Jr. lived with his mother until she passed away in her mid-90s. Richard Jr. continued to live in this house until he died in 2005. The family scrapbook told of a visit in the early years to see the Pope. They were a very devout family. (Gloria Boles.)

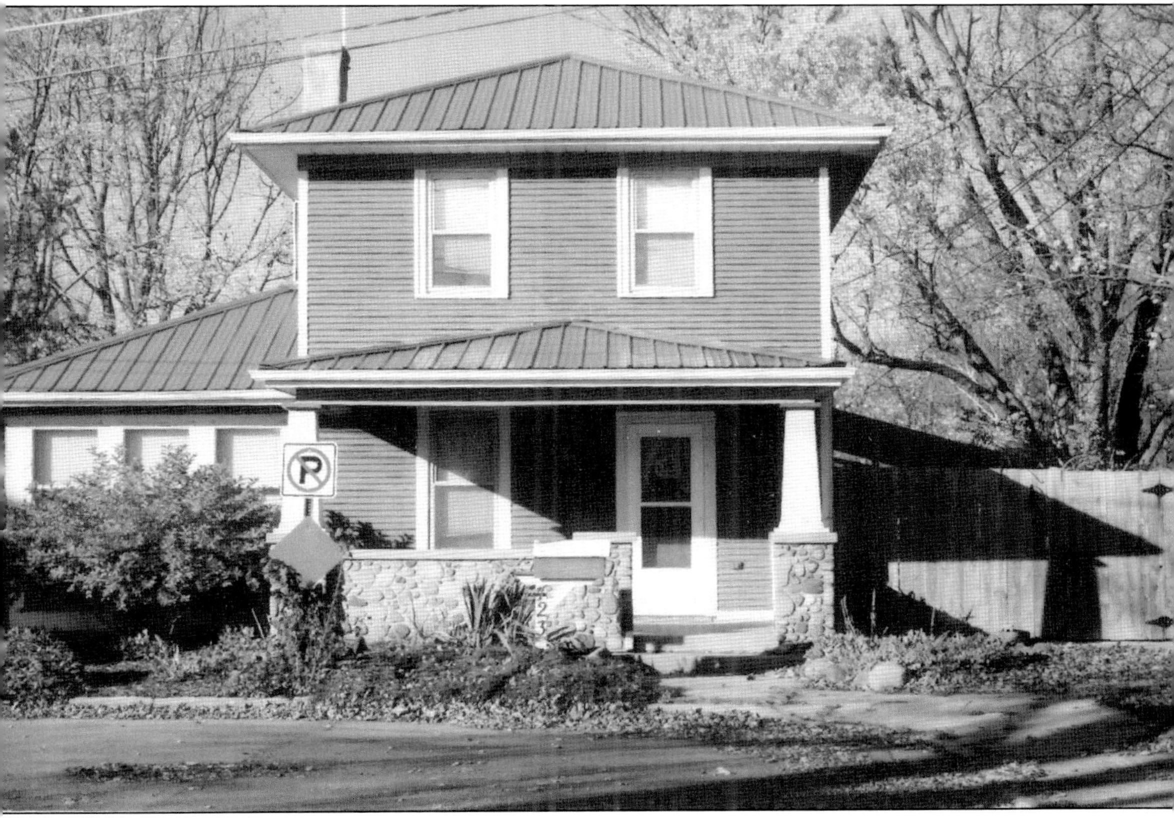

This is a "Sears in a Box" mail order structure at 423 High Street. Sears, Roebuck, and Company sold these houses by mail order beginning in 1918. They advertised easy assembly, with 750 pounds of nails and paint. The "American dream" arrived in scores and scores of boxes. Building paper, lumber, nails, and framing materials were included in the first shipment. The final shipment brought millwork and a bathtub. Boxes were loaded into two boxcars and hauled by steam engine trains. They were delivered all over the country. A horse or mule dragged wagonloads to large lots averaging 47 by 144 feet. Though the cost of the completed homes was low, prices for materials were not. Cypress shingles, bronze door hinges, glazed windows, granite bathtub, and other materials came in all styles, sizes, and prices. Between 1926 and 1929, the kit homes from Sears sold at prices ranging from $2,923 to $3,324. In 1940, Sears, Roebuck, and Company got out of the business of selling kit homes. (Stevia Webster and Deborah Hastings, *Fort Wayne Journal Gazette*, 2007.)

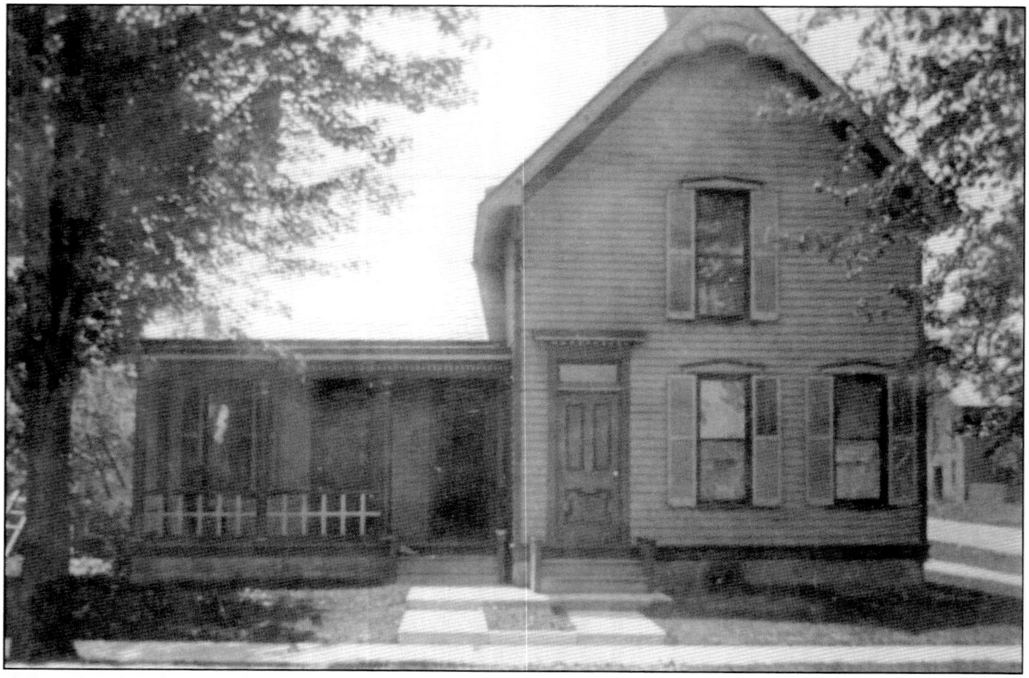

After the Civil War, this house was moved to its present location on Main Street. It once sat where the Wabash depot was located. (St. Louis Catholic Church and Jeff Hoffman.)

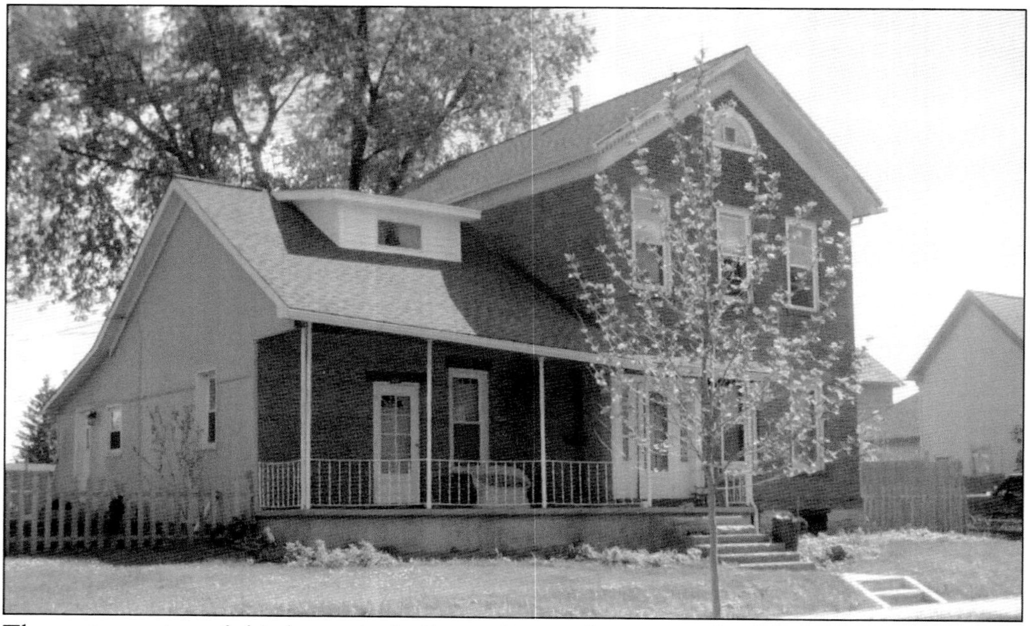

The main section of this house is similar to the two houses on the following page, although the wing on the side of the house creates a different look. It is located at 610 West Main Street. The three houses have a window in the peak of the gable, three side-by-side windows on the second story, and a door on the left or right with two windows side by side on the lower level. (Stevia Webster.)

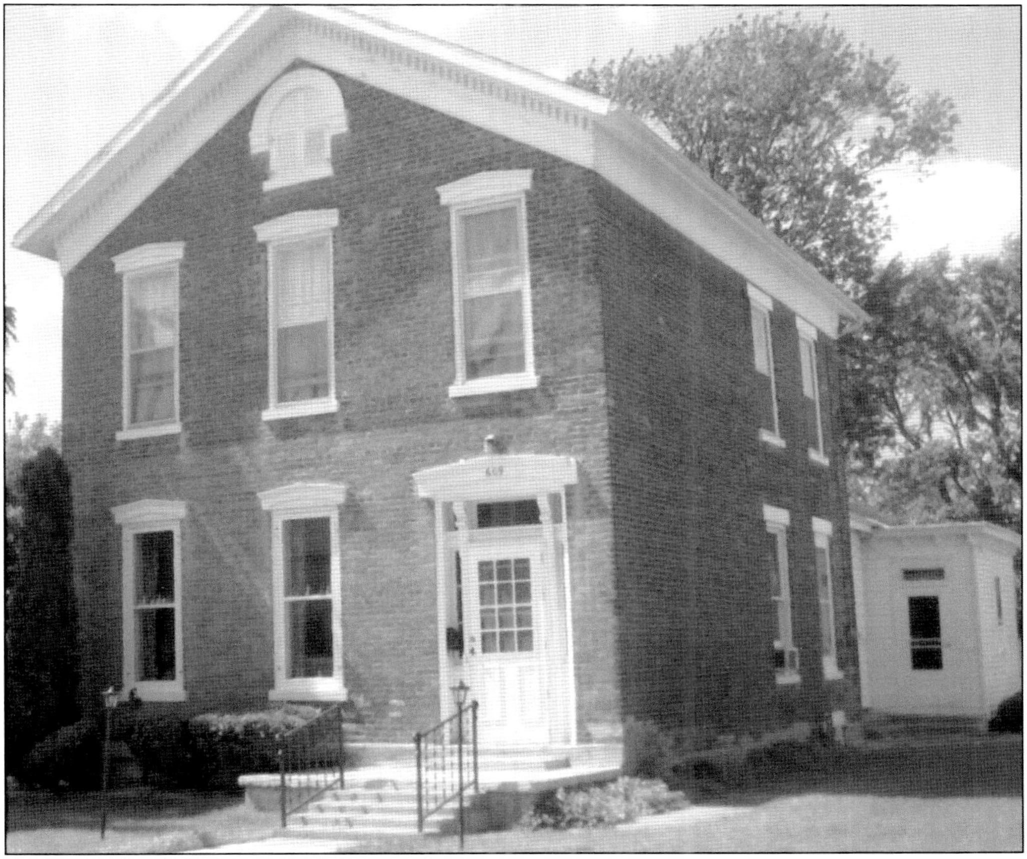

West Main Street is one of the oldest streets in the town and home to some of the oldest houses in New Haven. These two houses are located at 609 West Main Street, above, and 627 West Main Street, below. Both houses are similarly designed except for porches and additions to the rear of the buildings. (Both, Stevia Webster.)

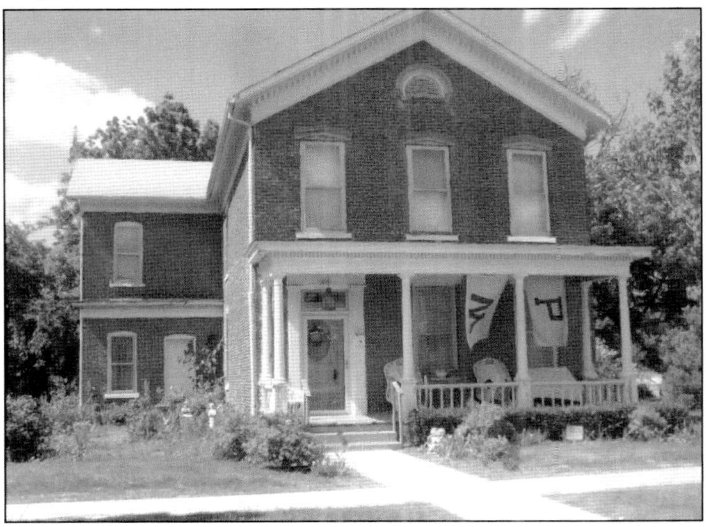

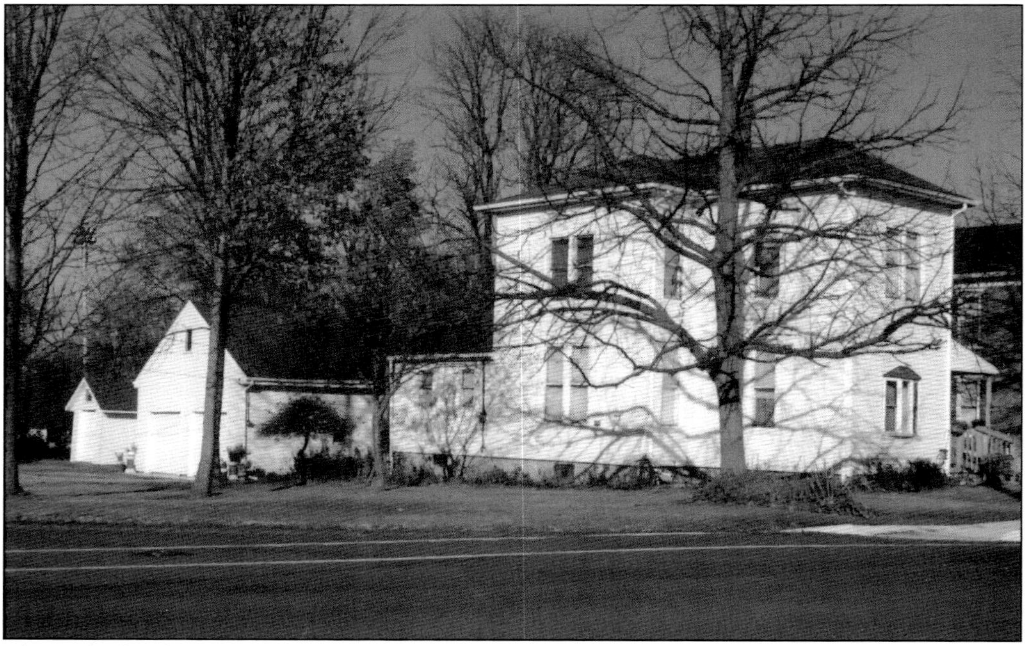

This is the last house at the northwest end of West Main Street, located at 603 West Main Street. It is the residence referred to in the 1937 train accident on pages 22 and 23. The description talks about the tree that protected the house from damage and part of the train trucks landing between the garage and house. The tree is gone and the outbuildings are different. (Stevia Webster.)

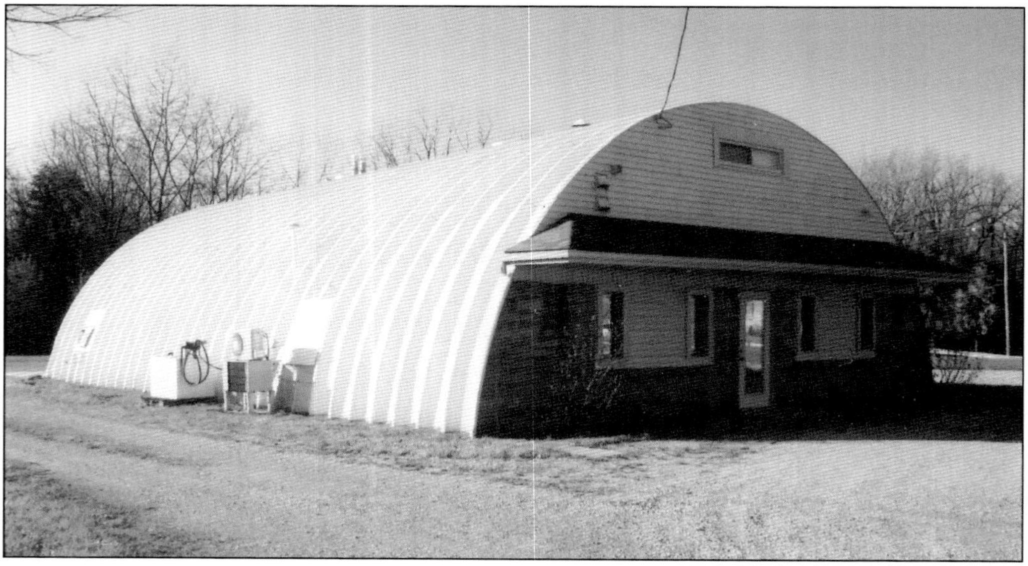

About 160,000 Quonset huts were constructed during World War II. They were easy to ship and install overseas, and the military used them to house troops in Guam. Huts were used as temporary postwar housing too. Fort Wayne had a Quonset hut village on the west side of town. After the war, huts were sold to the public for $1,000 each. One sits at the end of Main Street. Across the country, Quonset huts are used as outbuildings and as military museums featuring World War II memorabilia. (Stevia Webster).

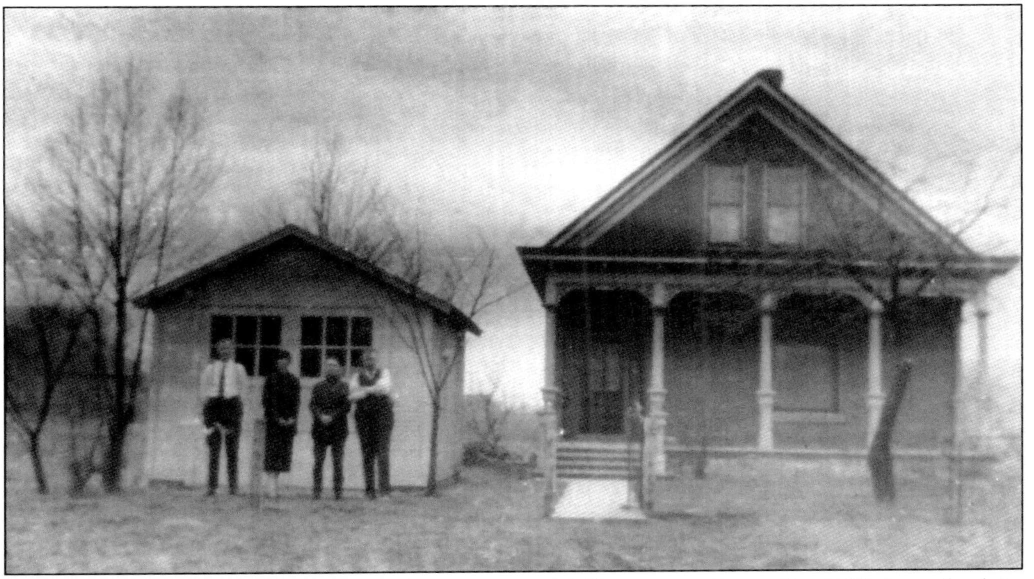

Louis Jacquay resided in this house at the west end of Bell Avenue, pictured in 1927. It was built in 1911. A one-of-a-kind house in New Haven, it was designed with concrete fretwork and columns in the front of the house. In the back of the property are the remains of the Wabash and Erie Canal. Standing from left are Louis Jacquay, Clara Jacquay, unidentified, and Louis Jacquay, Jr. The house no longer stands. (St. Louis Catholic Church and Jeff Hoffman.)

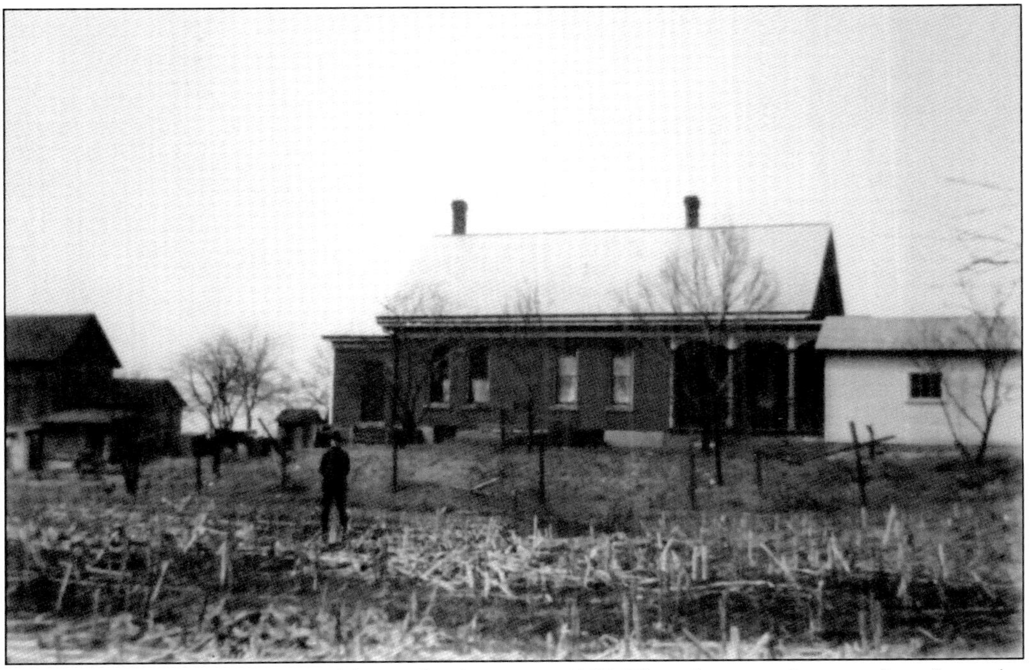

Louis Jacquay stands in the field near his house in 1927. This photograph was taken from the south, looking north. None of these buildings are standing now. (St. Louis Catholic Church and Jeff Hoffman.)

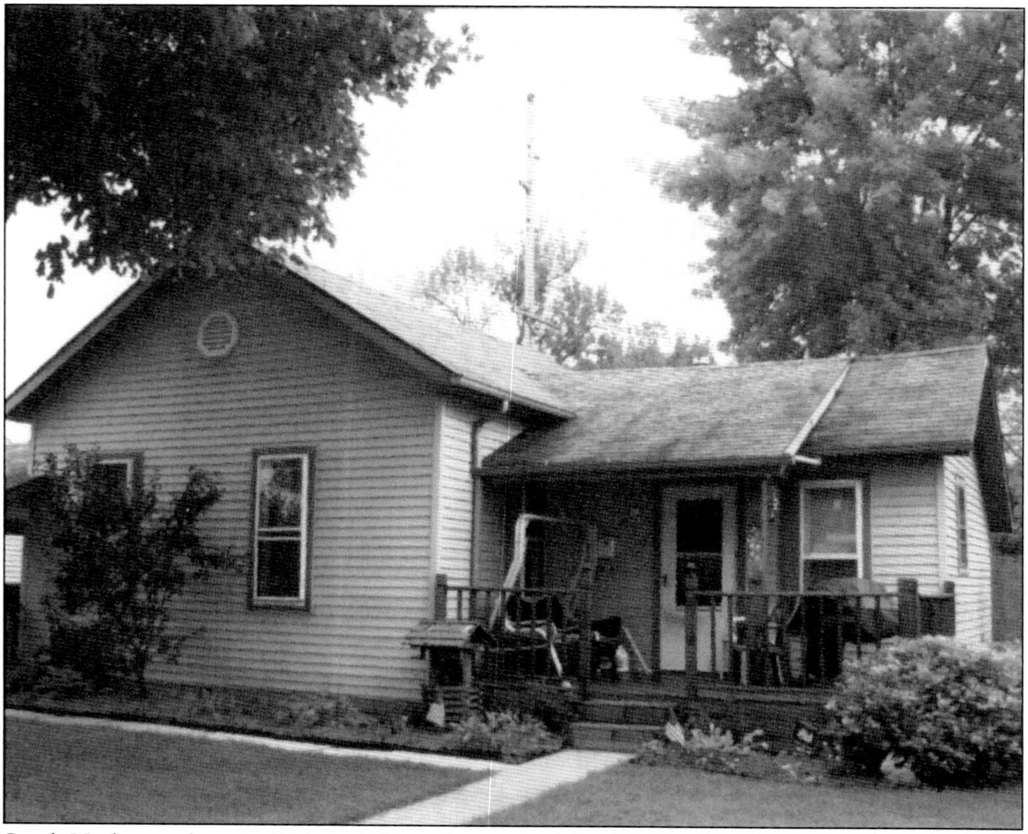

Sarah Harlor was born in Ohio in 1873 and moved to New Haven when she was four years old. She lived on Center Street in 1930 and later in this house at 530 South Street. At 3 feet, 10 inches tall, she joined the circus when she turned 12 and stayed with it for 45 years. During that time, Sarah married Frank Shade, who was 4 feet, 2 inches tall. Later Sarah married Dan Flood. They stayed with Sarah's brother Jesse Harlor when visiting New Haven. Sarah came back to live in New Haven during the last years of her life and died at age 72. (Mike Fromholt and Stevia Webster.)

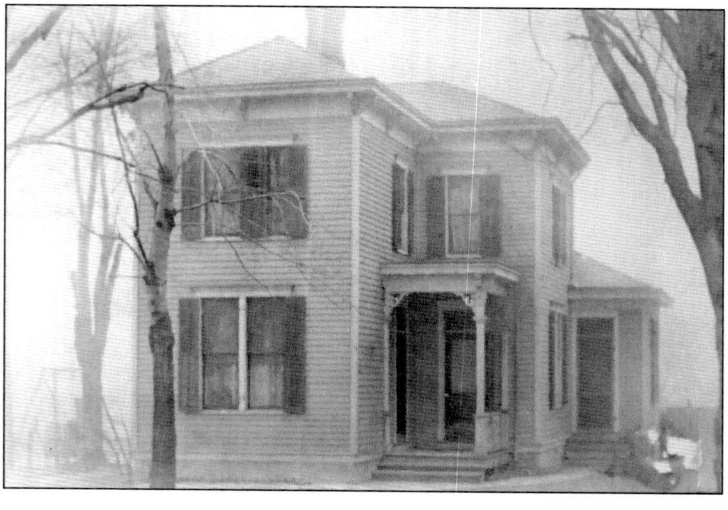

This house was built between 1898 and 1899. It stood between Ann Street and the end of Powers Street. (Todd Baron and *Allen County Times*, 1992.)

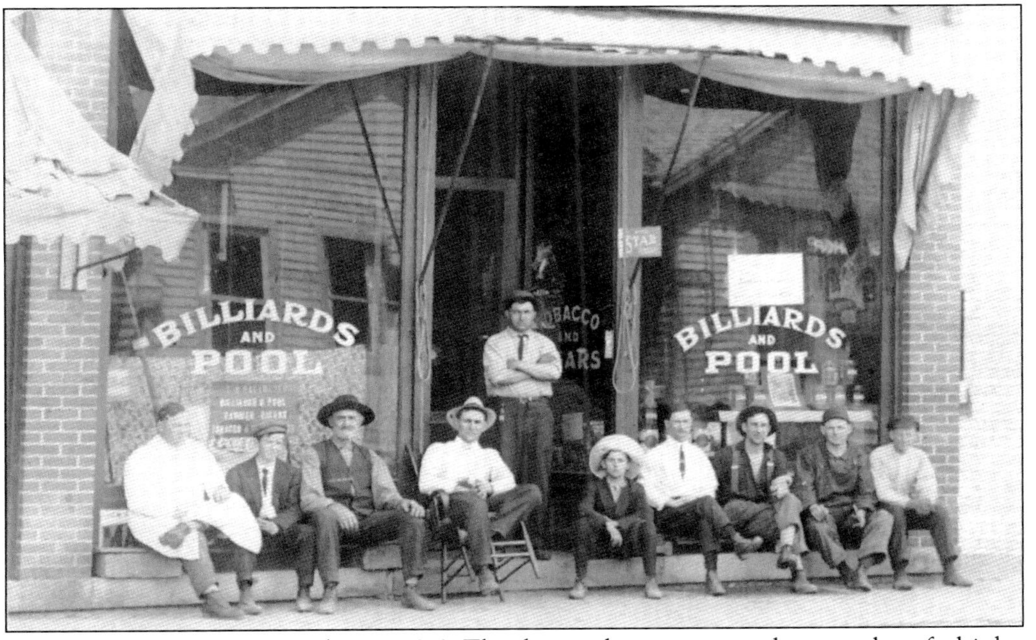

The photograph above was taken in 1910. The shop is the cigar store where candy, soft drinks, cigars, and tobacco were sold. The store was located at 432 Broadway Street, where the Moose lodge is located today. Look carefully at the reflections in the windows, as the buildings across the street can be seen. (Todd Baron.)

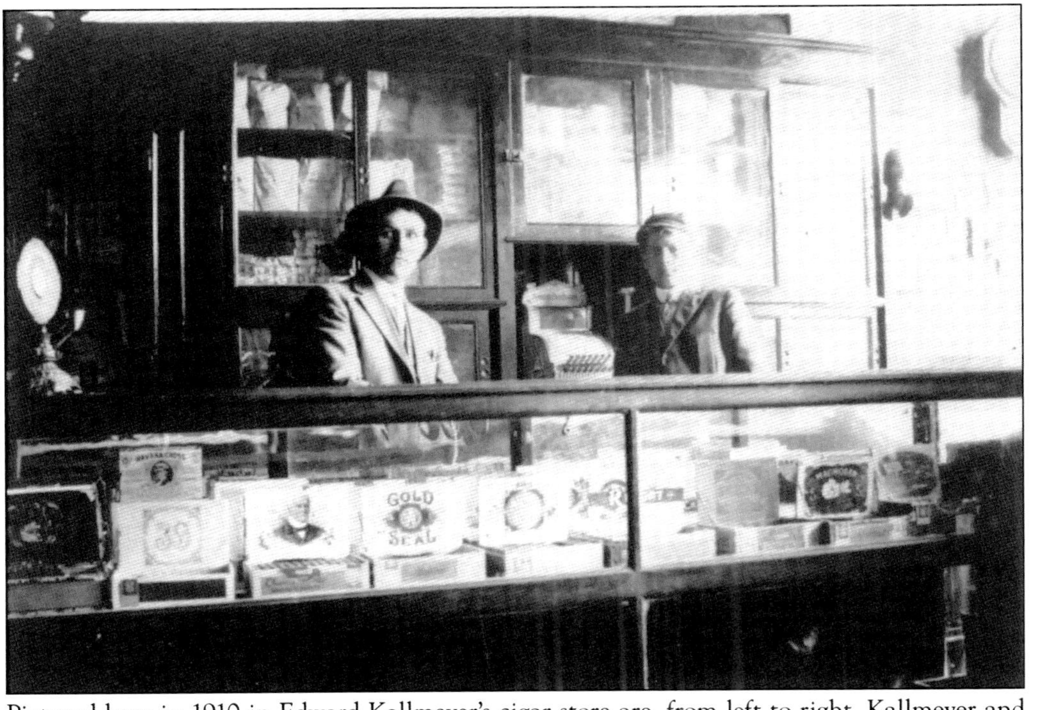

Pictured here in 1910 in Edward Kallmeyer's cigar store are, from left to right, Kallmeyer and Clair Cour. (Todd Baron.)

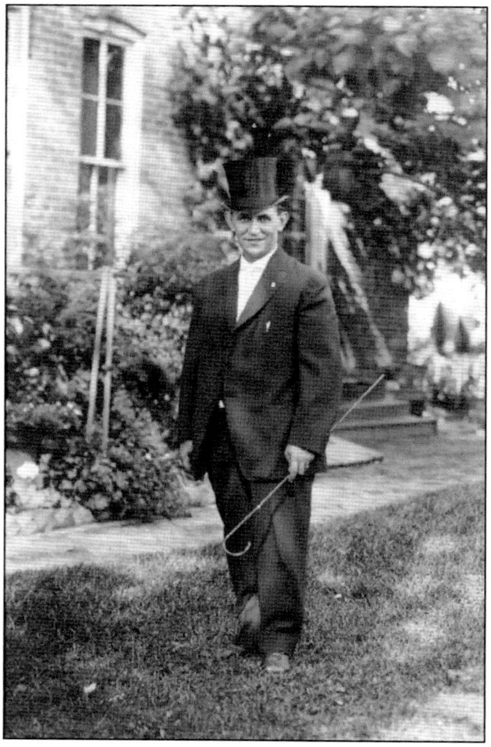

Joseph Kallmeyer visits the home of Amelia and Henry Kallmeyer in this photograph. Rudolph Lupkin, husband of Mary Kallmeyer Lupkin, of New Haven, constructed this two-story brick home, which stood at 501 Green Street in 1872 on land purchased for $400 by Mary's mother, Regina Kallmeyer. Regina was a widow who planned to marry Henry Beckman in October 1872 and move into the new house. Members of the Kallmeyer family occupied the home until 1972 when Catherine Kallmeyer, who had been living there, sold the property. The house today appears much like it did in this photograph taken in the early 1900s. The side porch is now enclosed. In 1966, the Edward Kallmeyer family celebrated the 100th year of their home on Summit and Green Streets. Below, Joseph A. Kallmeyer poses in his World War I uniform. (Both, Todd Baron.)

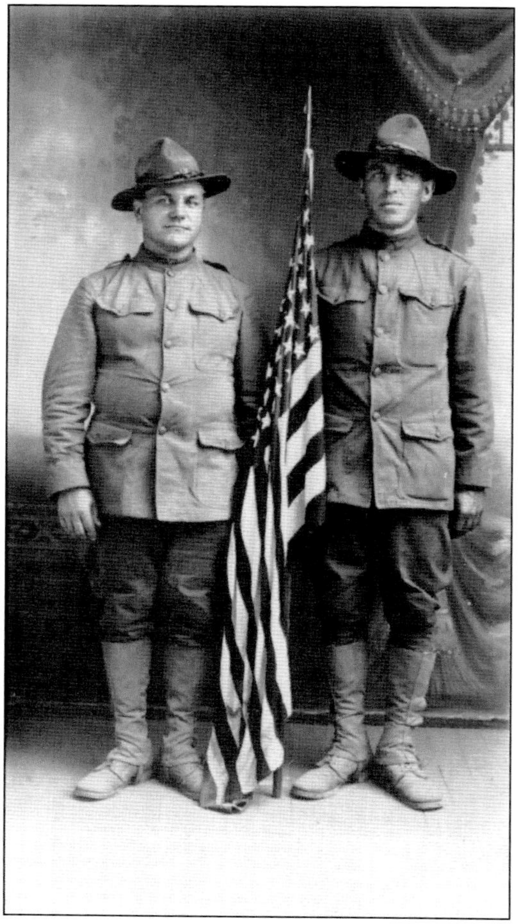

This is a formal picture of Joseph A. Kallmeyer. (Todd Baron.)

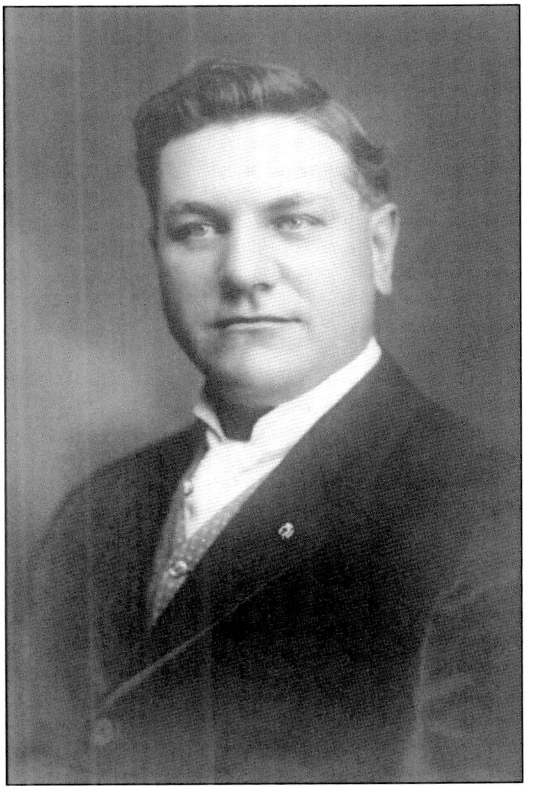

The Kallmeyer family, young and old, gathered at their family farm. It is threshing day, and 18 people are in the photograph. Men, women, and children had chores to accomplish. Horses and machines of today make farm work easier than in the old days. (Todd Baron.)

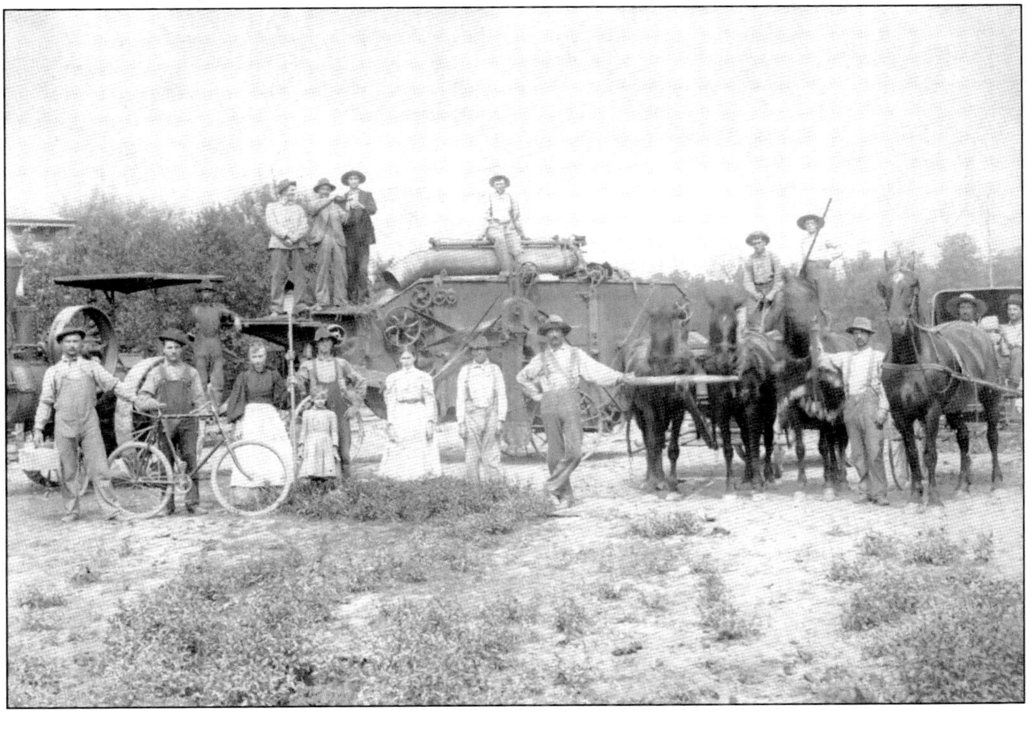

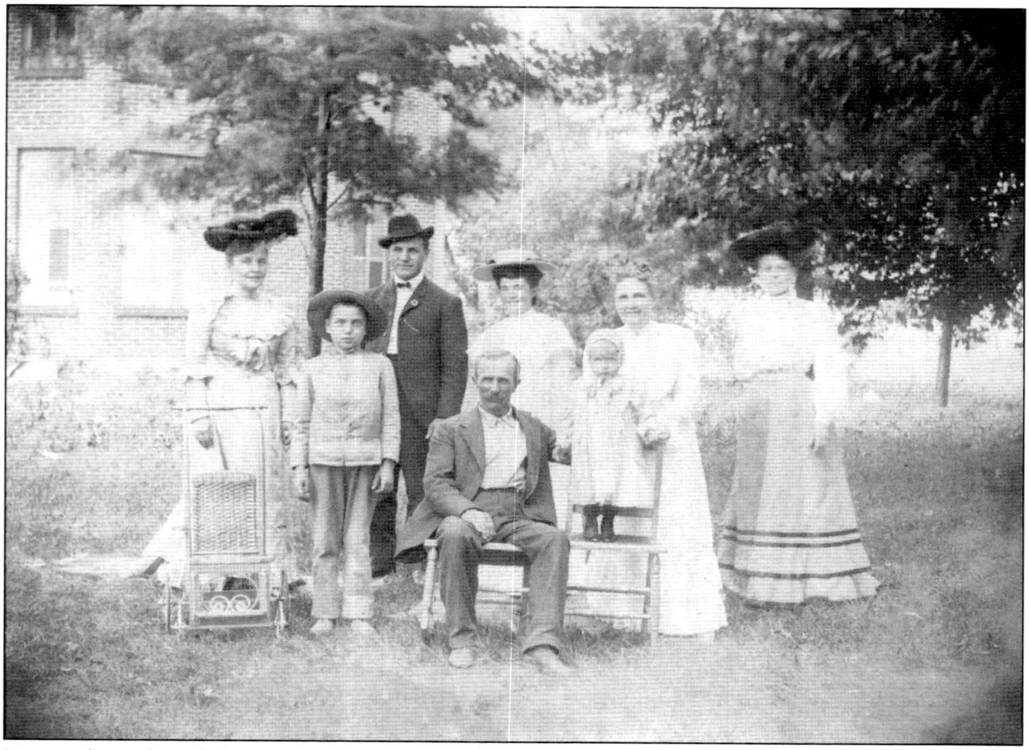

Pictured are, from left to right, (first row) Fred Mehring, Henry Kallmeyer, and Jackson ?; (second row) Maude Capps, Joseph Kallmeyer, Hortense Capps Kallmeyer, Marie Capps, and Virginia ?. (Todd Baron.)

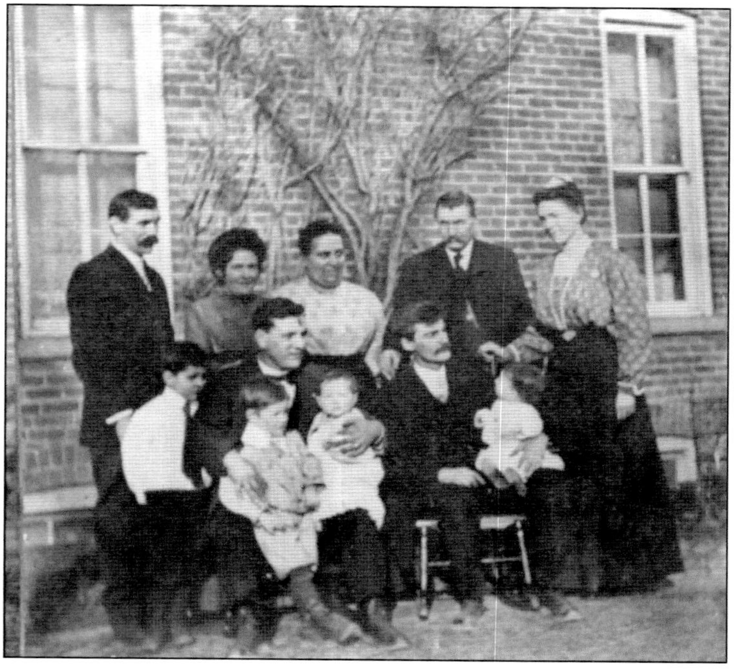

In a photograph taken at the Kallmeyer home on 501 Green Street are, from left to right, (first row) Edward, Joseph, Bernard, and Robert Kallmeyer and Justin Adams holding Louis Adams; (second row) Edmund Kallmeyer, Hortense Caps Kallmeyer, Amelia Rich Kallmeyer, Henry Kallmeyer, and Mary Kallmeyer Adams. (Todd Baron.)

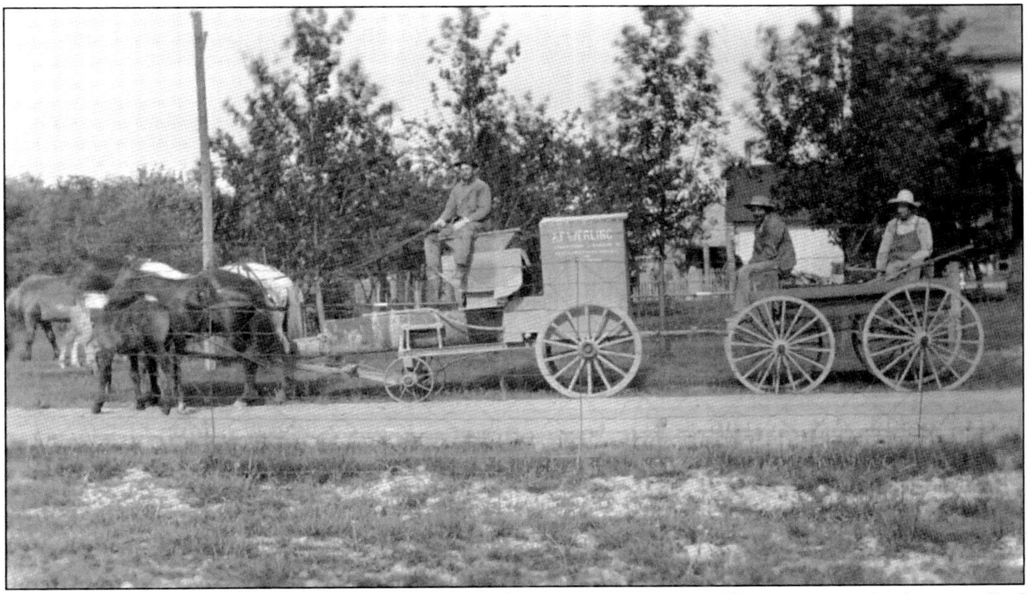

Alfred Werling is pictured with his cement crew, his cement mixer, and his wagons, which are pulled by two horses. He worked throughout Allen County. His residence was in New Haven. (Todd Baron.)

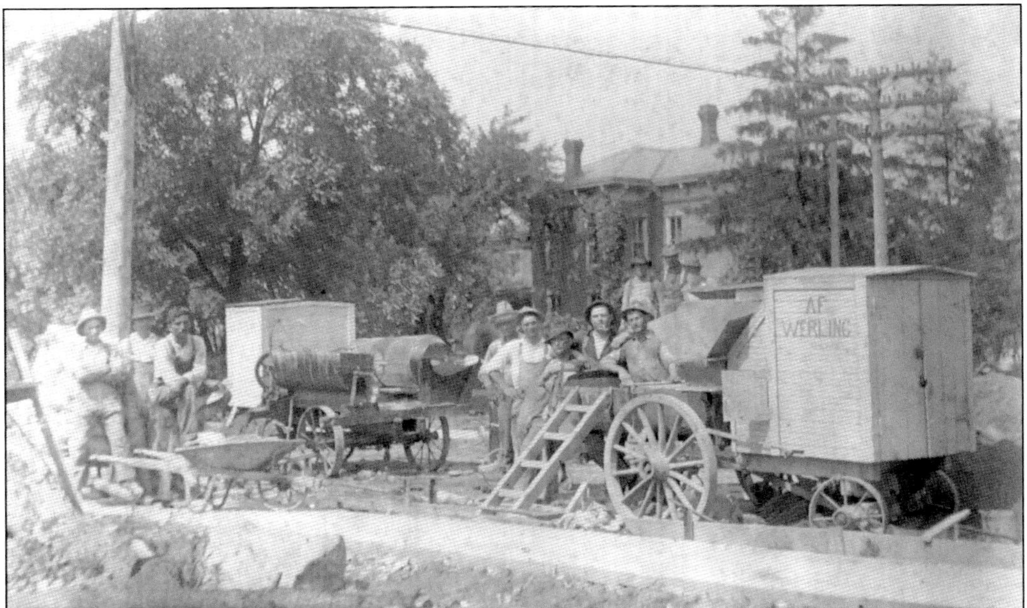

Alfred Werling is working with his cement crew on East Main Street in New Haven. The location may be in front of Harper's Funeral Home. This photograph is from 1910. The crew was installing curbs or sidewalks as the roads were not paved until after 1915. (Todd Baron.)

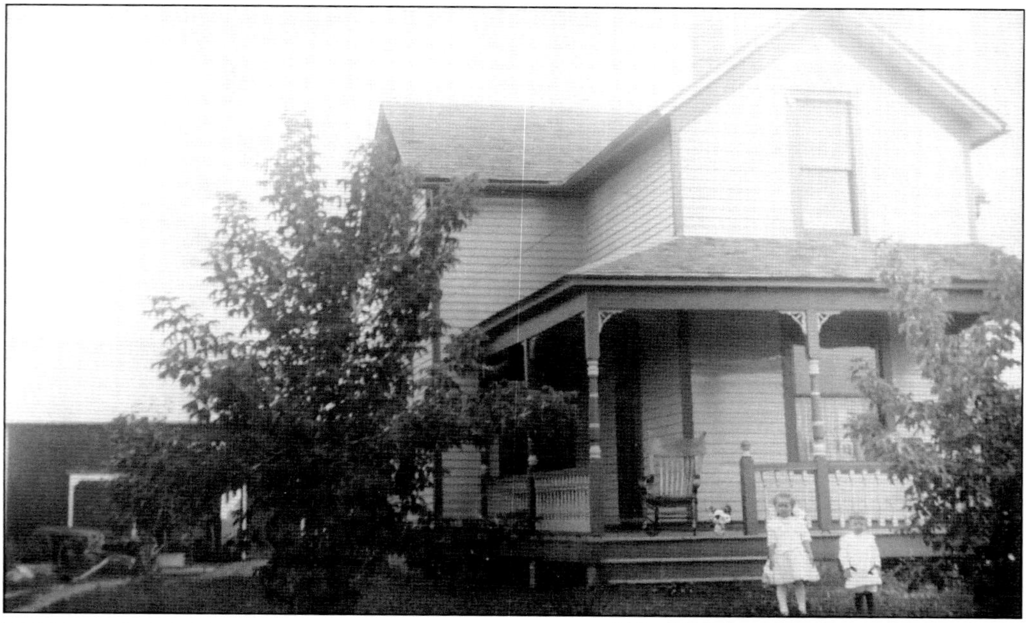

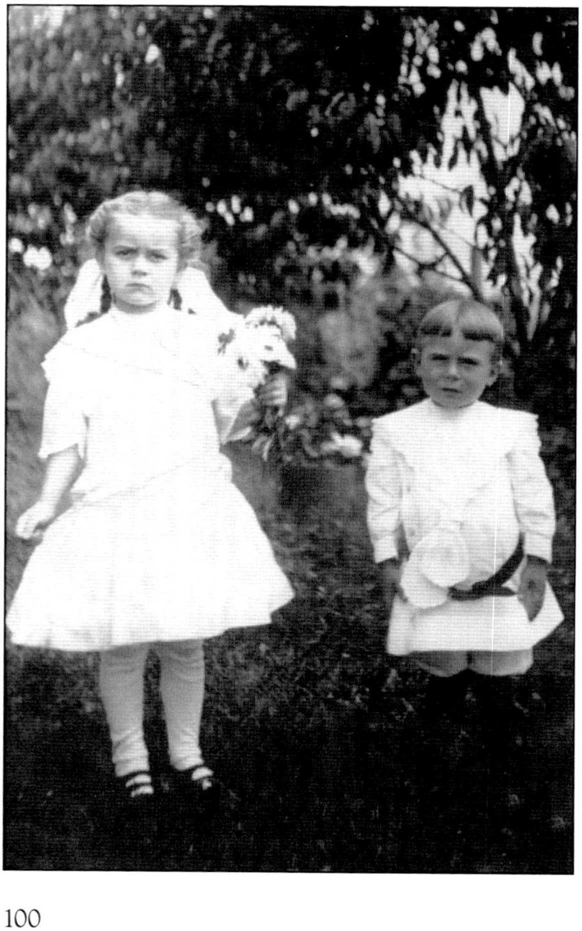

Alfred Werling lived at 1051 Rose Avenue in a house that no longer stands. The two children in this photograph may have been his; their names are unknown. The photograph at the left shows them again in more detail. The little girl holds flowers and the smaller child appears to be a boy. These photographs were taken in 1910. (Both, Todd Baron.)

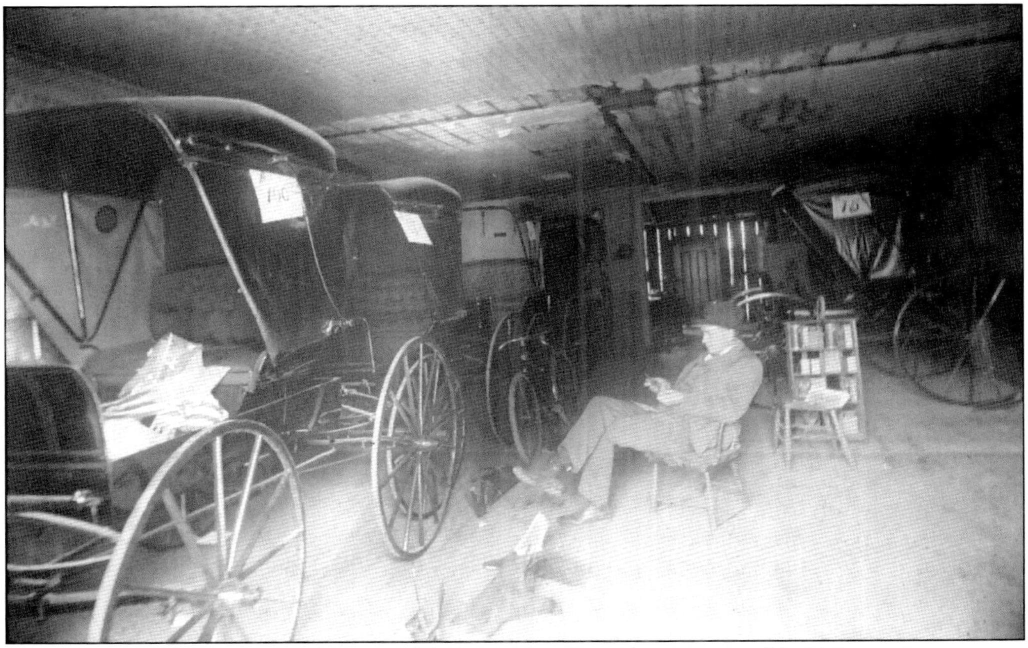

A. L. Rich sits in the buggy shop possibly located on Broadway Street. (Todd Baron.)

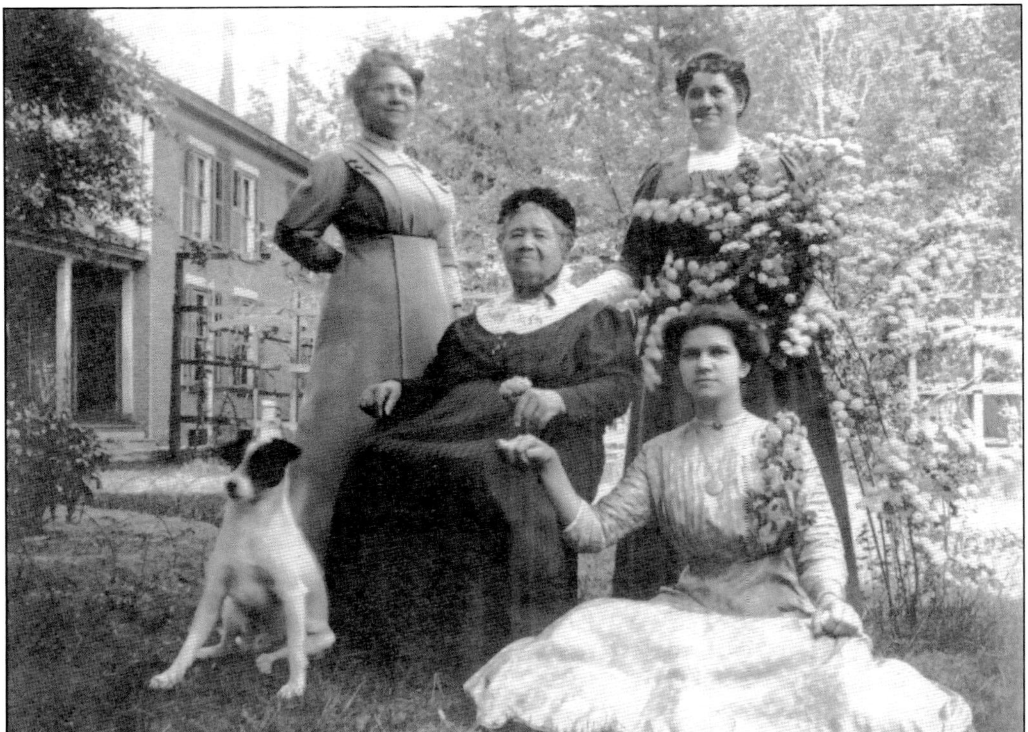

Pictured are, from left to right, (first row) Grandma Rich and Catherine Schoehl; (second row) Mrs. Joseph Rich and Mrs. ? Seida. The location of the house is unknown. (Todd Baron.)

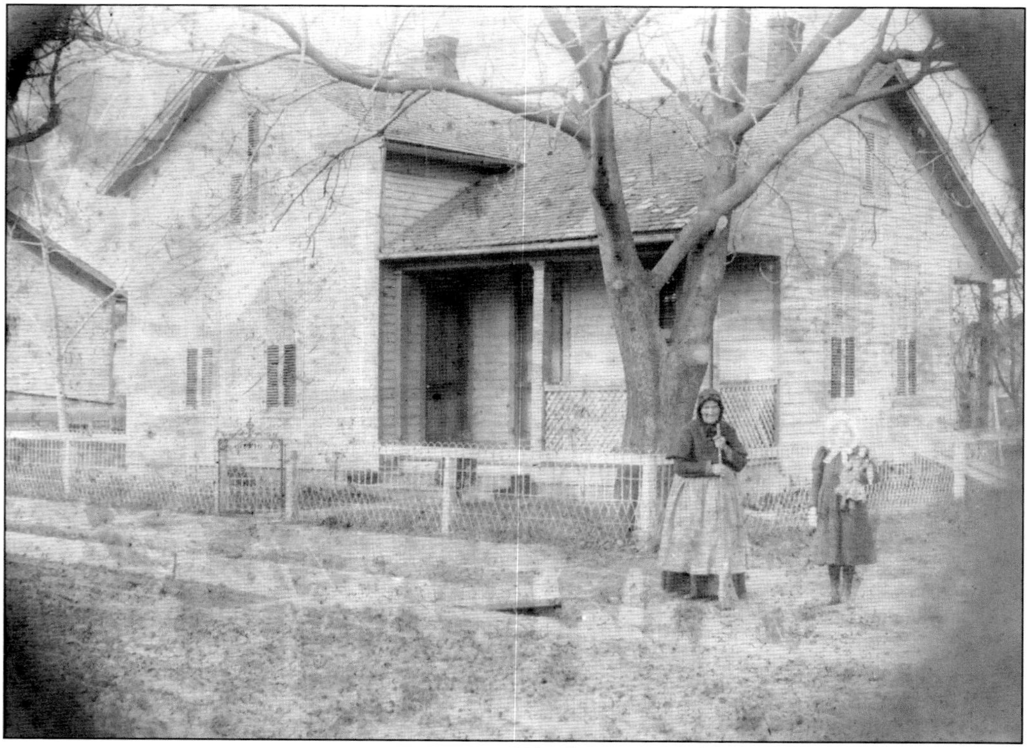

The location of this house is unknown. The older woman is Grandmother Rich and the child holding the doll is Margaret Moriarty. (Todd Baron.)

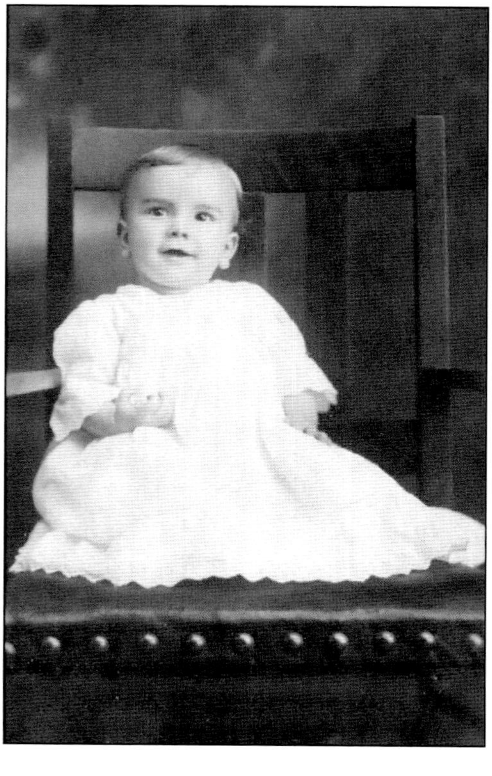

This baby is Master Lorenz Schaaf. He was a professional wrestler, worked in a circus, and on the railroad. He was in the concrete construction business for 35 years. He belonged to the New Haven Area Historical Association and communicated with the railroad company to help lay plans to acquire the Wabash depot. He died when he was in his 80s. (Todd Baron.)

Homer Harper is pictured here in 1910. A funeral business was in existence as early as 1872, owned at that time by Henry Tenge from whom a Mr. Lowell purchased the business. Edward Harper, Homer's great-great-grandfather purchased the business from Lowell in 1889. Under Harper's ownership, the business operated from a remodeled house on 939 East Main Street. In the 1980s, it was relocated to 740 State Road 930 East. (Todd Baron and *Fort Wayne News-Sentinel*, 1983.)

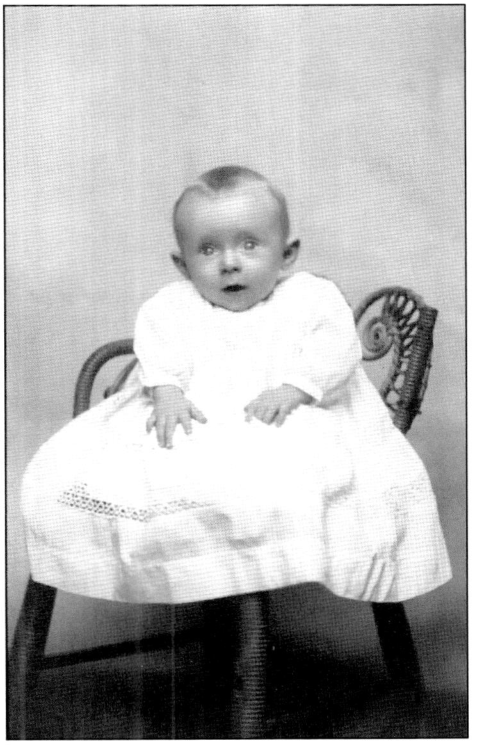

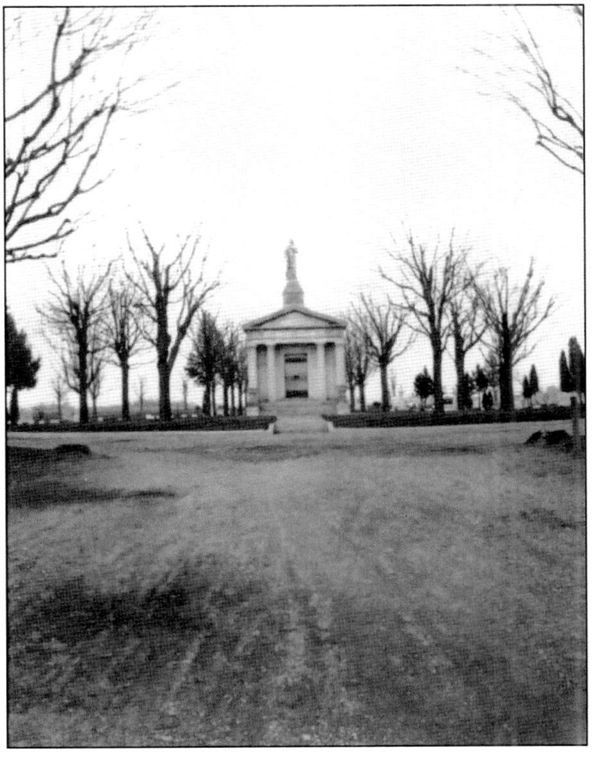

The old pioneer burying grounds was supplanted by the Odd Fellows cemetery on Hartzell Road. Established in 1875, it occupied part of the Miller farm near where the old Miller cemetery was situated. Many of the graves from Jesse Adams's farm were removed to the new grounds, including those of David and Rachel Miller, John Dougall, Levi Hartzell, Joseph Townsend, Richard Barrow, and many more. (Jo Anne Smith and Allen County Library.)

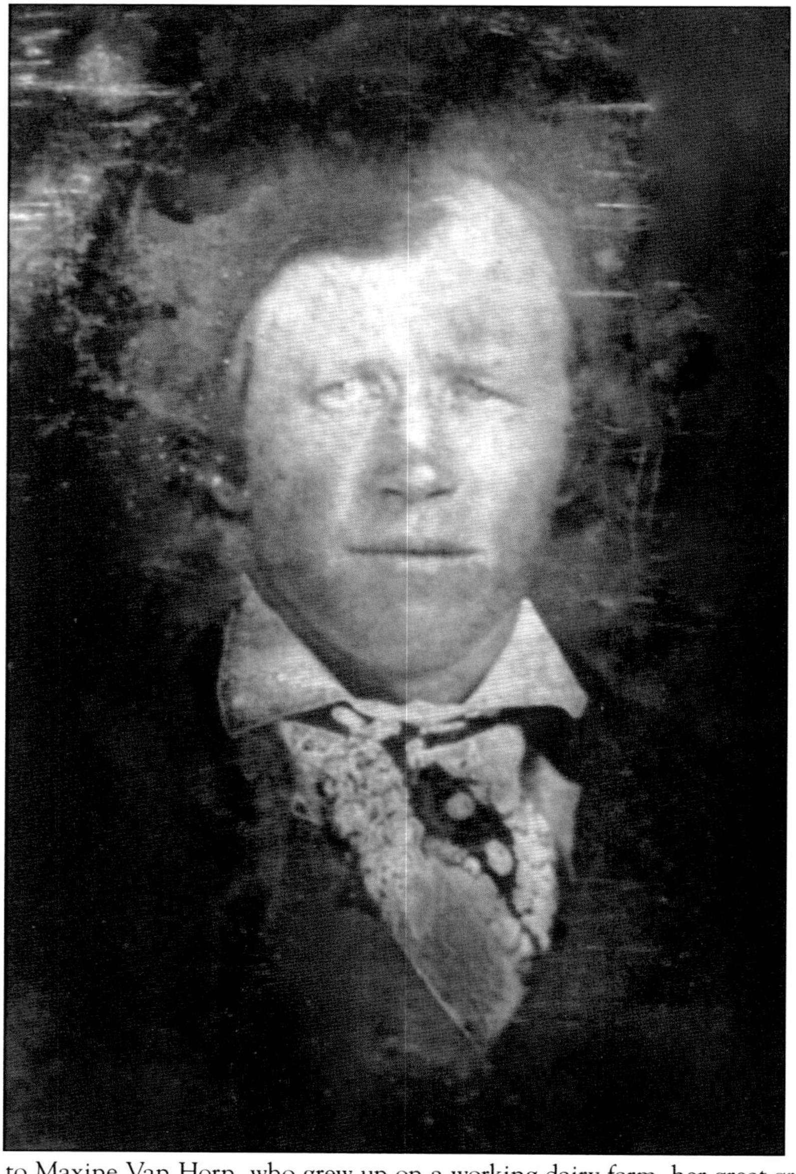

According to Maxine Van Horn, who grew up on a working dairy farm, her great-grandfather, Adolphus Wolf, pictured above, came to America from Germany in the 1800s. He moved to the New Haven area and helped dig the Wabash and Erie Canal. He bought 800 acres for a $1 an acre and married Martha Ulias. They had 12 children, but only four lived to adulthood. Maxine's grandfather, George Wolf, survived. Her father, Elias Wolf, maintained the farm on Harper Road. Maxine was born on the farm in 1921. In 1928, Elias decided to go into the dairy business. He reinvented some of the outbuildings, purchased 13 dairy cows, and bought milk from several neighbors. It was a family-run business, and Maxine and her brother had their jobs. Maxine and her father delivered milk six days a week, twice a day in the summer and once a day in the winter. They left the house at 3:00 a.m. and arrived home at 6:30 a.m. Her dad picked her up after school to deliver milk for the evening route, which took four hours to finish. Milk sold for 10¢ a quart and 5¢ a pint. (Maxine Wolf Van Horn.)

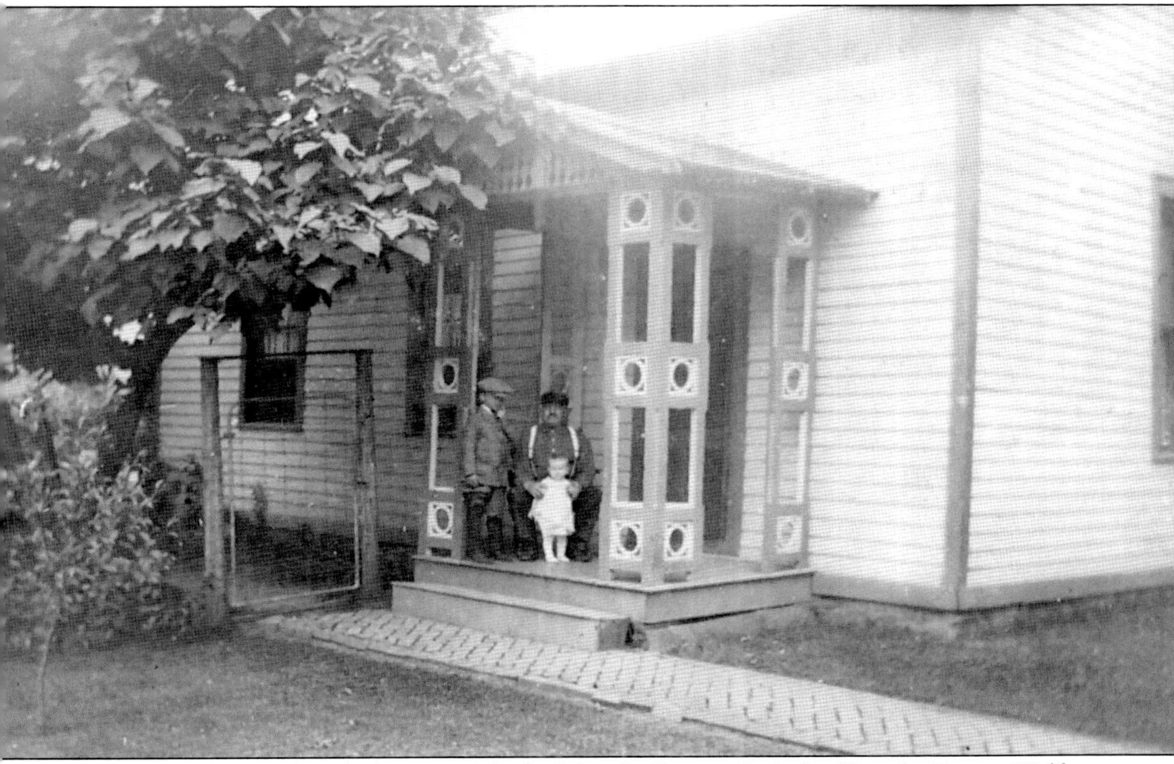

This school is discussed in the history of the St. John the Baptist Catholic Church. George Wolf, Maxine Wolf's grandfather, moved off the farm and bought the schoolhouse at 1008 Powers Street. George Wolf did not want electricity in the new house though Maxine's father, Elias Wolf, wanted to install it for him. Maxine's maternal grandmother was Charlotte Hannah Adams Wolf, making Maxine the great-great-granddaughter of Jesse Adams, founder of Adams Township. The people in the photograph from left to right, are brother George Wolf; grandfather George Forman Wolf; and Maxine Jeanette Wolf Van Horn. In later years, Maxine had two more brothers, Don and Ned Wolf. Don was executive vice president of Hardware Wholesalers, Inc., of Fort Wayne. He also served as national president of Big Brothers Big Sisters International and was the cofounder and president of the organization in Fort Wayne. (Maxine Wolf Van Horn.)

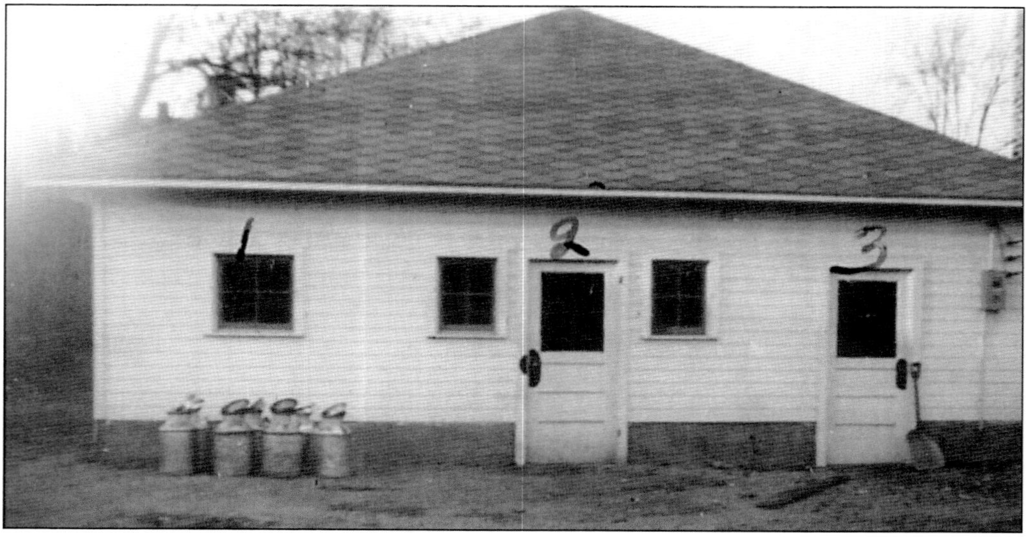

George and Maxine Wolf's father constructed a new dairy building in New Haven on Maxine's grandfather's, Elias, property, which was at 1008 Powers Street. The new dairy had pasteurized milk. It also had a new automatic bottler and capper. Production expanded to include white and chocolate milk, whipped cream, cottage cheese, buttermilk, butter, and eggs. When Maxine was 16 years old she worked in the dairy making cottage cheese. Maxine never learned to milk the cows; she said she did not know if she was too smart or too dumb to learn how. Her mother died at 52 with a bad heart, and her father died at 58. Maxine married Alfred William "Bill" Van Horn in 1942; he served in World War II. She and her husband raised her two younger brothers. In the photograph below, Van Horn is in the back row, the last soldier to the right. (Both, Maxine Wolf Van Horn.)

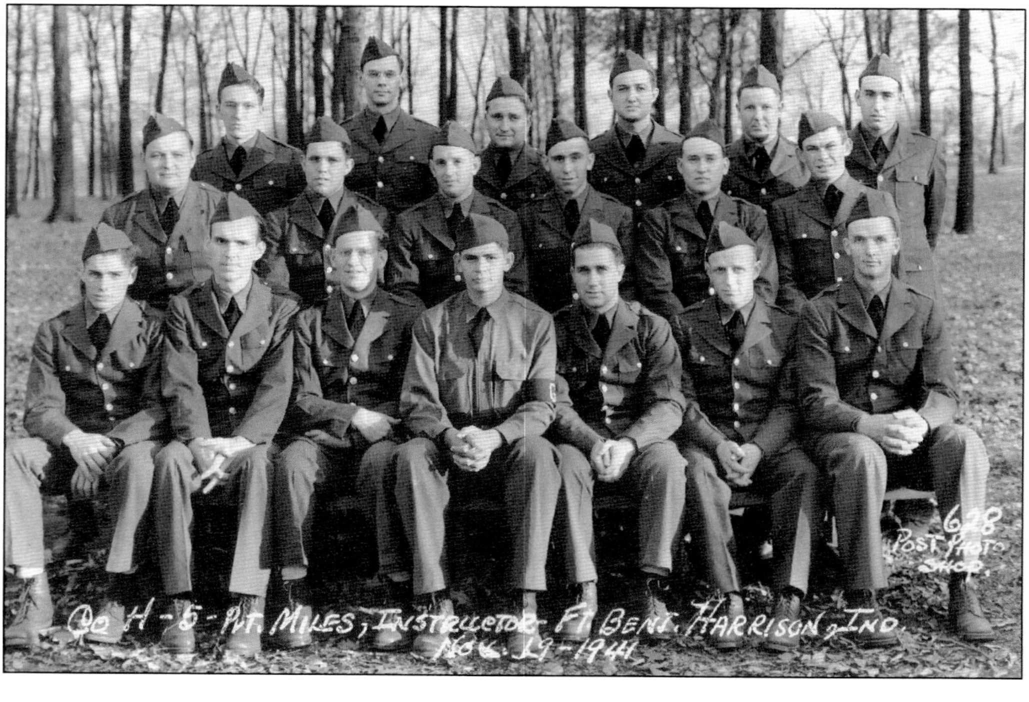

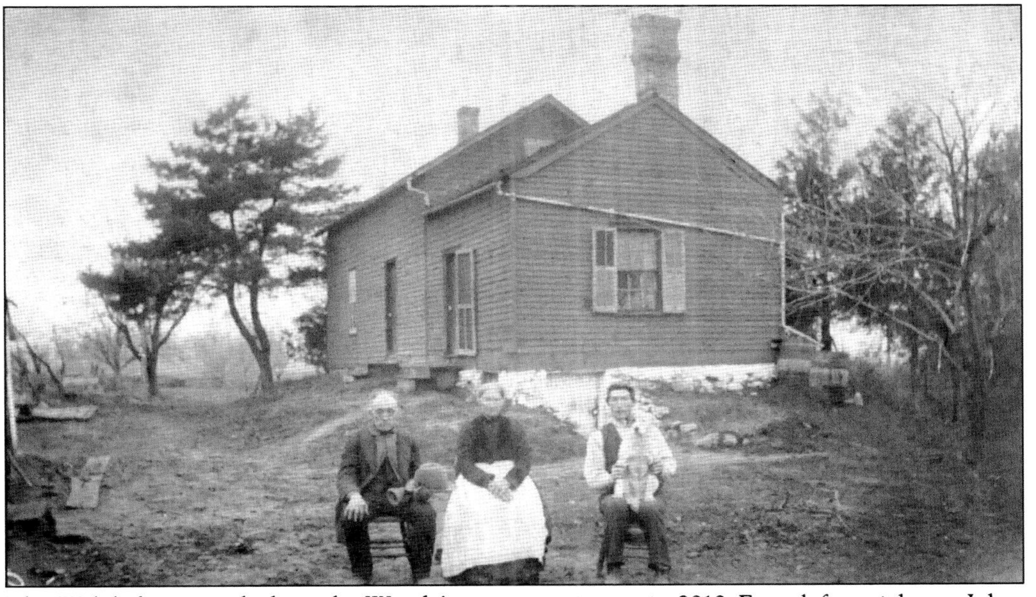

The Welph farm stood where the Wendy's restaurant is now in 2010. From left to right are John, Margaret, and Henry Welph. Granddaughter Catherine Pranger told this story when she was 91 years old: When she was living on part of grandfather John Welph's farm along Lincoln Highway, he had three sons and was anxious to acquire three 80-acre tracts of land, one tract for each son. (Mary Ketzler as told by her mother, Lotti Pranger.)

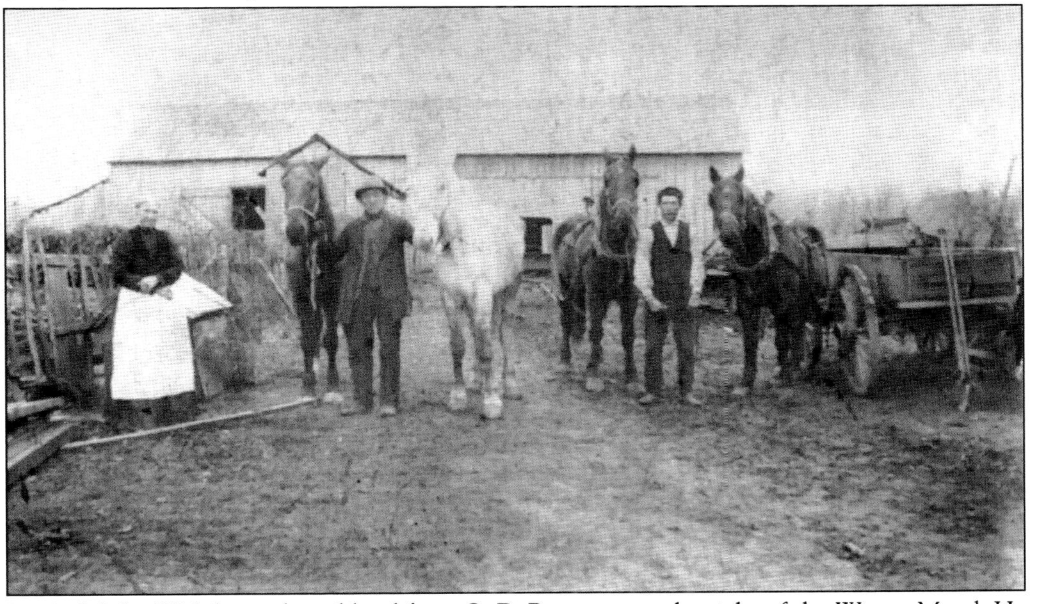

In 1845, John Welph purchased land from O. D. Rogers, now the sight of the Wayne Motel. He paid for the land in gold, which he toted over in a copper kettle. On the way, there was a tollgate located at the east corner of O. D. Rogers's farm. The toll was 5¢ for a team and wagon and 3¢ for a horse and rider. In those years, the land along Old New Haven Avenue or later U.S. Highway 30 was green and tranquil with a narrow road for horses and wagons. (Mary Ketzler as told by her mother, Lotti Pranger.)

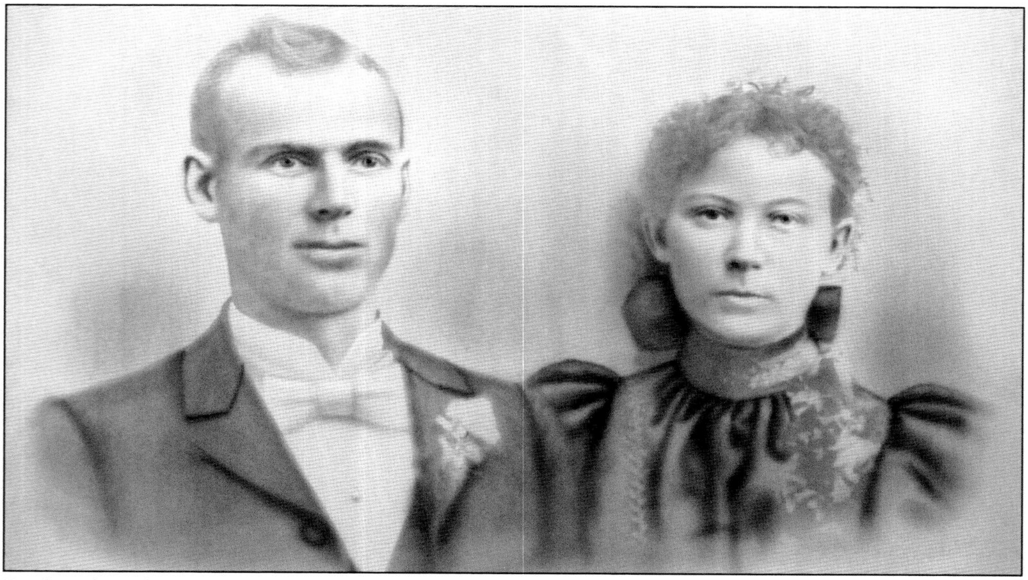

Fred and Catherine Pranger started their life together in 1895 in a small house on the Pranger homestead. Later they farmed 200 acres along Lincoln Highway, east of Adams Center Road. Fred built a barn in 1904 and a house facing Lincoln Highway in 1912. The interurban train ran past their house. Fred and Catherine's daughter, Louise "Lotti" Pranger, was born in 1912 in their farmhouse on Lincoln Highway, then called Old New Haven Avenue. The coast to coast Lincoln Highway did not begin until 1914. Lotti said she and Fred were self-sustaining, even during the Depression. They never went hungry. Everyone congregated at the farm; it was a neighborhood gathering point in the evening when chores were finished. Baseball and hayrides were popular entertainment and down the highway was an open-air dance pavilion that later became Bells Skating Rink when Joseph Bell bought it in 1926. Bells Skating Rink still operates today. (Above, Patricia Davis; below, Mary Ketzler as told by her mother, Lotti Pranger.)

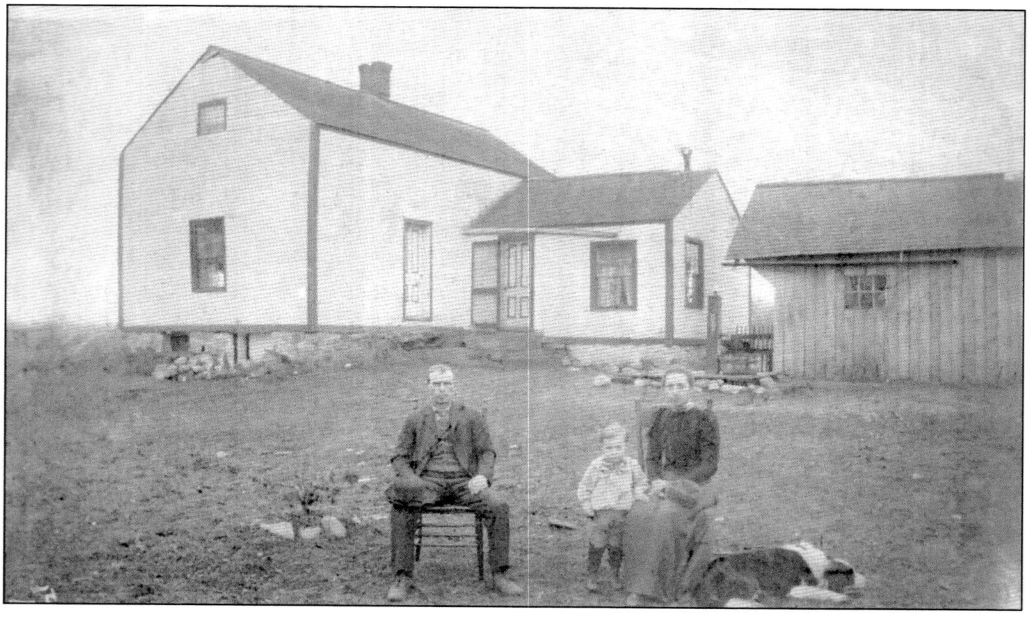

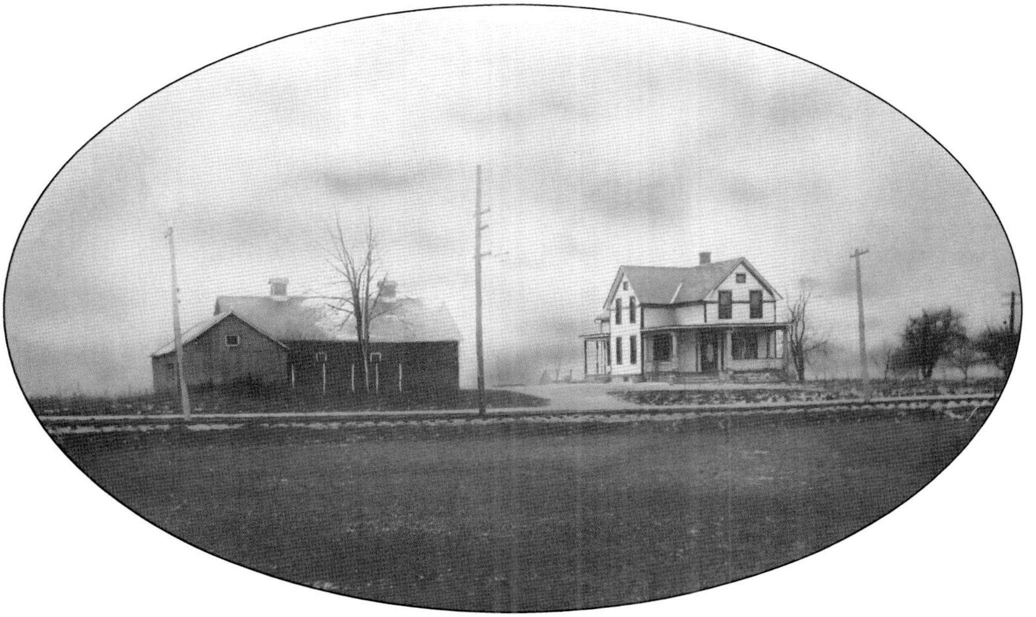

The interurban train tracks ran along the electric poles, but they are gone now, as well as the Pranger family home. In 1930, the state took ground to widen the highway and again in 1958 to build a dual-lane highway. The barn had to be razed for the highway. Carter Lumber now stands where the Pranger farmhouse and barns once stood. Lotti and her siblings walked into New Haven to St. John's school. She has many memories back to when she was four years old when the family bought their first car. New Haven Avenue was being paved so her father would drive the car over plowed ground to get to Maumee Avenue. She said it was really bumpy. In the photograph below is the Fred and Catherine Pranger family in 1904. Lotti, who was not yet born, says it was not unusual to trot out the horses when a family picture was taken. (Above, Patricia Davis; below Mary Ketzler and Lotti Pranger.)

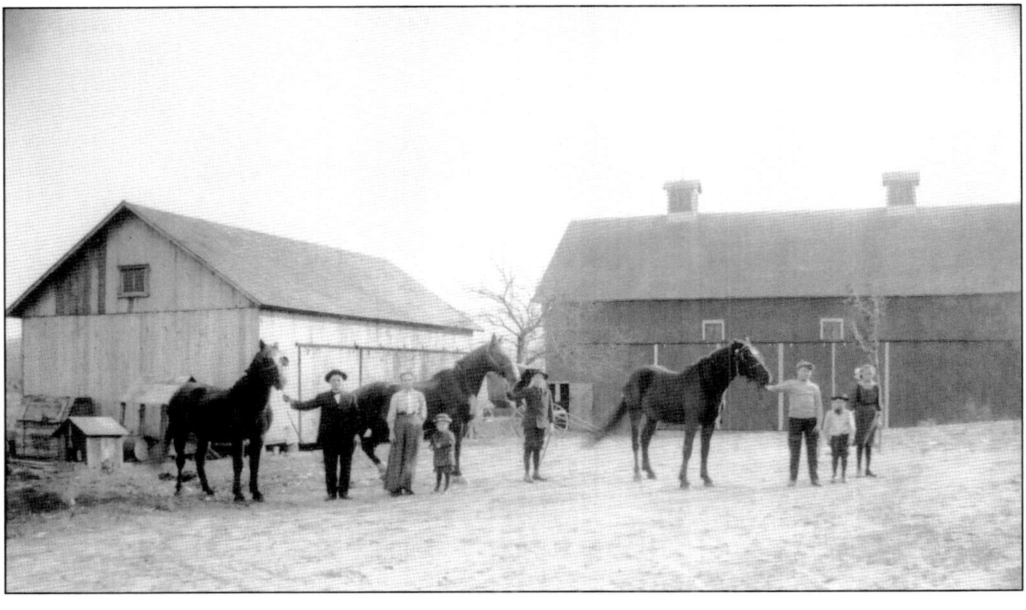

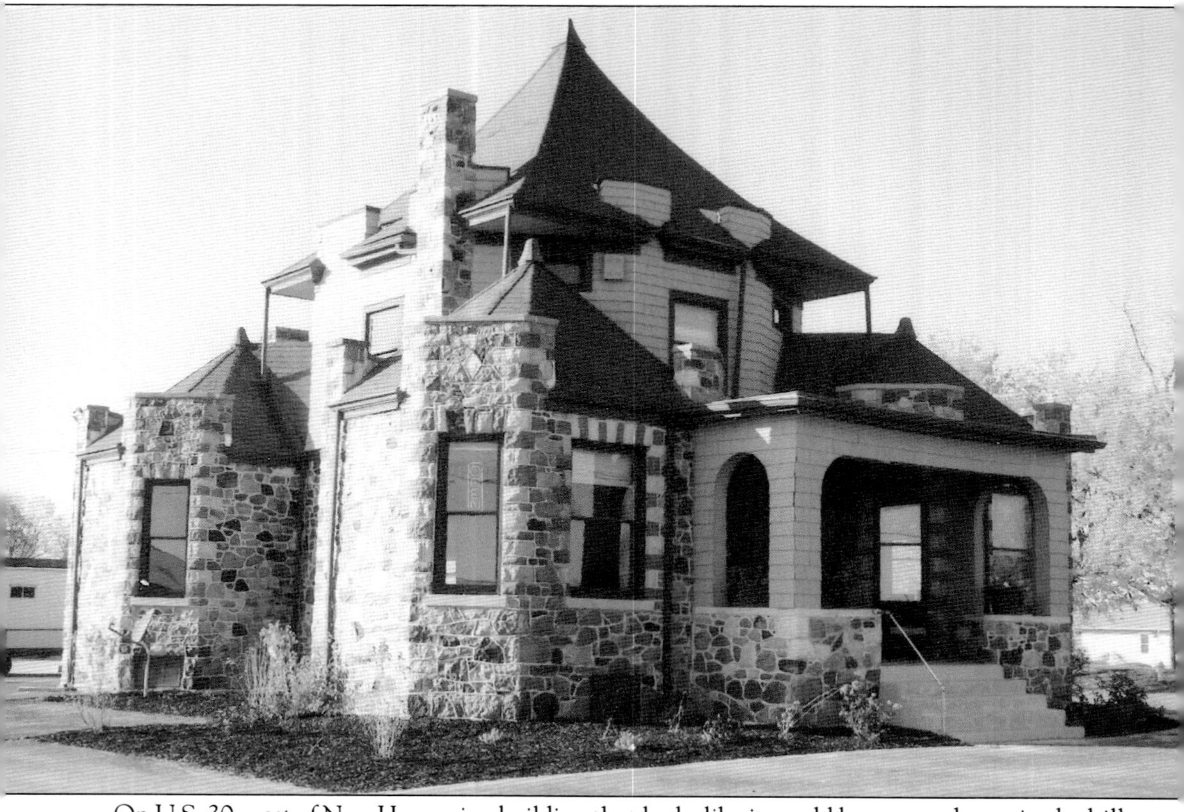

On U.S. 30, west of New Haven, is a building that looks like it would be more at home in the hills of Bavaria or in Paris or London. Children and adults alike probably have referred to this building as "the castle" since it was built in 1907. William and Caroline Holterman decided to build a home for themselves and their two children, Louis and Emily. The stones used for construction were gathered from the beds of the Maumee, St. Joseph, and St. Mary's Rivers and were laid by a Scottish-Canadian stonemason. Michael Hawfield, director of the Allen County Historical Museum, said "I would guess they used stone from the local riverbeds because of its availability and it being free for the taking." He explained that the castle's architecture reflects the neo-Gothic–style churches and monasteries built in the 12th and 14th centuries. New Gothic is a recent imitation of that style. However, the Holtermans' home also was the center of a thriving business. Holterman was an international chicken breeder and chicken feed salesman. Buyers came from Japan and other countries to choose prize roosters and hens to upgrade their flocks. (Stevia Webster and Lois Emenhiser, *Neighbors Correspondent*, March 1988.)

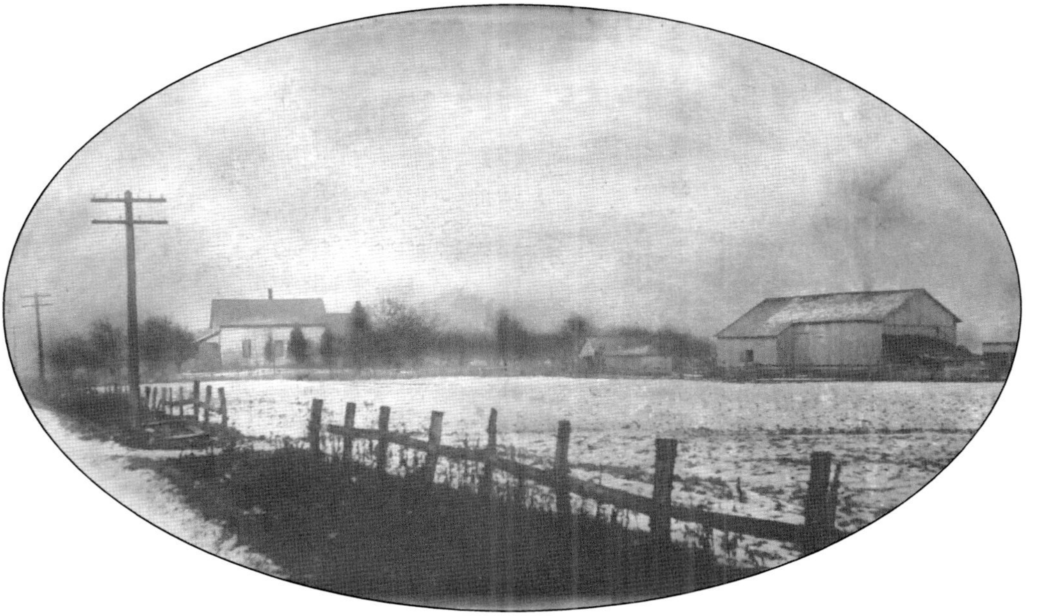

This is the farm and house of Paul and Marie Morrell. The snow-covered lane with the rail fence is now U.S. Highway 30, west of New Haven. The road was either dirt or stone since highways were not paved here until 1913. The barn and buildings have been gone for many years. (Patricia Davis.)

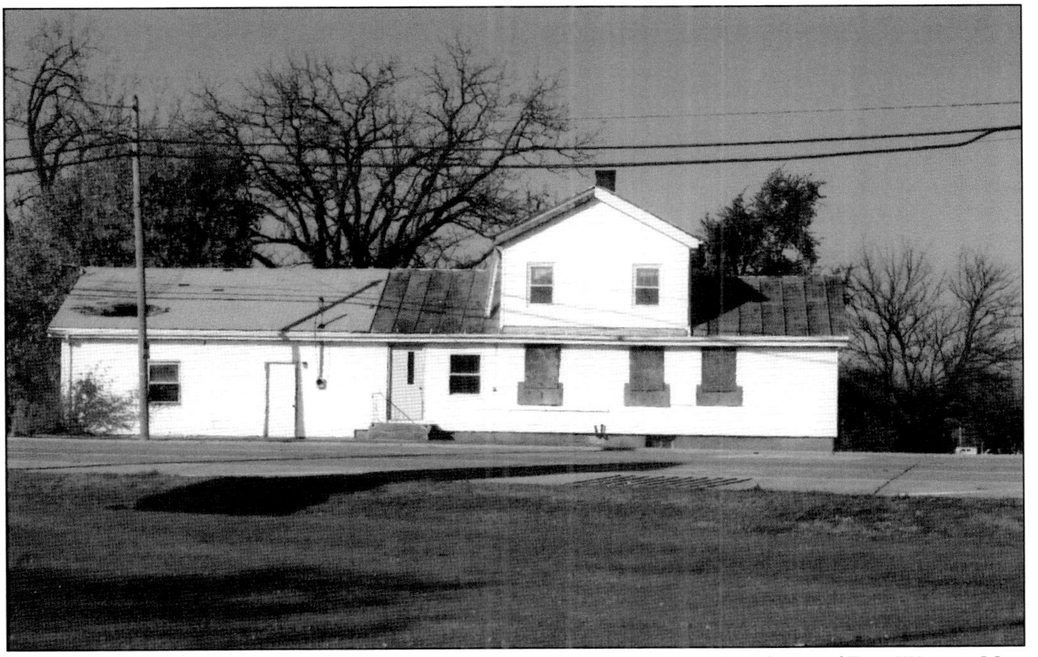

Hilda Hamilton's father purchased this farm in 1906. In 1903, the right-of-way of Fort Wayne, Van Wert, and the Lima Traction Company's interurban train was through this farm. That right-of-way was still theirs in 1994. The house sits at 2011 Highway 30 East where in early years the property housed a stagecoach stop. (Hilda Hamilton and Stevia Webster, *Allen County Times*, 1994.)

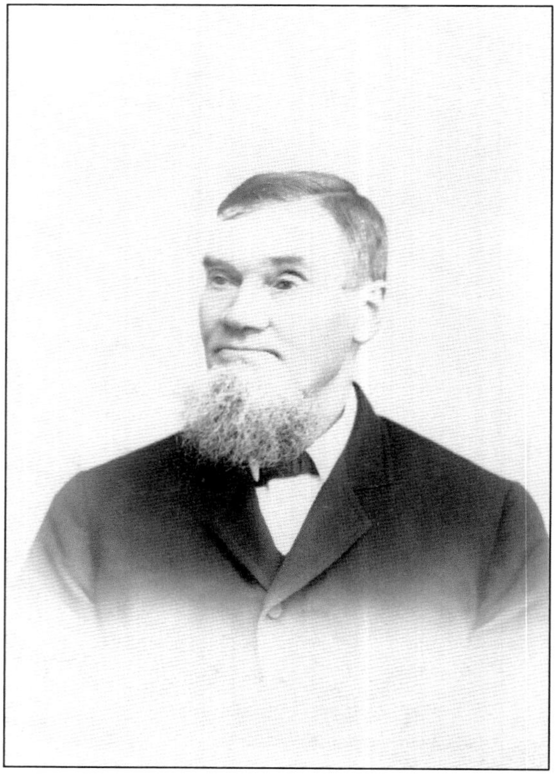

In 1850, Gerhard Rebber immigrated from the farming region outside Hanover, Germany. He and others who lived along Moeller Road had lost their farming land in Germany when it was expropriated for a shooting range. Their land is part of a nature park outside of Celle, Germany. He was part of the swelling tide of German immigration that came to Allen County. Gerhard purchased land on Moeller Road in 1856. The first farmhouse from the 1850s era was a farmstead that was built further north on the property along the creek. Rebber first thought Moeller Road would be built along the creek and the old Native American trails. Rebber married Sophie Bradtmuller. He is listed as a member of St. Paul's Lutheran Church on Barr Street until 1853 when Martini Lutheran Church was founded on the west end of Moeller Road. It was indeed "the model German Lutheran parish" as it was labeled in the 1889 history of the Valley of the Upper Maumee River. (Both, Donn Werling and *Old Fort News*.)

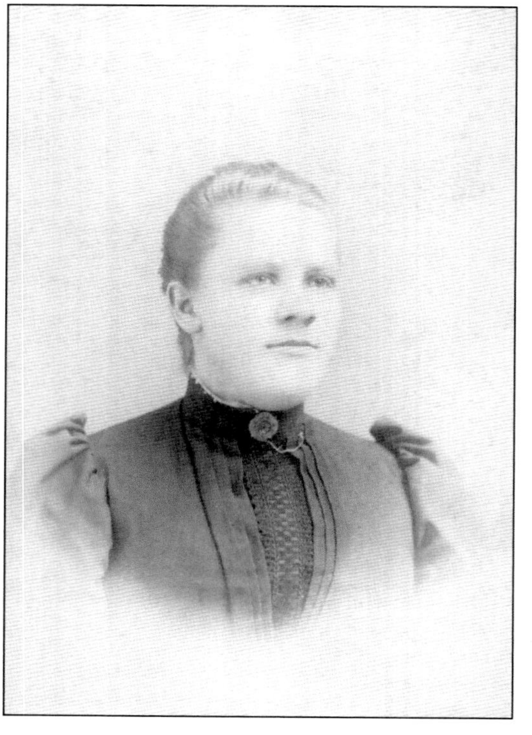

In 1895, Ernst Rebber, son of Gerhard and Sophie Rebber, and Flora Stock were married and built a new modern Victorian house closer to Moeller Road where it sits today. Moeller Road was not the paved road it is today but a graded, dirt-covered country lane at the time. Martin Stock, Flora's brother, designed the new house. (Donn Werling and *Old Fort News.*)

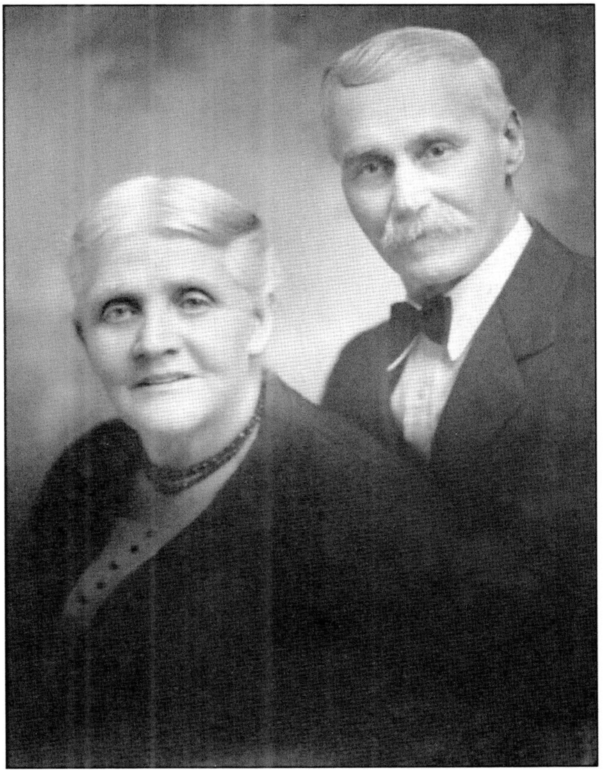

A view of the front, south-facing side of the house shows Ernst and Flora Rebber holding their twins, Erwin and Albert. Daughter Martha and son Gerhard are standing at center. This photograph was taken in 1903. (Donn Werling and *Old Fort News.*)

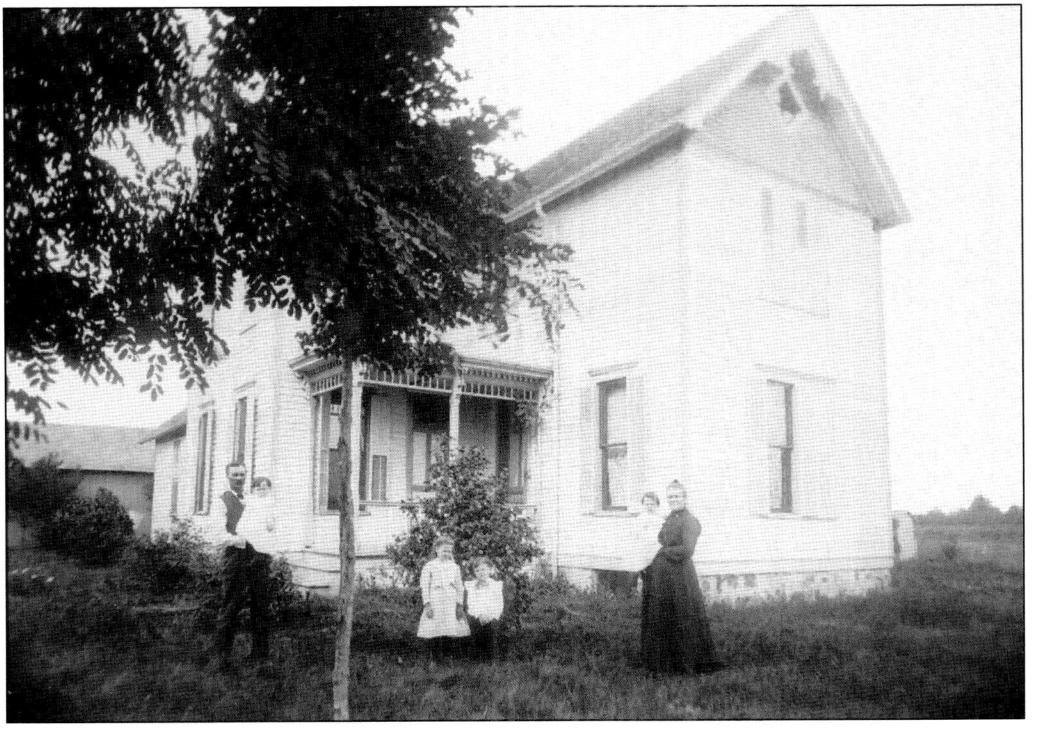

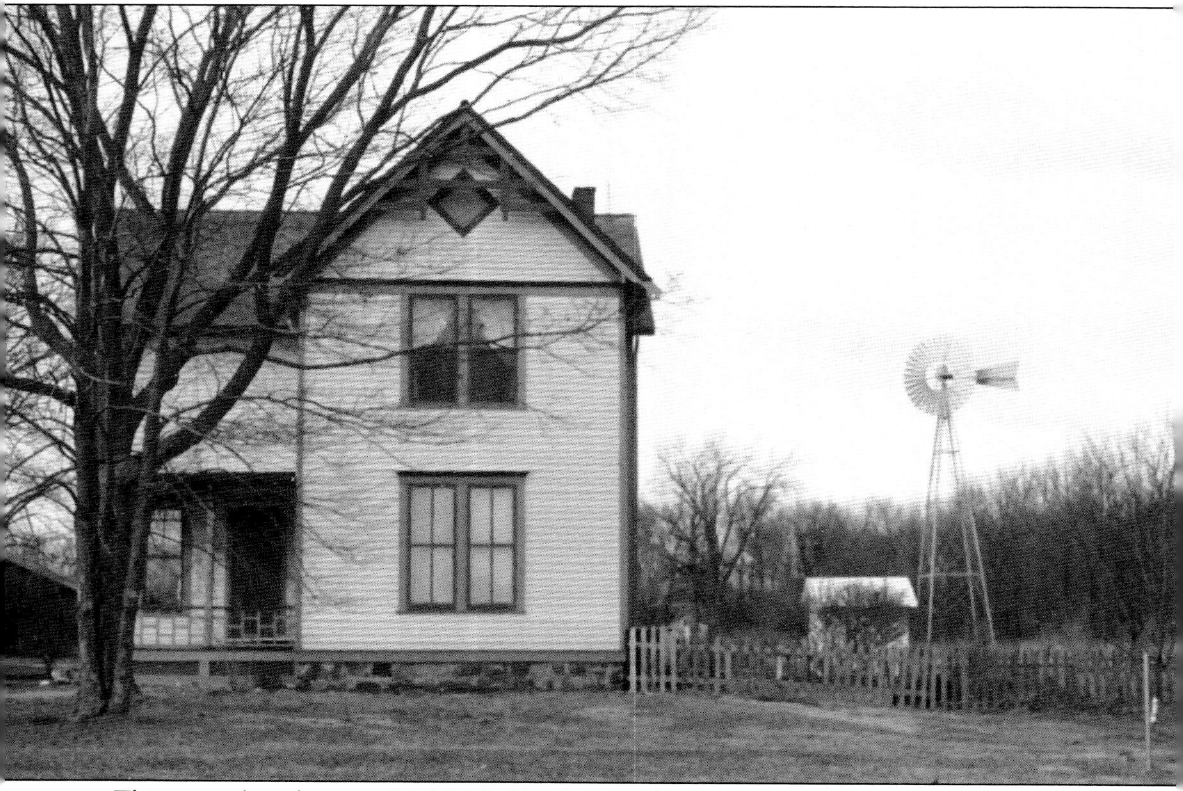

This is another photograph of the Rebber home. The original linen architectural drawings were found in the 1980s while cleaning the house. The floor plans show the original function of each room. It was a generous house with an enclosed front parlor and the kitchen and bedroom in the back of the house. At the head of the steps on the second floor is a parlor with a stove to warm the room so the three bedroom occupants could dress in a heated room. It was used as a playroom or a sort of upstairs family room. To the right of the house sits the milk house, next to the windmill. Since refrigeration was not yet invented in the early 1900s, milk was kept cool using 50-degree groundwater from the hand-dug well; the windmill pumped and circulated cold water around the milk cans. The milk house and windmill stand today, though the windmill no longer operates. Donn Werling purchased the farm of his birth, where his great-grandfather, Gerhard Rebber, bought land in 1856 and built his house and outbuildings. (Donn Werling and *Old Fort News*.)

The old original 1850s-era smokehouse and buggy garage, to the left side of Pauline Plothe, was moved from the location of the homestead house to the new Victorian home. At one end of the building is a large bay for the surrey with the fringed top that the grandparents rode in to church or town. Two-thirds of the smokehouse was devoted to smoking or preserving food using both cast iron and copper kettles for rendering lard and making sausages or boiling down apples into butter. (Donn Werling and *Old Fort News*.)

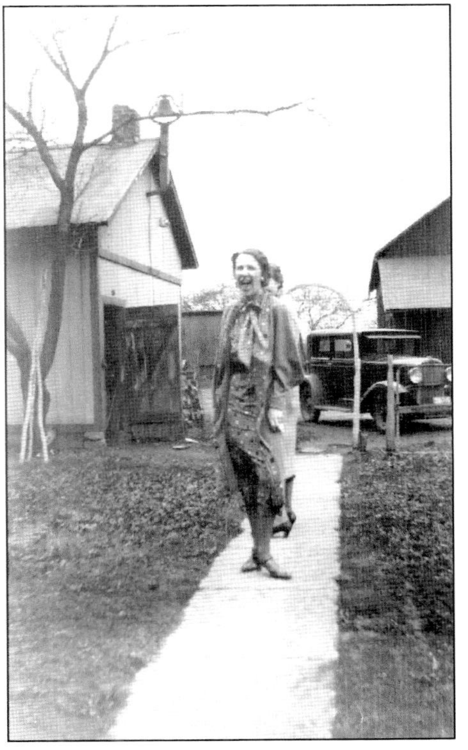

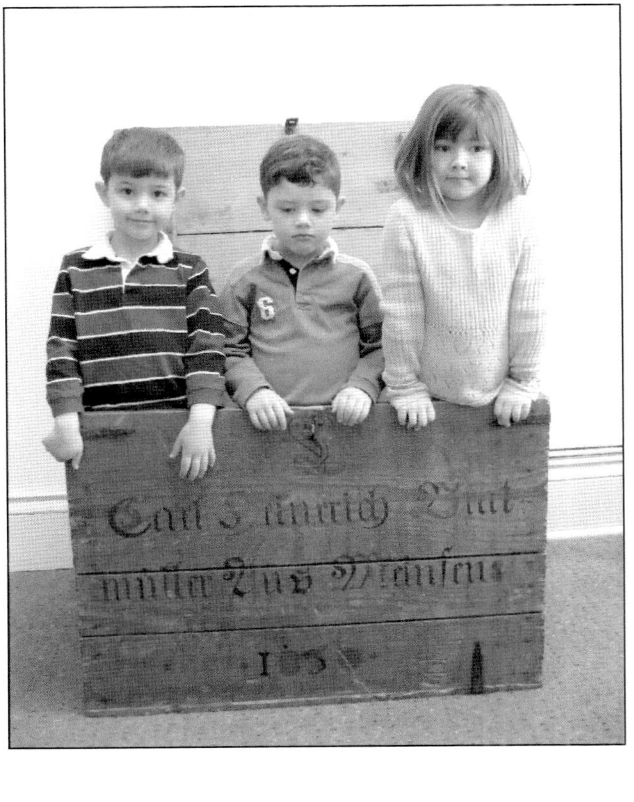

This is the original 1850 immigrant trunk of Carl Heinrich Brat Mueller Aus Meifen, or Carl Heinrich Bradtmuller. His great-great-great-great-grandchildren standing in the trunk are, from left to right, Addison, Elliot, and Jordyn Hanni. (Donn Werling and *Old Fort News*.)

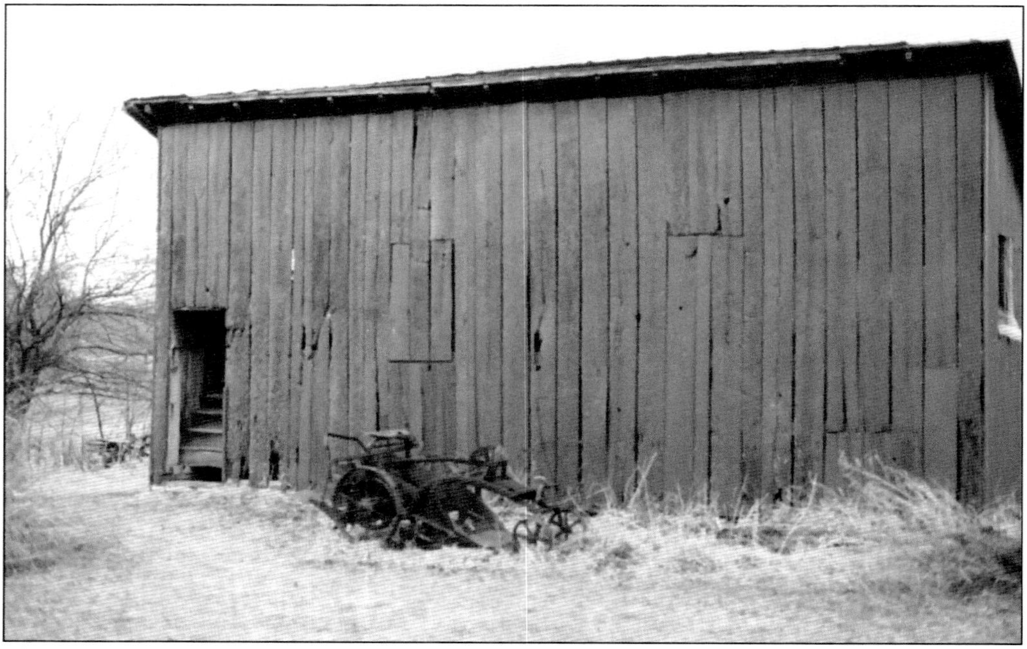

The grain and feed were stored on the second floor of the hog barn. An old potato digger sits in the front. On the land stands an original 7-acre woodlot, which is a remnant of the old growth forest of the Maumee Valley. Maybe they shaded the Native Americans who once lived here. (Donn Werling and *Old Fort News*.)

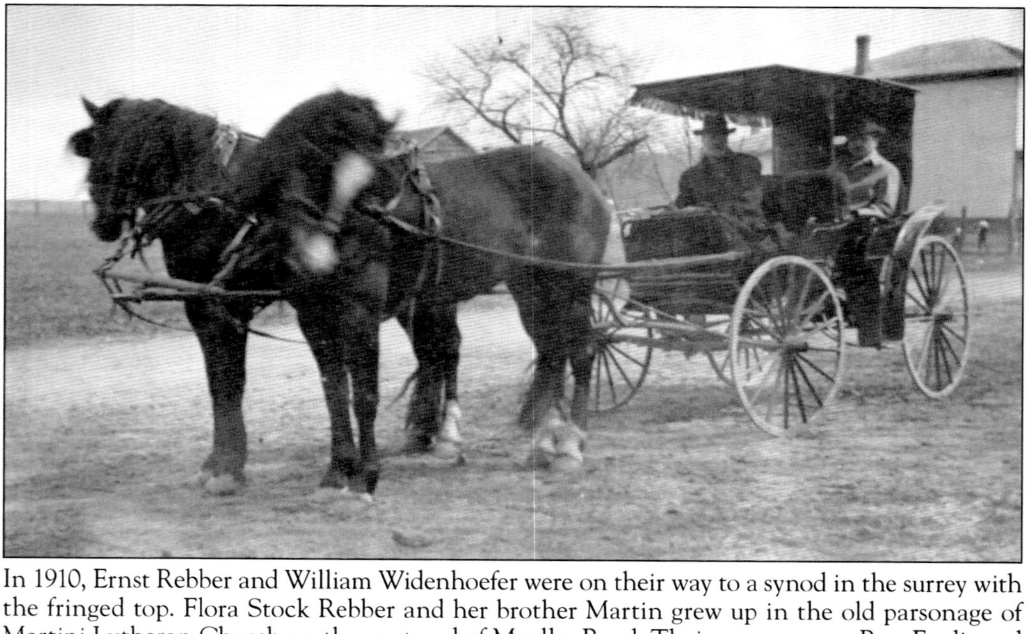

In 1910, Ernst Rebber and William Widenhoefer were on their way to a synod in the surrey with the fringed top. Flora Stock Rebber and her brother Martin grew up in the old parsonage of Martini Lutheran Church on the west end of Moeller Road. Their parents were Rev. Ferdinand and Mrs. Stock; Ferdinand was the beloved parish minister who became a pastoral counselor for both Allen and Adams County. He pastored for 60 years beginning in 1861. (Donn Werling and *Old Fort News*.)

Frederick and Sophia Rodenbeck were married in 1897. Their farm was located on the north side of Moeller Road, east of and bordering Adams Center Road. The east side of the acreage bordered the Rebber farm. The house, built in 1840, was the third oldest frame house in Adams Township. The farmhouse sat back half a mile from Moeller Road. (Natalie Seltz and *Old Fort News*.)

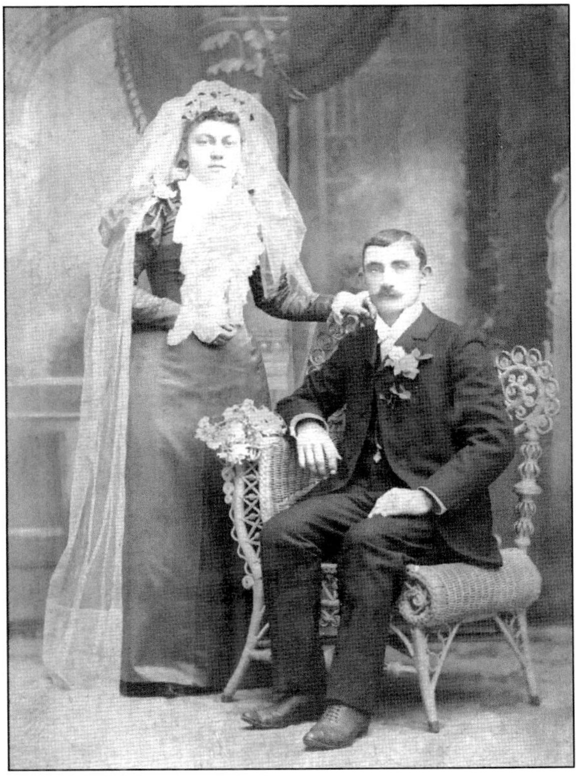

In 1901, this photograph was taken behind the Rodenbeck house. From left to right are Frederick, Walter, and Sophie holding baby August. The brick building to the left is the summer kitchen and to the right is the milk house. In the summer, families cooked in the summer kitchen so the house would stay cool. (Natalie Seltz and *Old Fort News*.)

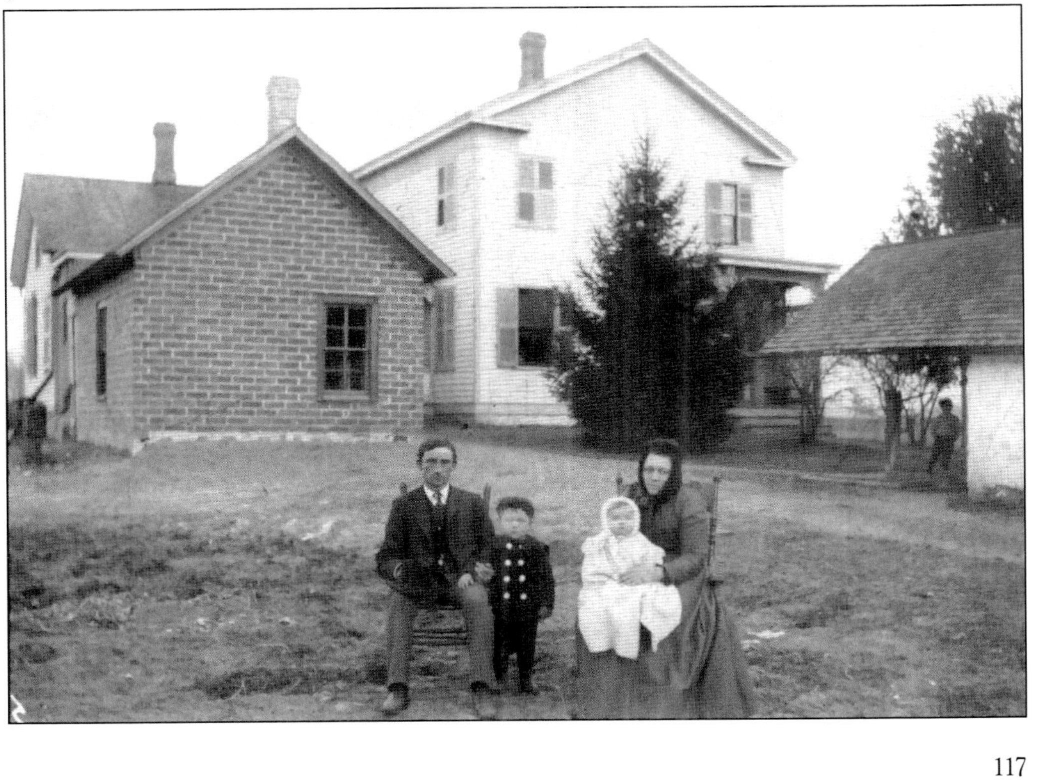

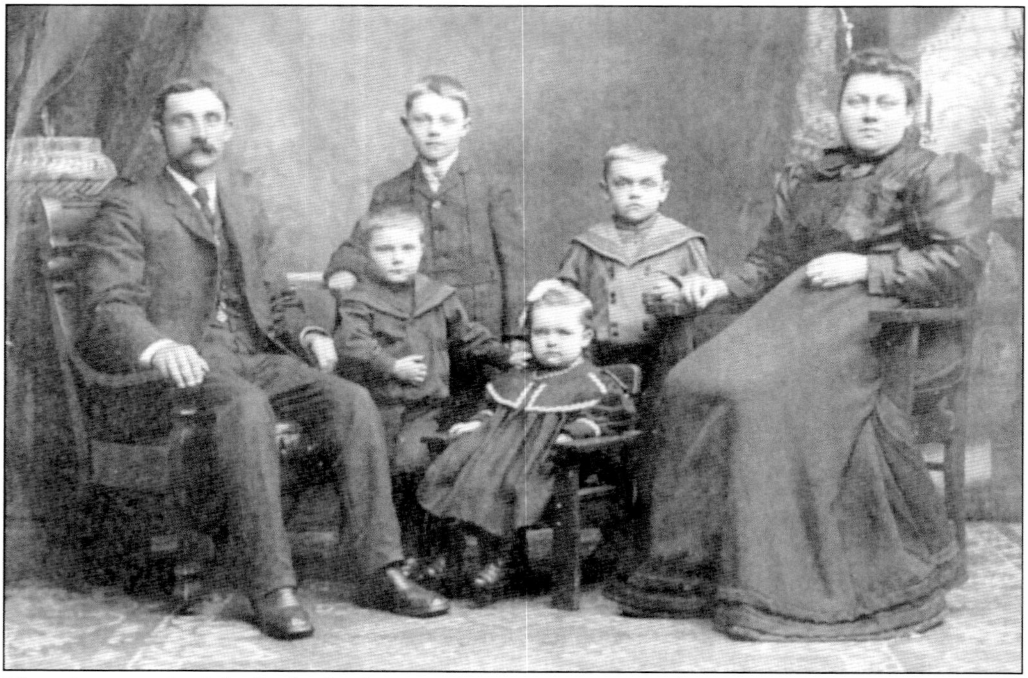

This photograph of the Rodenbecks was taken in 1906. Pictured are, from left to right, (first row) Frederick, August, Ella, and Sophie; (second row) Walter and William. Clara, the youngest, was born in 1909 after this photograph was taken. (Natalie Seltz and *Old Fort News*.)

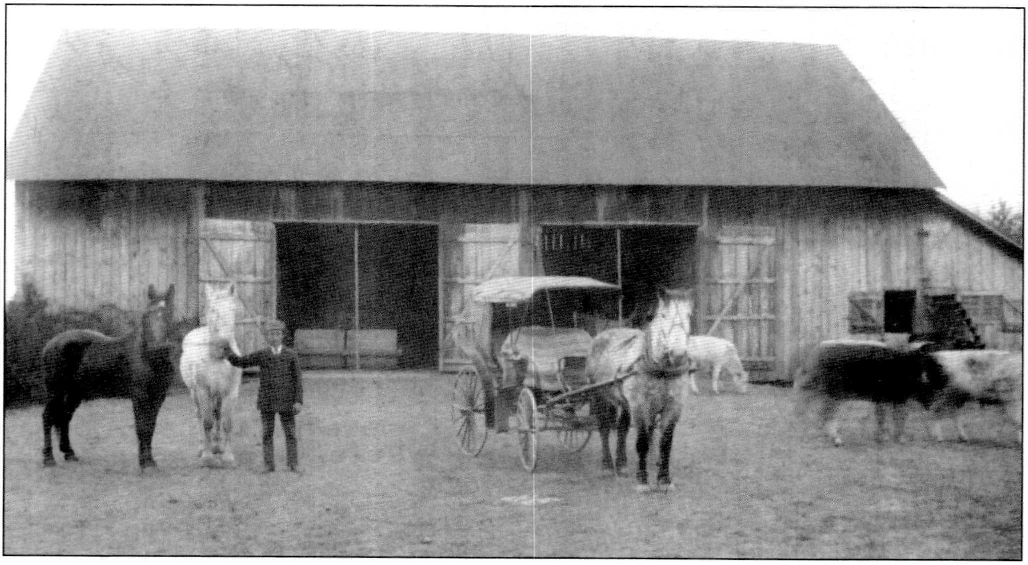

Here is the Rodenbeck farm barnyard in 1903. Frederick Rodenbeck is posed with two horses. A field roller can be seen inside the barn. On the floors, behind the doors on the right, hay and grain was stacked on the barn floor waiting to be threshed when the threshing machine was not busy. The big barn was never painted so the sides were well-weathered. There were very high double doors at two places so the large wagons, loaded with hay or grain, could get in. (Natalie Seltz and *Old Fort News*.)

Frederick Rodenbeck was of average height, slender, and had wavy black hair. Icicles hung from his moustache after he had been out in cold weather. He played in the local farmer's band that mostly performed for Democratic rallies. Rodenbeck wore a snappy uniform and played the coronet. He was secretary of a farmer's insurance company and was a trustee in his home church. (Natalie Seltz and *Old Fort News*.)

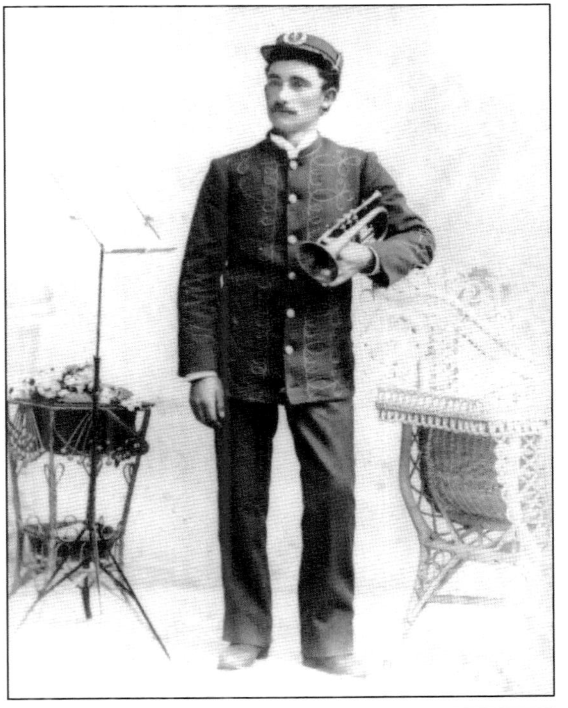

Sophie was of average height, had black hair, and was quite plump. Clara, Sophie's youngest child, does not remember very much about her mother since she died of typhoid fever in 1913 when Clara was five years old. The whole family had typhoid except two children. Sophie left five children for her husband, Frederick, to care for. The photograph shows flowers and her picture at her funeral. (Natalie Seltz and *Old Fort News*.)

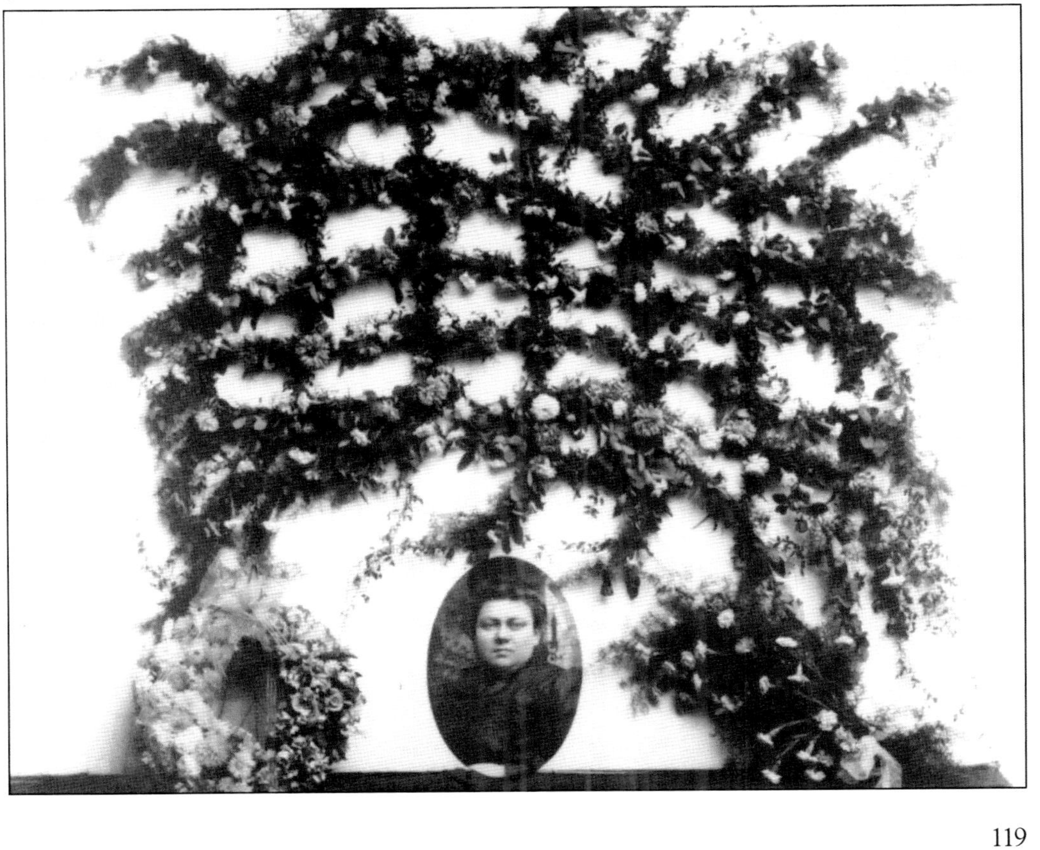

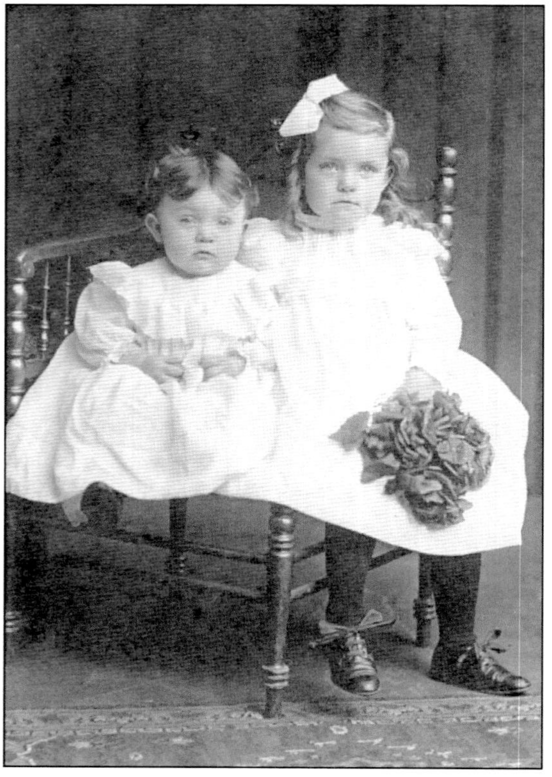

This photograph of Clara and Ella Rodenbeck was taken in 1909. Clara was the youngest child in the family. Her mother, Sophie, died when Clara was five years old. All of the children had to take responsibilities. While growing up Clara had many daily chores. The stories of the Rodenbeck farm are told in these few pictures and are inspired by Clara's memories. She reflects upon the wonderful days and explains the evolution of the seasons and what transpires on a farm throughout the year. Clara graduated from Lutheran Hospital School of Nursing in 1931. She traveled to China as a nurse deaconess with the Lutheran church. She met and married Eugene Seltz, who was a missionary for the Lutheran church in China. While coming home on furlough, their home in China was invaded by Japan. They settled in Minnesota until 1959, when they moved back to China. They stayed in China between 1959 and 1971. After coming home, they settled and retired in Minnesota. (Both, Natalie Seltz and *Old Fort News*.)

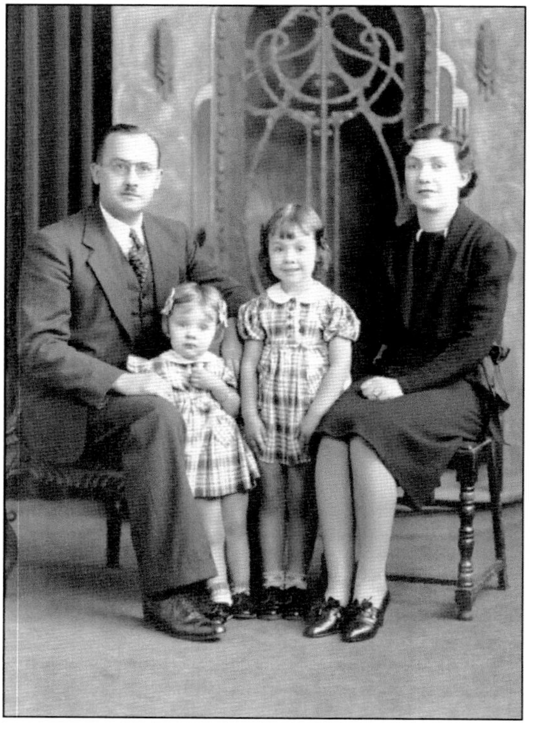

Six

French Settlement in Jefferson Township

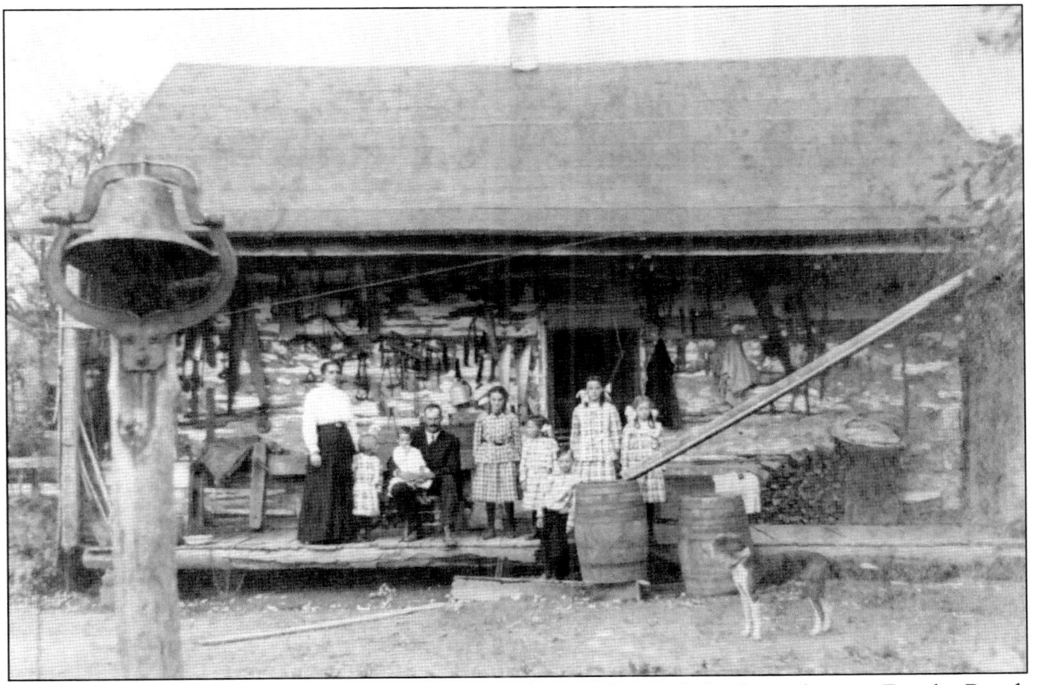

In 1913, the Converset family had its picture taken in front of the log cabin on Franke Road. Mother sewed the children's matching clothes. Notice the farm tools hanging on the front cabin wall. They also recovered soft rainwater from the cabin roof, routing it to the downspout and then the barrels. Pictured are, from left to right, Agnes Rorick Converset, Sylvia, Joe holding Julian, Frances, Rose, Leo standing by the rain barrel, Florence, and Alice. (St. Louis Catholic Church and Jeff Hoffman.)

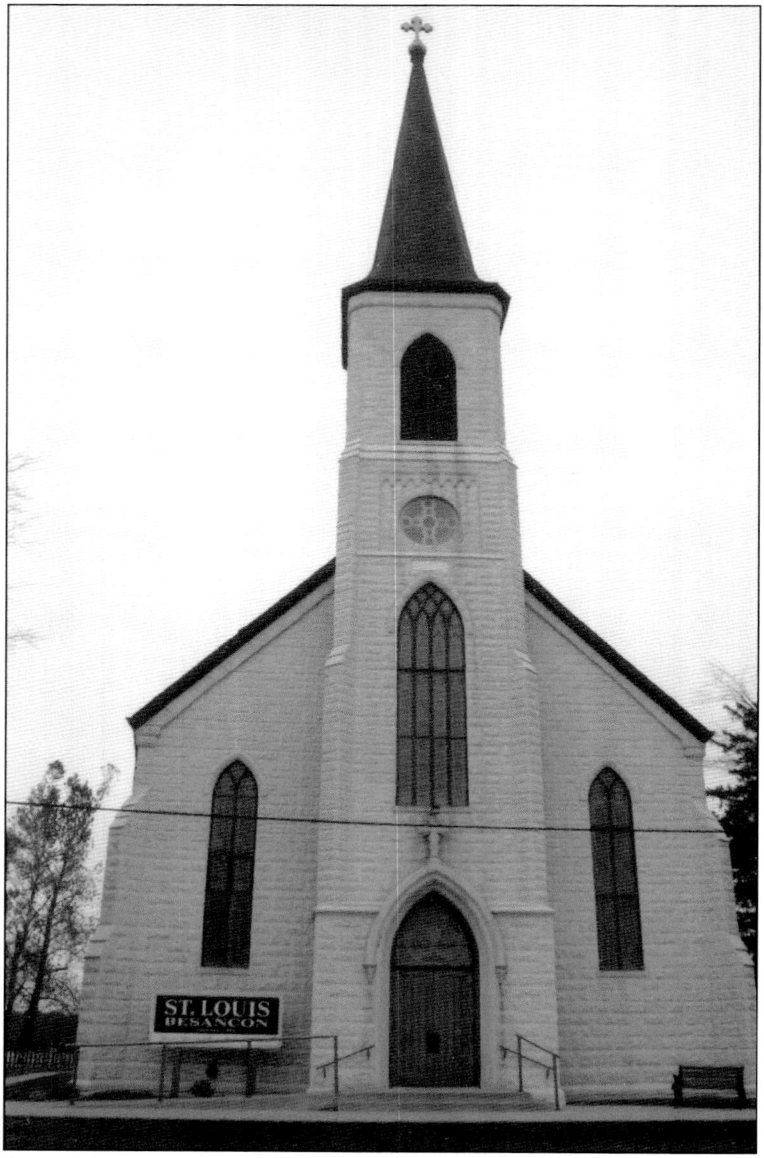

A small settlement known as "New France" grew in Jefferson Township. In 1851, St. Louis Catholic Church was founded under the direction of Father Bessonies. The complex of buildings around the church became known as "Besancon," after the city in France from which much of the congregation had immigrated from due to economic times and the Napoleonic wars. The first St. Louis Catholic Church building was a log cabin. In 1871, the present building was constructed around the old cabin. When the new brick church was finished, the log cabin was taken apart and removed through the front door. In the 1920s, a procedure called "shamrocking" was done, in which a thin coat of material that looked like limestone was applied to the outside bricks. It was attractive and helped preserve the bricks. In 1913, a school opened. The original church was built on a dirt road that is now Lincoln Highway, east of New Haven. The following pages highlight some of the settlements and people of Jefferson Township. (St. Louis Catholic Church and Jeff Hoffman.)

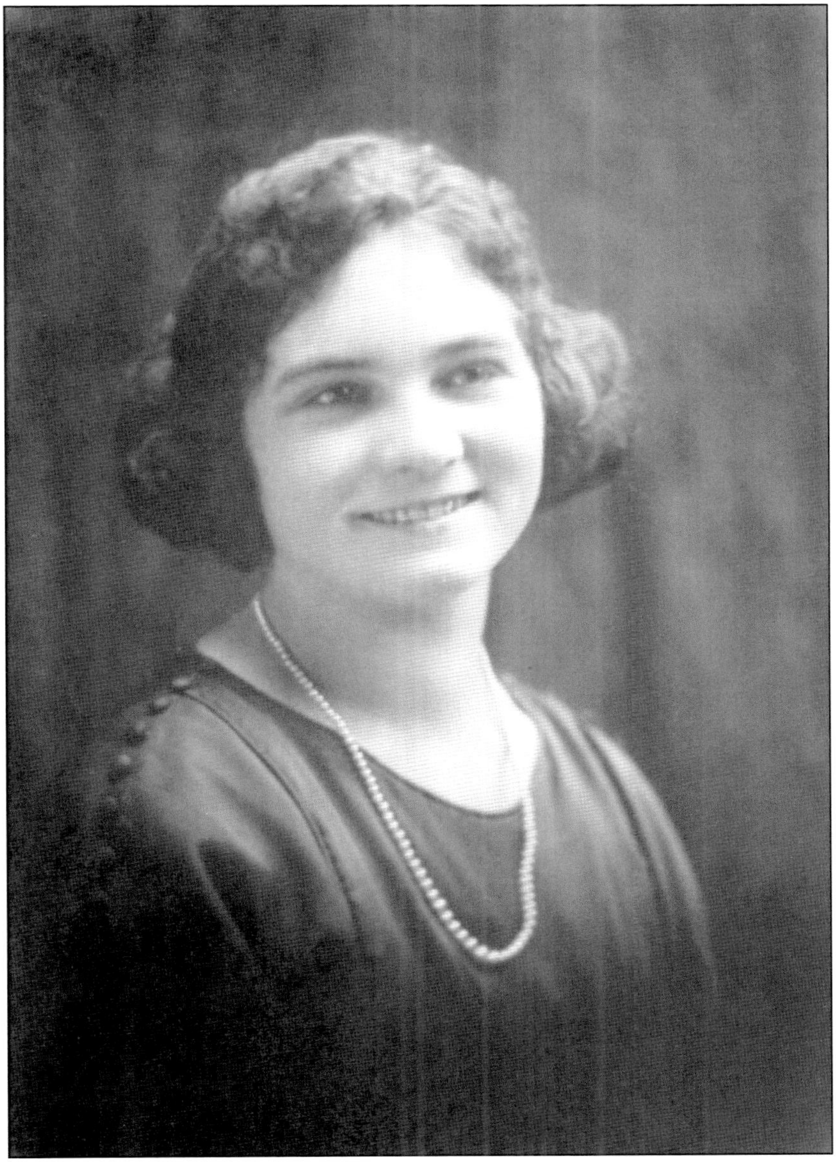

Maples was platted in 1853, named for settler Lewis S. Maples. Gladys Nail, pictured here at age 21, was born in 1903 to John and Juliette Coulardot Nail in a home near the Pennsylvania Railroad in Maples. She was their fourth child. At age five she started school at a one-room schoolhouse. Gladys graduated from New Haven High School in 1920. Although she was not 18, the school trustee let her substitute teach. Nail enjoyed teaching and, beginning in 1921, taught for 10 years. She met Allen Lomont in 1929, and they married in 1930. In 1931, the Lamonts purchased an 80-acre farm and lived there until 2003. Their son Mick purchased the home in 2003. The property had been in the Lomont family since Claudia Francis settled in 1850 from Besancon, France. The Lomonts raised seven children; in 1942 the eldest died in a farm accident at age 10. The children attended St. Louis School in Besancon. The St. Louis Catholic Church dedicated a room to the memory of Gladys Nail because she founded the historical group in the church. She died in 2003 at 100 years old. (St. Louis Catholic Church and Ed Lomont.)

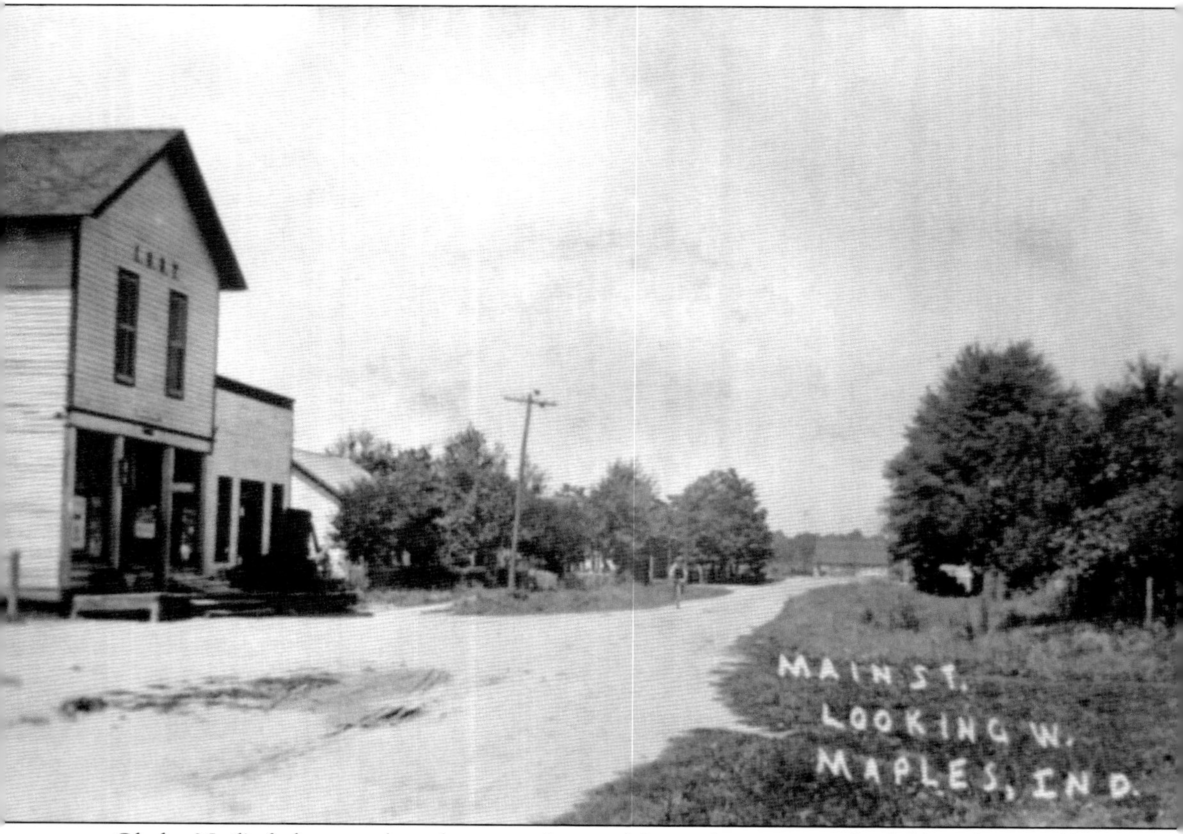

Gladys Nail's father purchased a general store (above the store on the left) and post office in Maples. He named it Nail General Store. According to Gladys, "[The store] was broken into and the safe blown. There was boxes dumped out, and money all over the floor. We spent hours getting the store back into order. The thief was never caught. Another time Father was almost stabbed by an enraged man who had come to the store looking for work. He did not like what my dad had asked him to do, so he pulled a knife and made a dive for Dad. He missed, ran, and was never seen again." (St. Louis Catholic Church and Ed Lomont.)

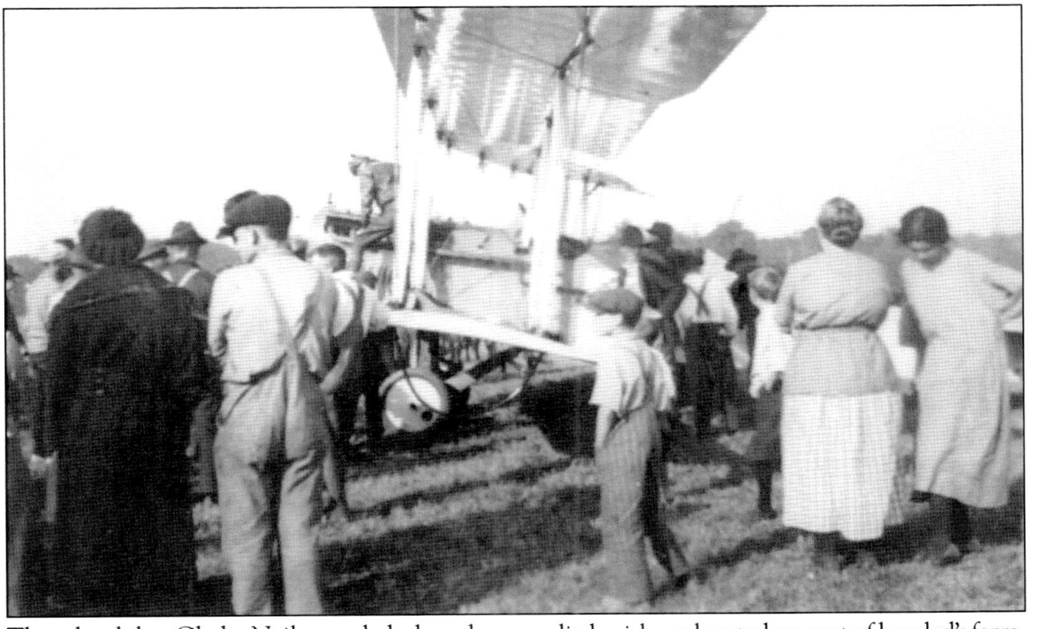

The school that Gladys Nail attended when she was a little girl was located on part of her dad's farm. He owned 465 acres, which was the largest farm in Jefferson Township. One day the children were surprised by an airplane landing in the schoolyard. It seems it sprung a leak in the oil line. This was the first time Gladys saw an airplane. (Ed Lomont, life story of his grandmother, Gladys.)

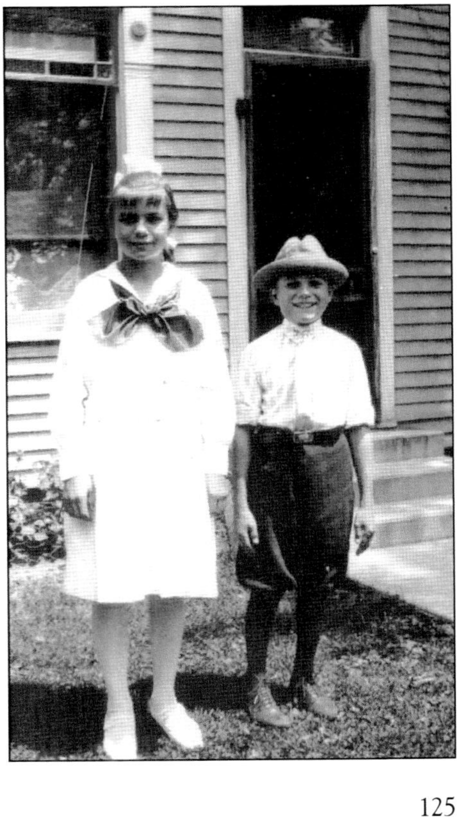

Gladys Nail had nine siblings. Younger siblings Lela and John, born in 1909 and 1911, stand in front of the family home, which burned down in 1925. Gladys recounted another family tragedy: "In 1915 my sister Geraldine was drawing gas for the family car. Some neighbor boys had been playing with a hand mirror near the shed. They were shining the mirror in her eyes. She came running into the store crying. Her apron was on fire . . . We finally got the flames out but her clothes were about half-burned off her . . . She died the next morning." (Ed Lomont, life story of his grandmother, Gladys.)

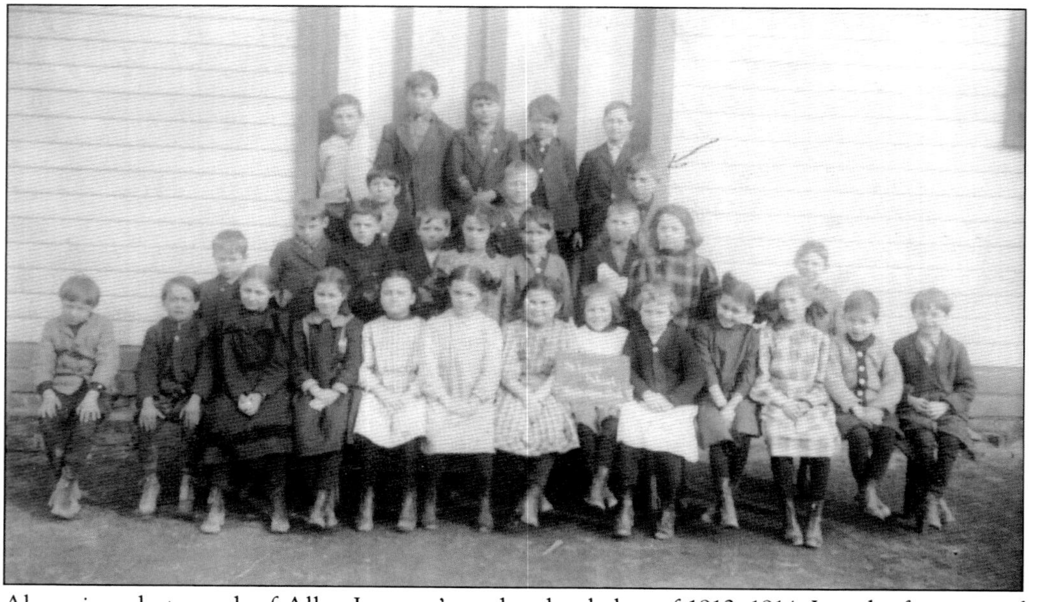

Above is a photograph of Allen Lomont's grade-school class of 1913–1914. It is the first year of classes in the St. Louis Catholic School. Beatrice Frane is in the center of the first row wearing a checked dress. In the second row from the top is Allen Lomont, the last boy at the far right. Some of the children's names, in no particular order, are Everette Lothame, Lilliaca Rousel, Marcella Coulardot, and Mae Coulardot. All others are unidentified. (Ed Lomont, life story of his grandmother, Gladys.)

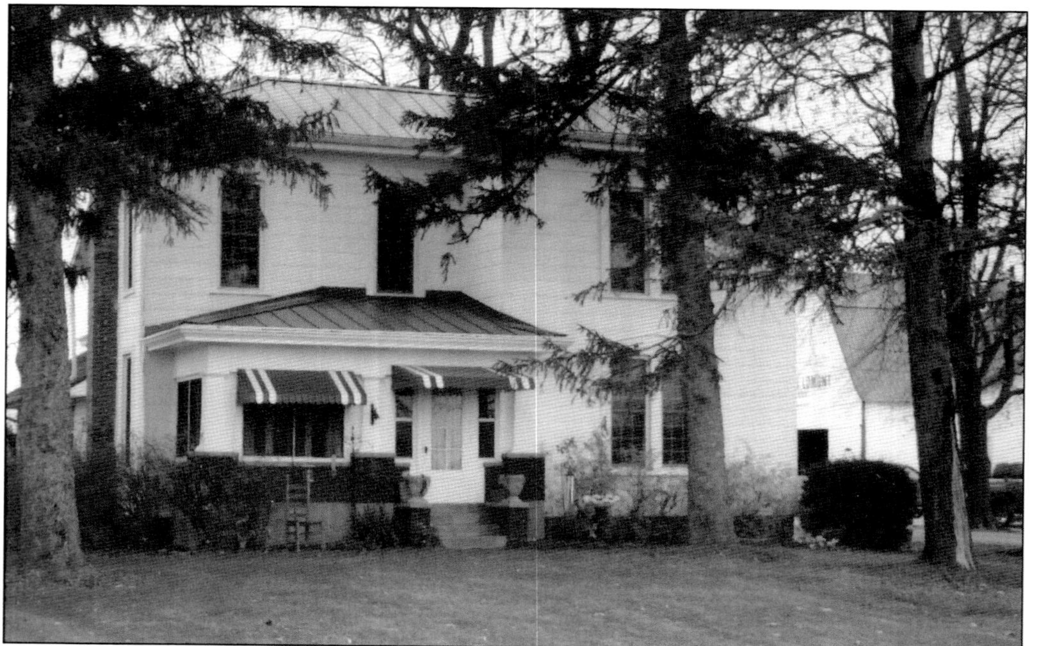

Allen and Gladys Lomont's home was located close to the St. Louis Catholic Church and U.S. Highway 30. The Lomonts raised seven children. The property has been in the Lomont family since 1850. (Stevia Webster.)

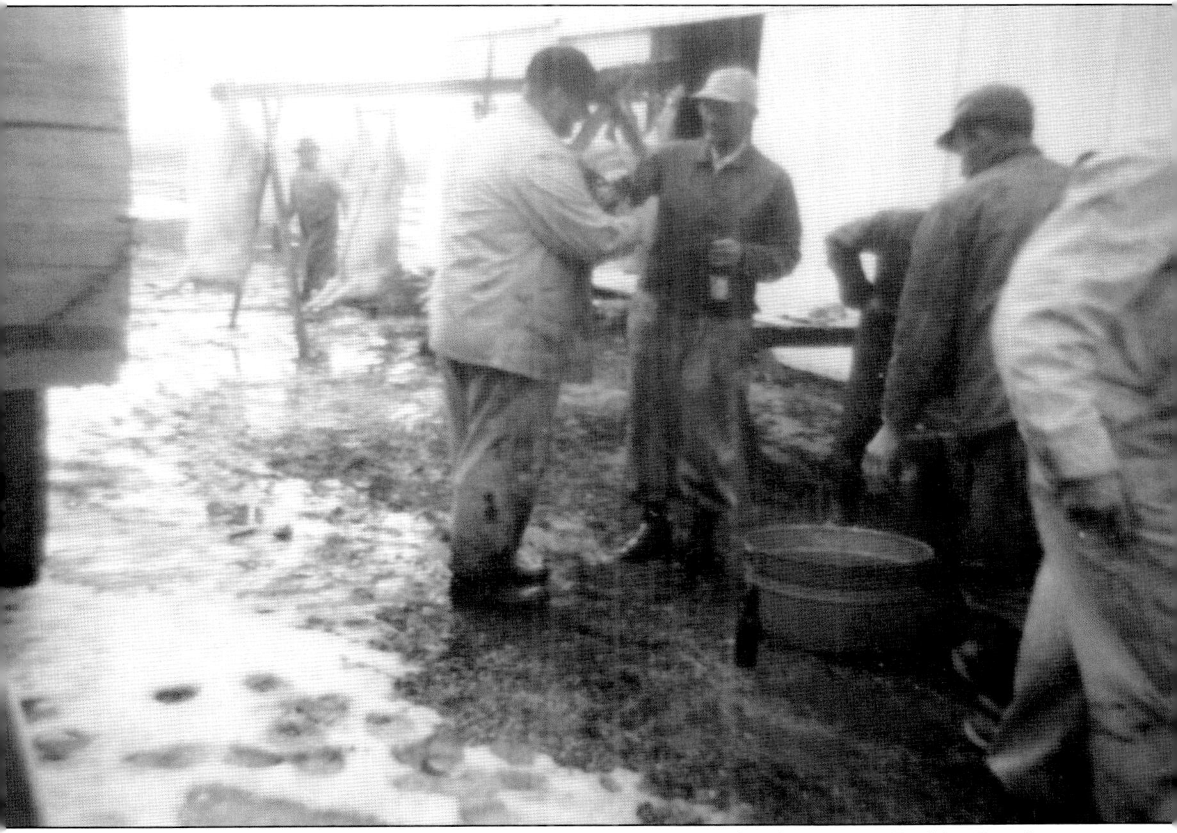

Hog butchering day on the Bacon farm was a very busy one. The farm is on Fackler Road in Jefferson Township. In 1838, Harvey's great-great-grandfather, Socrates Bacon, homesteaded the land and built a farm. Walter Bolyard stands between the hogs. Standing at the front are, from left to right, Harvey Bacon Jr., Harvey Bacon Sr., and Elmer Giant. Harvey Bacon Sr. was born in 1897. He attended No. 8 district schools and Monroeville High School and served in World War I. He married Bertha Bolyard at St. Louis Catholic Church in Besancon. They moved to his father's farm on Fackler Road in 1928, and bought the farm from his parents, Albert and Lucy Bacon. Harvey Sr. retired from International Harvester in 1962 and died of pneumonia in 1978. Harvey Bacon Jr. graduated from Hoagland High School in 1943. He married Velma Hart at St. Louis Catholic Church in 1945. They moved to the Bacon homestead, which they bought from his father in 1976. They built a new home on the property. He worked for the Allen County Cooperative in New Haven. (St. Louis Catholic Church and Jeff Hoffman; information from the *Descendants of the Bacon Family*.)